Searching for a Cultural Diplomacy

Explorations in Culture and International History Series
General Editor: Jessica C. E. Gienow-Hecht

Volume 1
Culture and International History
Edited by Jessica C. E. Gienow-Hecht and Frank Schumacher

Volume 2
Remaking France
Brian Angus McKenzie

Volume 3
Anti-Americanism in Latin America and the Caribbean
Edited by Allan McPherson

Volume 4
Decentering America
Edited by Jessica C. E. Gienow-Hecht

Volume 5
Practicing Public Diplomacy
Yale Richmond

Volume 6
Searching for a Cultural Diplomacy
Edited by Jessica C. E. Gienow-Hecht and Mark C. Donfried

Searching for a Cultural Diplomacy

Edited by
Jessica C. E. Gienow-Hecht
and Mark C. Donfried

berghahn
NEW YORK • OXFORD
www.berghahnbooks.com

Published in 2010 by
Berghahn Books
www.berghahnbooks.com

First paperback edition published in 2013

Library of Congress Cataloging-in-Publication Data

Searching for a cultural diplomacy / edited by Jessica C.E. Gienow-Hecht and Mark C. Donfried.
p. cm. — (Explorations in culture and international history series ; v. 6)
ISBN 978-1-84545-746-4 (hardback alk. paper) — ISBN 978-1-84545-994-9 (institutional ebook) — ISBN 978-1-78238-079-5 (paperback) — ISBN 978-1-78238-080-1 (retail ebook)
1. Cultural relations. 2. World politics—1945–1989. I. Gienow-Hecht, Jessica C. E., 1964– II. Donfried, Mark C., 1978–
D843.S36 2010
327.1—dc22

2010023852

British Library Cataloguing in Publication Data

A catalogue record for this book is available from the British Library

Printed in the United States on acid-free paper

ISBN 978-1-78238-079-5 paperback
ISBN 978-1-78238-080-1 retail ebook

Contents

ACKNOWLEDGMENTS

With a project as interdisciplinary and international as one that searches for a cultural diplomacy, there is necessarily a challenge of overcoming the physical, methodological, and ideological distances that exist between the many people involved. In this case however, the shared interest in and enthusiasm for this crucial aspect of international relations provided a steady foundation, allowing the project to proceed very smoothly. Our foremost gratitude therefore goes to the essayists, whose combined work provides a new insight into the range and the influence of cultural diplomacy across the globe.

Some of the essays from this book are based on papers that were presented at the conference "Culture and International History III" hosted by the Goethe University in Frankfurt am Main. We would like to thank the primary sponsor of this conference, the Fritz Thyssen Stiftung, and in particular Dr. Frank Suder, without whose major contribution the conference could not have been initiated. We also thank the US Embassy for the generous grant assistance they provided for our international scholars. Also vital to the success of this conference was the staff of the Goethe University Gästehaus, above all Frau Maria Reinhardt. Similarly, the staff of the Center for North American Studies was of enormous help. We would particularly like to thank our student assistant there, Annika Poppe.

For their hard work in managing the conference and then proofreading, formatting, editing, and sub-editing contributions, we owe a debt of gratitude to the interns at the Institute for Cultural Diplomacy, namely: Mariusz Bartoszewicz, Castle Sinicrope, Leila Mukhida, Matthew Nobblit, and Sam Powney. At the University of Cologne, Jochen Molitor went out of his way to format and edit all notes and bibliographies while Carolin Fischer served as a patient and diligent assistant during the copyediting process. And once again, Wayne Moquin compiled the index with a keen eye for detail.

We are very grateful to the anonymous reviewers appointed by Berghahn Books for their thoughtful comments, and to the essayists for their willingness to share their ideas and make numerous revisions. Jaime Taber proved to be an excellent copyeditor. Special thanks also go to Marion Berghahn at Berghahn Books for all the hard work, enthusiasm, and encouragement she has invested in our research and this publication. Were it not for her support and interest in our project, this publication would not have been possible. Chapeau, once again!

Cologne and Berlin, July 2010

Contributors

Maki Aoki-Okabe is a research fellow at the Institute of Developing Economies at the Japan External Trade Organization. She is the author of several papers on regional integration in East Asia, focusing especially on Japan and Thailand. As a visiting research fellow in Thammasat University in Thailand from 2007 to 2009, she conducted research on Thailand's regional cooperation policy in the post–cold war era, which is her PhD dissertation topic at the University of Tokyo.

Mark C. Donfried is the director and founder of the Institute for Cultural Diplomacy (ICD). After completing his undergraduate studies in European history and French at Columbia University, he pursued graduate research at the Institut des Études Politiques, where he wrote his thesis on "la diplomatie du jazz." He then worked as an analyst at the Cultural Services of the French Embassy in New York, the Mergers and Acquisitions Department of Credit Suisse First Boston, and the Deutsche Gesellschaft für Auswärtige Politik. In 2001 he founded the ICD, an independent, nonprofit, nongovernmental organization based in New York City. The ICD has since opened a European headquarters in Berlin, where Mark is presently a visiting professor at Humboldt University. His recent research and publications focus on civil society–based cultural diplomacy.

Jennifer Dueck, who earned a D.Phil. in History at the University of Oxford, was awarded the Leigh Douglas Memorial Prize by the British Society for Middle Eastern Studies for her doctoral thesis on culture and politics in French Mandate Syria and Lebanon. Currently a Post-Doctoral Research Fellow at Corpus Christi College, University of Oxford, Dr Dueck has held positions in Middle Eastern history at the University of Cambridge and the London School of Economics.

Her recent book, entitled *The Claims of Culture at Empire's End: Syria and Lebanon under French Rule* (Oxford: OUP/British Academy, 2010) deals with the dynamic power struggles for control over cultural institutions in Syria and Lebanon during the years leading up to decolonization. Her ongoing research focuses on understanding cultural and educational networks in the Middle East, as well as assessing the impact of mission-driven educational programmes in this highly-contested region.

JEAN-FRANÇOIS FAYET is a master-assistant at the University of Geneva (general history), visiting lecturer at the Graduate Institute of International Studies (HEI, Geneva), and researcher at the Swiss National Science Foundation. He is the author of numerous publications on Soviet foreign policy, communism, and anti-communism, including *Karl Radek (1885–1939): biographie politique* (Bern: Lang, 2004); *Archives d'histoire, histoires d'archives* (Lausanne: Antipodes, 2006); *Le totalitarisme en question*, (Paris: L'Harmattan, 2008); *Histoire(s) de l'anticommunisme en Suisse* (Zurich: Chronos, 2008). He also serves on the editorial boards of *The International Newsletter of Communist Studies* and *Twentieth Century Communism.*

ANNIKA FRIEBERG is currently teaching at Colorado State University in Fort Collins. She received her PhD at the University of North Carolina-Chapel Hill, and her dissertation is entitled *The Project of Reconciliation: Journalists and Christian Activists in Polish-German Relations, 1956–1972*. In 2004–2005, she spent a year and a half in Poland and Germany researching her topic with a yearlong scholarship from DAAD, and a residential fellowship at the Institut für Europäische Geschichte in Mainz. She has also published several articles, most recently "Transnational Spaces in National Places: Early Activists in Polish-West German Relations" in *Nationalities Papers,* and is currently working on a book manuscript based on her dissertation.

JESSICA C. E. GIENOW-HECHT is a professor of international history at the University of Cologne. She has been a Heisenberg fellow of the Deutsche Forschungsgemeinschaft at the Goethe-Universität in Frankfurt am Main, as well as a John F. Kennedy fellow at the Center for European Studies and a visiting fellow at the Charles Warren Center for American History, both at Harvard University. She previously taught at the universities of Virginia, Bielefeld, Halle-Wittenberg, Harvard, Frankfurt, and Heidelberg, and at the Hertie School of Governance in Berlin. Her first book, *Transmission Impossible: Ameri-*

can Journalism as Cultural Diplomacy in Postwar Germany, 1945–1955 (Baton Rouge: Louisiana State University Press, 1999), was co-awarded the Stuart Bernath Prize and the Myrna Bernath Prize, both given by the Society for Historians of American Foreign Relations. Her second book, *Sound Diplomacy: Music and Emotions in Transatlantic Relations, 1850–1920,* was published by the University of Chicago Press in 2009 and won the Choice Outstanding Academic Title Award. She is the editor of the book series Explorations in Culture and International History (Berghahn Books).

Yoko Kawamura is an associate professor on the Faculty of Humanities at Seikei University, Tokyo. Her special field of interest is culture in international relations in both theory and practice, and her focus is on finding a historical perspective on the foreign cultural policy of the Federal Republic of Germany. She has co-authored several books on international cultural relations and has also contributed an essay on Japan's international cultural relations to Kurt-Jürgen Maaß's *Kultur und Außenpolitik* (Baden-Baden: Nomos Verlagsgesellschaft 2005). She studied international relations and worked as a research assistant of German studies at the Graduate School of Arts and Sciences, University of Tokyo.

Anikó Macher is preparing her PhD in twentieth-century history under the direction of Professor Pierre Milza at the Institut d'Etudes Politiques de Paris (L'histoire de la diplomatie culturelle franco-hongroise de 1945 au début des années 1970). In 2006–07 she worked in the archives departments of the Council of Europe in Strasbourg and the European Parliament in Luxembourg. She is currently completing studies on Hungarian propaganda in the 1950s and the activities of Eastern and Central European exiles in the early days of the cold war. Her published work includes "Les paradoxes de la politique culturelle étrangère de la Hongrie de 1956 à 1963," in *Les politiques culturelles étrangères des démocraties populaires,* ed. A. Marès (Paris, Institut d'Etudes Slaves, 2007) and "L'histoire de la diplomatie culturelle franco-hongroise de 1945 à 1949, vue de Hongrie," in *La culture dans les relations internationales,* ed. F. Roche (Rome, Editions de l'Ecole Française de Rome, 2003).

Rósa Magnúsdóttir is an assistant professor of Russian history at the University of Aarhus in Denmark. She specializes in Soviet history and is working on a book exploring Soviet-American cultural relations in the post–World War II period.

Yuzo Ota, born in Yokohama, lived in nine different areas of Japan before the age of fifteen. This made him a cosmopolitan of sorts and helped him many years later to portray a cosmopolitan British scholar and a cosmopolitan Japanese psychiatrist with great sympathy in his books *Basil Hall Chamberlain: Portrait of a Japanologist* (Richmond, Surrey, UK: Curzon Press, 1998) and *A Woman with Demons: A Life of Kamiya Mieko (1914–1979)* (Montreal and Kingston: McGill-Queen's University Press, 2006) respectively. After working as a research associate at the University of Tokyo, his alma mater, he moved to Montreal, Canada, in 1974 to work at McGill University. He has taught Japanese history there ever since, except on sabbaticals such as the 2007–08 academic year, spent in Japan as a visiting professor at Waseda University. The eleven books he has published thus far relate mostly to his special interest in individuals, both Japanese and Westerners, who embodied the drama of cultural contact between Japan and the West.

Toichi Makita worked for many years for the Toyota Foundation, a private grant-making foundation, as a program officer for its international program, mainly assessing and following up grants to local scholars in Southeast Asia for research and projects. Later he received his PhD in international relations from the University of Tokyo. Currently he is a professor at J.F. Oberlin University, Ohio. His doctoral dissertation is about the Ford Foundation's overseas development assistance for Burma, India, and Indonesia in the 1950s–1970s. He has also authored several books and articles on local and international American and Japanese philanthropy and NGOs from a historical perspective.

Dr. James R. Vaughan received his PhD from the University of London and is currently a lecturer in International History at Aberystwyth University. He has published several scholarly articles on the subject of propaganda and public diplomacy in the Middle East and is the author of *The Failure of American and British Propaganda in the Arab Middle East, 1945–1957: Unconquerable Minds* (Palgrave, 2005). His current research focuses on the history of Anglo-Israeli relations and the attitudes of British political parties toward Zionism and Middle Eastern politics.

Introduction

SEARCHING FOR A CULTURAL DIPLOMACY

WHAT ARE WE SEARCHING FOR?

Culture, Diplomacy, Agents, and the State

Jessica C. E. Gienow-Hecht

In the past fifteen years, a growing body of studies has investigated the meaning of cultural diplomacy in the twentieth century. While much of this research continues to focus on the United States and the cold war,[1] some historians have begun to look at other "Western" countries, such as Germany.[2] Much of the US-centered research is based on the premise that cultural diplomacy became a key instrument of foreign policy in the nation's effort to contain the Soviet Union. As a result, the term "cultural diplomacy" has assumed a one-dimensional meaning linked to political manipulation and subordination, and it has also been relegated to the backseat of diplomatic interaction.

This book reflects the collective attempt to search for the meaning, inherent strategy, and history of one of the most confusing terms in modern diplomatic history. Our goal is to find a usable definition for cultural diplomacy and, also, establish a teleology for the term beyond the parameters of the cold war. As such, this book is designed for academics, students, public officials, and laymen interested in the field of cultural diplomacy.

The purpose of this introduction, and indeed of this book, is to cast a wider net, searching for the origins of cultural diplomacy—including its informal beginnings prior to World War I—its development as a political tool in the interwar period, its expansion during the cold war, and its global significance since the 1990s. The collection as a whole seeks to complement the existing preponderance of

Notes for this section begin on page 11.

studies dedicated to US information and exchange programs in Europe. "Searching for a Cultural Diplomacy" studies the significance of cultural diplomacy in regions outside of the more commonly cited transatlantic, i.e., European-American circuit. To analyze the general function, meaning, and definition of cultural diplomacy, we have deliberately abstained from a theoretical exploration and chosen a pragmatic approach: how do authors and actors use the term under highly variable circumstances?

The essays in this volume look at instances of cultural diplomacy around the world before and during the cold war. The sections are grouped according to region: the Soviet Union, Eastern Europe, the Middle East, and Asia. Within each region, we have applied a chronological approach in an effort to demonstrate how visions of cultural diplomacy may differ across time and space. Two methodological key themes emerge in all of these essays. First, how do states, regions, and governments organize cultural diplomacy? Which agents are involved in the process? Is it run formally or informally or both? Second, what exactly are nations trying to achieve via cultural diplomacy?

Summaries and Definitions

Following this introduction our volume begins with a short theoretical essay by the editors outlining the most pertinent problems facing both the analysis and the practice of cultural diplomacy today. Surveying the historical research, they identify two approaches in the field—concept and structure—that invariably play into our perceptions and actions in international cultural diplomacy. From this they develop a model of cultural diplomacy for future strategists operating in post-9/11 embassies and NGOs around the world. The editors argue that the more distance there is between the agent of a cultural diplomacy program and a political or economic agenda, the more likely the program is to succeed. Equally important, the more interactive the structure of the cultural diplomacy program is, the more likely it is to be successful. States need to employ a diversity of different vehicles of cultural diplomacy; short-term and long-term strategic goals will then be easier to fulfill, and bilateral and multilateral relations will be strengthened.

The book then proceeds with an update on the research regarding the cultural diplomacy policies of various communist countries during and before the cold war. The first section looks at recent findings pertaining to Soviet cultural diplomacy. An early portrayal of VOKS, the All-Union Society for Cultural Relations with Foreign Countries in the USSR, is at the heart of Jean François Fayet's essay. Created in 1925 in order to sponsor various pro-Soviet cultural groups, i.e., all those organizations maintaining relations with the USSR outside of the direct channels provided by the Communist Party, VOKS conducted activities targeted at intellectuals and the "progressive bourgeoisie." Seemingly a nongovernmental network, VOKS was closely supervised by state and party officials who hoped to create a sympathetic environment outside of the traditional spheres of political communist expansionism and to neutralize the most damaging campaigns against the USSR promoted in these circles. Above all, VOKS's activities aimed at disseminating a positive and controlled image of the USSR abroad, in order to rebuild the Soviet economy and restore the nation's diplomatic credibility.

In the next essay of this section, Rósa Magnúsdóttir retraces how the Soviet Union consolidated its propaganda efforts after World War II. Magnúsdóttir is particularly interested in showing how the state sought to represent itself in the United States and how Soviet authorities found themselves on the defensive side of the cultural cold war. Her essay breaks new ground in that it analyzes Soviet popular perceptions of the United States of America in order to show how a positive myth of America existed in contrast to the Soviet view of modernity and progress. Khrushchev's thaw, the "Spirit of Geneva," and discourses of peaceful coexistence opened up an assortment of problems for the Soviet state as delegates slowly realized the didactic nature of their own propaganda and the fact that their knowledge of America was both superficial and outdated. With increased access to American culture and people, the mission of making Soviet socialism attractive as an alternative to Western lifestyle became impossible to fulfill.

Cultural diplomacy in Eastern Europe forms the core of section two. Anikó Macher studies the forms, rhythms, and internal commitments of Western cultural presence in Hungary between the uprising in 1956 and the year 1963, and examines the end of the supervision of the "Hungarian question" by the UN Security Council. After the uprising in 1956 Hungarian domestic politics was characterized by a conflict between Stalinists and moderates headed by János Kádár, first secretary of the Communist Party. In this context, Western cultural institutions assumed critical importance. Notwithstanding the reestablishment of Soviet-inspired propaganda, Hungary clearly desired to establish cultural contacts with the West. In doing so, the country revealed an autonomous tendency among Warsaw-bloc countries. Hungarians used cultural contacts to continue their prewar contacts with European countries, such as France, whose political affiliation stood in sharp contrast to Hungary's.

Annika Frieberg's look at the Bensberg memorandum reveals a similarly clandestine approach. Drafted in 1966 by Polish and West German Catholics, the memorandum sought to inspire a peaceful dialogue between the two nations. Frieberg concludes that in the absence of an official diplomacy between West Germany and Poland, other societal institutions such as the media and the church gained more important roles in transnational relations. In the correspondences and contacts between the nonstate actors in Polish-German relations who belonged to the Bensberger Circle, it becomes clear how diplomacy and nonstate diplomacy were mediated through networking. The Catholic peace efforts between Poland and West Germany took on state proportions and structures, and contributed to a change of tone in official diplomacy that had long-term consequences for both Polish and German societies.

The Middle East has recently become a focus of the public debate around cultural diplomacy and forms the topic for the third section of this volume. Jennifer Dueck's essay analyzes international diplomatic power struggles arising from the use of cultural diplomacy in the French Mandate territories of Syria and Lebanon from 1936 to 1946. It examines the competition between various European governments and indigenous political leaders for control of cultural enterprises, and compares the ways government officials of different countries used culture to promote a specific diplomatic agenda. During this time, culture was a central, though often overlooked, weapon for influence in this highly contested region. As Dueck is able to show, the mandatory administrator, France, used education, publishing, cinema, community recreation, and the scout movement to entrench its diplomatic position. But these were not unilateral initiatives projecting highly controlled messages from French ruling authorities onto indigenous masses; rather, they depended on the cooperation of a plethora of nongovernmental and indigenous participants who had their own independent agendas. In the religiously diverse Levant, where the official French administration only dated back to the end of World War I, competition and negotiation for power over cultural institutions played a surprisingly prominent role in defining political and diplomatic allegiances. Moreover, other nations such as Germany, Italy, and Great Britain were competing for influence in the region. Since all of these nations wished to avoid open political or military conflict, cultural diplomacy assumed an unusually prominent role.

James Vaughan examines the conduct of foreign relations in the Middle East during the postwar decade and the formative years of the cold war, when, as he argues, cultural diplomacy came again to play an increasingly prominent role. Great Power ideological and political rivalries combined with the emergence of new technologies, mass media, and cultural practices to revolutionize the conduct of diplomatic relations in the region. State agencies and private actors from a broad range of countries embarked upon campaigns to mobilize forces in such diverse fields as education and exchange programs, science and technology, the arts, commercial publishing, the radio and cinema industries, and even international sport, hoping to advance their respective national interests. Focusing primarily on the cultural diplomacy programs of the United Kingdom and the United States of America in Israel and the Arab Middle East between 1945 and 1958, Vaughan exposes the irony that, as the turbulent political conditions prevalent in much of the Arab world after 1945 forced Western policymakers to seek 'cultural' alternatives to traditional diplomatic channels, Western failure to ameliorate conditions at the political level made the successful conduct of cultural diplomacy immeasurably more difficult.

Our last section turns to cultural diplomacy in Asia, notably Japan, an area especially dependent on an international stability due to its lack of fossil fuels and other natural resources.[3] Analyzing early forms of informal cultural diplomacy, Yuzo Ota introduces us to Nitobe Inazô (1862–1933), one of the Japanese pioneers in interpreting Japanese culture for the foreign audience. Thanks to their exceptional knowledge of the English language and familiarity with Western culture, members of Nitobe's generation emerged as Japan's major actors in cultural diplomacy for foreigners. However, Nitobe and other Japanese of his generation had a shallow understanding of Japanese culture, and their interpretations for foreign audiences were full of contradictions and ambivalences. They had often internalized Western values to a significant extent, and not infrequently they were ignorant and even contemptuous of many aspects of their own cultural tradition. Still, in the face of foreigners who took it for granted that Japan had been a barbaric country prior to contact with Western civilization, they felt the need to defend Japanese culture as something unique, profound, and spiritual. Japan's emergence as one of the most affluent countries in the world has likely worked to generate a more positive and sophisticated appreciation of its culture as a whole—to counter the view that components of traditional culture, such as Zen and Kabuki theater, are the only authentic aspects of Japanese culture.

Finally, Maki Aoki-Okabe, Yoko Kawamura, and Toichi Makita offer a comparative study of Japanese cultural diplomacy in Asia and German cultural diplomacy in post–World War II Europe. Focusing on cultural diplomacy exercised within a regional framework, they ask why national policymakers engage in regional cultural cooperation. As they show, in Japan and Germany this cultural cooperation began as a means of reintroduction into postwar international society. Burdened by defeat and national division after the end of the war, Germany's cultural policy aimed for both the rehabilitation of national prestige and reconciliation with neighboring nations. While under Allied occupation, the Japanese government favored cultural diplomacy similar to Germany's. But unlike Germany's regional approach, the target countries of Japanese cultural policy throughout the cold war were the US and Southeast Asian nations, rather than immediate neighbors such as South Korea and China, with whom Japan shared a turbulent and traumatic past. Thus Japan's cultural diplomacy developed in a seemingly "distorted" manner, even more so when compared with West Germany, which engaged in cultural relations with France. This "disproportion" reflects the struggle, inherent in Japanese policy making, to redefine their cultural identity within the framework of an international society.

These glances at initiatives and inquiries from around the world do not aim at providing a complete or representative picture of cultural diplomacy. Rather, they are *Streiflichter,* flashlights into the depth and complexity of the topic. They show that the intentions inherent in cultural diplomacy depend very much on the cultural mindsets of the actors involved as well as the immediate organizational and structural circumstances. Cultural diplomacy in a country like Poland, for example, pursued goals completely different from those of cultural diplomacy in a neighboring country such as Hungary. Strategies of cultural diplomacy in one and the same region or era differed greatly according to their respective historical context. During the cold war, for instance, Western countries tended to employ information programs as a device to support their political goals. Individual East European nations, in contrast, did exactly the opposite. While some nations prefer to officially dissociate NGO activities from public diplomacy, others, such as Japan, Germany and Great Britain, have often organized NGOs in order to complement the activities of the state government. The essays in this collection support this argument: they stress how regional determinants influence the making and meaning of cultural diplomacy, and thus attempt to generate a more universal understanding of the term and its inner workings.

Three Schools of Thought

All authors in this volume grapple with definitions of cultural diplomacy along structural and conceptual lines, with Fayet on the one extreme (state control and propaganda) and Yuzo Ota on the other (no state involvement, personal visions). Here is where the nexus between organization and desire becomes most visible. Depending the course of their stories, the more authors perceive state involvement and clear-cut state interest, the more likely they are to link cultural diplomacy to propaganda-like activities. The less visible the state remains, the sooner they are willing to move their definition closer to cultural relations and benevolent long-term strategy. This is all the more surprising since the actions of nongovernmental actors, as the essays by Frieberg and Ota show, are often more radical and controversial than those pursued by state officials, even though both declare to act in the name of their country.

Basically, then, we can distinguish three schools of thought: One set—or school—of authors grapples with the tension between propaganda and diplomacy. To Fayet, cultural diplomacy in the Soviet Union from the 1920s onward took the dimension of cultural propaganda work, organizing tours by Soviet artists, scholars, and exhibitions outside Russia while welcoming foreign journalists and representatives of international humanitarian organizations. Rósa Magnúsdóttir's analysis of Soviet postwar effort likewise addresses cultural diplomacy in a formal manner, but on a par with US cultural diplomacy: while the respective outgrowth after 1945 may have differed, its mechanisms, targets and motivations were mutually interchangeable. James Vaughan's definition of cultural diplomacy is clearly aligned with Rósa Magnúsdóttir's and Fayet's, but the results he presents are far less encouraging. All three authors see the use of culture as "an instrument of state policy"[4] with limited private participation.

Another set of authors accentuates the use of cultural diplomacy as an instrument to work at the exclusion of politics. Jennifer Dueck's essay on French involvement in the Middle East shows that cultural diplomacy extended well beyond the empire and lacked the colonial baggage of the civilizing mission. Anikó Macher's study finds that while officials used the terms "cultural diplomacy" and "propaganda" interchangeably, cultural diplomacy's origins were nonetheless neither propagandistic nor new: instead, it represented a means to establish ties with countries that were politically unpalatable.

A third trend defines cultural diplomacy beyond the realm of the state. Maki Aoki-Okabe, Toichi Makita, and Yoko Kawamura categorize cultural diplomacy into two different types: the promotion abroad of "national culture" and interactive international cultural exchange. As their essay shows, the structure of the cultural diplomacy agency can be extremely heterogeneous. Japanese NGOs participating in cultural diplomacy were actually initiated and primarily funded by the government. As a result, the NGOs' interactive cultural programs were very similar to the official government policy on cultural diplomacy, and one finds close collaboration between the public and private sectors, even though the whole idea of an NGO is that it is free of governmental influence. Frieberg's definition is even more radical: in her essay, cultural diplomacy entails diplomatic activities by nonstate actors who, in the name of a nation, people, or larger ethical question, attempt to accomplish a change in foreign relations. Yuzo Ota takes perhaps the most extreme approach: like Frieberg, he is keenly interested in nongovernmental actors, but he even dismisses the necessity of state activity. To him, cultural diplomacy is any undertaking to promote the culture of a country by people who identify themselves with that country.

Collectively, the authors try to walk a fine line between propaganda and information, between state institutions and nongovernmental organizations. What complicates the definition of cultural diplomacy is the fact that unlike in other areas of diplomacy, the state cannot do much without the support of nongovernmental actors such as artists, curators, teachers, lecturers, and students. The moment these actors enter, the desires, the lines of policy, the targets, and the very definition of state interests become blurred and multiply. What is more, these actors frequently assume a responsibility and an agenda of their own, regardless of the program or organization to which they are assigned. While the degree of state involvement remains negotiable, the criteria of "state interest"—defined in the broadest possible terms and to the extent that informal actors likewise represent the state — remains stable. In itself, cultural diplomacy has no political meaning or leaning, no special advocacy nor any particular constituency. In addition, people previously not associated with state interest or governmental affairs can direct its mechanisms. For all these complications, however, in the end cultural diplomacy is an action and an instrument quite like classical political diplomacy—a tool and a way of interacting with the outside world.

Endnotes

1. Volker R. Berghahn, *America and the Intellectual Cold Wars in Europe: Shepard Stone between Philanthropy, Academy, and Diplomacy* (Princeton: Princeton University Press, 2001); Laura A. Belmonte, *Selling America: Propaganda, National Identity, and the Cold War* (Philadelphia: University of Pennsylvania Press, 2007); Walter Hixson, *Parting the Curtain: Propaganda, Culture and the Cold War, 1945–1961* (New York: St. Martin's Press, 1997), Kenneth Osgood and Brian Etheridge (eds.), *The United States and Public Diplomacy: New Directions in Cultural and International History* (Leiden and Boston: Brill, 2010).
2. Johannes Paulmann, ed., *Auswärtige Repräsentationen: Deutsche Kulturpolitik nach 1945* (Cologne: Böhlau, 2005); Eckard Michels, *Von der Deutschen Akademie zum Goethe-Institut: Sprach- und auswärtige Kulturpolitik, 1923–1960* (Munich: Oldenbourg, 2005); Ulrike Stoll, *Kulturpolitik als Beruf: Dieter Sattler (1906–1968) in München, Bonn und Rom* (Paderborn: Schöningh, 2005).
3. Anny Wong and Kuang-Sheng Liao, *Japan's Cultural Diplomacy and Cultivation of ASEAN Elites* (Hong Kong: Hong Kong Institute of Asia-Pacific Studies, 1991).
4. Jessica C. E. Gienow-Hecht, "On the Divison of Knowledge and the Community of Thought: Culture and International History," in *Culture and International History*, ed. Jessica C. E. Gienow-Hecht and Frank Schumacher (New York: Berghahn Books, 2003), 3–41, here 4.

Bibliography

Belmonte, Laura A. *Selling America: Propaganda, National Identity, and the Cold War.* Philadelphia: University of Pennsylvania Press, 2007.

Berghahn, Volker R. *America and the Intellectual Cold Wars in Europe: Shepard Stone between Philanthropy, Academy, and Diplomacy.* Princeton: Princeton University Press, 2001.

Gienow-Hecht, Jessica C. E. "On the Diversity of Knowledge and the Community of Thought: Culture and International History." In *Culture and International History.* Ed Gienow-Hecht and Frank Schumacher. New York: Berghahn Books, 2003, p. 3–26.

Hixson, Walter. *Parting the Curtain: Propaganda, Culture and the Cold War 1945–1961.* New York: St. Martin's Press, 1997.

Michels, Eckard. *Von der Deutschen Akademie zum Goethe-Institut: Sprach- und auswärtige Kulturpolitik, 1923–1960.* Munich: Oldenbourg, 2005.

Osgood, Kenneth and Etheridge Brian, ed. *The United States and Public Diplomacy: New Directions in Cultural and International History*, Leiden and Boston: Brill, 2010.
Paulmann, Johannes, ed. *Auswärtige Repräsentationen: Deutsche Kulturpolitik nach 1945.* Cologne: Böhlau, 2005.
Stoll, Ulrike. *Kulturpolitik als Beruf: Dieter Sattler (1906–1968) in München, Bonn und Rom.* Padernborn: Schöningh, 2005.
Wong, Anny and Kuang-Sheng Liao. *Japan's Cultural Diplomacy and Cultivation of ASEAN Elites.* Hong Kong: Hong Kong Institute of Asia-Pacific Studies, 1991.

THE MODEL OF CULTURAL DIPLOMACY

Power, Distance, and the Promise of Civil Society

Jessica C. E. Gienow-Hecht and Mark C. Donfried

The State of Research

Cultural diplomacy has become an increasingly perplexing and controversial term, one that is often used interchangeably with "public diplomacy," "cultural exchange," and "propaganda."[1] The confusion arises from the fact that cultural diplomacy is very different from other sorts of diplomatic interactions. It is not government-to-government communication but, even in its strictest sense, communication between governments and foreign people. Cultural diplomacy, according to the 1959 definition of the US State Department, entails "the direct and enduring contact between peoples of different nations" designed to "help create a better climate of international trust and understanding in which official relations can operate."[2] Thus cultural diplomacy is a matter of traditional foreign policy, but only indirectly.

In current historiography, cultural diplomacy often denotes a national policy designed to support the export of representative samples of that nation's culture in order to further the objectives of foreign policy. In the United States, the term has come to be closely associated with the policies of the cold war. In 1960, Frederick Barghoorn defined it as the "manipulation of cultural materials and personnel for propaganda purposes," and a "branch of intergovernmental propaganda."[3] Former cultural diplomat Richard Arndt

Notes for this section begin on page 25.

sharply distinguishes between cultural relations and cultural diplomacy. The former "grow naturally and organically, without government intervention—the transactions of trade and tourism, student flows, communications, book circulation, migration, media access, intermarriage—millions of daily cross-cultural encounters." The latter, in contrast, involves formal diplomats in the service of national governments who employ these exchanges in the support of national interest.[4]

In the Anglo-American world, authors often differentiate between cultural diplomacy and public diplomacy. Public diplomacy, according to documents published by the State Department in 1987, entails "government-sponsored programs intended to inform or influence public opinion in other countries; its chief instruments are publications, motion pictures, cultural exchanges, radio and television."[5] British historian Nick Cull even sees cultural diplomacy as a subset of actions and programs under the general heading of public diplomacy. Cultural diplomacy, he states, represents the attempt "to manage the international environment through making its [that nation's] cultural resources and achievements known overseas and/or facilitating cultural transmission abroad."[6]

One of the central unresolved questions emerging from all of these and many more attempts to define the matter concerns agency. Who is in charge? Whose desire to export and interact qualifies as "state interest"? In other words, is cultural diplomacy really diplomacy at all, and does it have a place in diplomatic history? One can argue, with Manuela Aguilar, that as long as cultural diplomacy constitutes a policy designed to encourage public opinion to influence a foreign government and its attitudes toward the sender country, it belongs in the framework of diplomacy.[7] But what happens if the policy changes, if foreign governments cease to be of critical importance in this policy, and if the exporters are not recruited from the inner circle of a state's foreign office?

While definitions remain shaky, there is, to be sure, no shortage of publications pertaining to the history and function of cultural diplomacy. Indeed, one might argue that the history of cultural diplomacy, particularly in modern times, has already been told: the US Department of State, for example, created a new tool for the conduct of relations with foreign nations in the 1930s when it founded the Division of Cultural Relations and, at the same time, established a program designed to stimulate cultural and educational exchange between the United States and various Latin American countries.[8] In the early stages of the cold war, the US government, along with a host of private organizations, churches, and foundations, became the key propagandist of American values and consumer goods, bringing what Harry Truman labeled "a full and fair picture" of American life to Europe and, eventually, the Third World. Both Soviet and American policymakers realized that to "win the minds of men" in Europe and to convince people of the "right" ideology, they had to appeal more to their cultural identity than to their political identity. Both superpowers deliberately employed psychological warfare and cultural infiltration to weaken the opponent and its client states on the other side of the Iron Curtain.

As a result, between 1945 and 1989–91, cultural productions became the most powerful tools for the promotion of ideological goals and strategies. Educational exchange programs, grants to American-sponsored schools abroad, cooperation with other exchange efforts, special educational travel projects, and the reception and orientation of foreign visitors were just some of the programs devised by the US government. Never before or afterward did governments, hegemonic powers, NGOs, or private individuals invest as much money, energy, and thought in the promotion of the arts, academic exchange, or cultural self-presentation. Nor have Europeans benefited from as many state-subsidized performances, exhibitions, and shows since these decades.

Thanks to the release of countless governmental and nongovernmental records, we have in-depth knowledge of US cultural diplomacy during the cold war. US institutions, information programs, and cultural exchanges created after 1950, such as the United States Information Agency and the Fulbright program, aspired to export American culture, including literature, music, art, and science, abroad while simultaneously stimulating academic exchange. Due to the fact that much of this propaganda war concerned Europe and the division of Germany, Soviet and American policymakers dedicated more time, more activities, and more money to the cultural cold war in Central Europe, notably Germany, than in any other region or continent.[9]

Recent research has given us some insight into the cultural diplomacy of other countries, such as the German Federal Republic and the Soviet Union during the cold war.[10] The resulting research has not done much, however, to revise the US-centered approach or quell uneasiness with the issue of cultural diplomacy.[11] While our knowledge of both Soviet and American propaganda activities has enhanced our understanding of cultural diplomacy—and US cultural diplomacy in particular—during the cold war, it has limited our understanding of the general nature of cultural diplomacy. To put it differently, the US involvement in the cold war, its institutions, and its ideological preconceptions—not to mention its focus on Europe—has influenced everything we know and think about the cultural side of foreign relations. Our perspective and behavior during the cold war significantly shaped our understanding of the term "cultural diplomacy" so that it entails the geopolitical, ideological, and economic objectives of US national interest and security, the actions of government officials and bureaucracies, the instruments they used, notably mass communication technologies, and their ultimate target: the public opinion of millions of people around the world.[12]

But what happens to our understanding of cultural diplomacy when the parameters of time and location change? While it is true, as Kenneth Osgood says, that "US psychological programs had a global reach,"[13] each program, target, mission, or strategy represented just one out of many at a particular point in time. What mechanisms, strategies, messages, and agents do we encounter if we look at a different actor, a different region, or a different period? What elements of our understanding of cultural diplomacy remain in place if there is a change in the sender or the target audience? In short: what is the essence of cultural diplomacy across time and location?

Two Approaches: Concept and Structure

If we consider time and location to be critical variables in the carrying out of cultural policies, then two avenues remain through which to consider the significance of cultural diplomacy: concept and structure. The conceptual approach looks at motivations: what do nations, rulers, governments, and citizens desire to achieve by familiarizing others with their culture? What is the content of their programs? Historically, we can retrace these motivations to ancient times, and their genesis shows how the US's efforts in the twentieth century were in many ways neither unique nor produced by the mechanics of the cold war. Since antiquity, nations, states, and rulers have initiated strategies to sell a positive image abroad or to create a dialogue with other people.[14] The sixteenth century marked one of the heydays of cultural diplomacy. Jesuits such as the Italian Matteo Ricci entered China on a mission to defy Asian xenophobia by sharing knowledge and bringing Western ideas into harmony with Chinese thought.[15] The religious order also formed the informal cultural arm of the French court abroad: all the formal diplomats of

France at Louis XIV's court were Jesuit pupils. Indeed, they were also instrumental in exporting the French language. Less than a century after Ricci's voyage to China, the Sun King began exporting and radiating French works of art and intellect around Europe in the form of books, newsletters and gazettes, and human envoys. The tradition of exporting French universalism continued under Napoleon Bonaparte, who, determined to reinforce French power by exporting and blending French education and culture, established new educational and judicial systems in Italy and Germany.[16]

The structural approach, in turn, addresses the setup of cultural diplomacy. Who are the responsible agents of cultural diplomacy, and how do they correlate with state interest? The historian David Potter has retraced a "private face" in Anglo-French relations as early as the sixteenth century. British and French families established acquaintances, friendships, and extended visits, all of which gave rise to liaisons between leading clans that crossed both national and cultural frontiers. These friendships were not motivated by blood relations but by personal interest: British families would board their children in France to "finish" them, introduce them to society, and familiarize them with French, the emergent international language for diplomats.[17] Here, the government's interest played a role only inasmuch as these children were prepared for state service and state liaisons.

In a parallel development farther south, informal connections assumed a decisive political twist. Spanish ambassadors dispatched to Italian posts, notably Venice, likewise acted as cultural intermediaries and bridges, often serving as contact agents between Spanish and Italian artists such as Titian and Tintoretto. Unlike in the present, the ambassadors' portrayal of cultural imperialists had little to do with the expansion of Spanish life and products to the rest of the world. Quite the contrary, one of their primary functions was to organize the import to Spain of Renaissance artifacts such as books, paintings, and relics. This attitude appalled Italians everywhere: to them, Spanish imperialist nobles (capitalists, in contemporary terminology) stole Italian art in the interest of their state.[18]

These motivations and structures differed profoundly from the twentieth-century model, and the following centuries saw numerous other varieties of cultural diplomacy as well: the British in India and the Middle East, the Germans in Africa, and the French in Indochina all supported/pushed their own culture abroad as a powerful tool to strengthen trade, commerce, and political influence, and to recruit intellectual elites for their own purposes abroad. In many cases, governments encouraged but did not fund the ventures of missionaries, philanthropists, academics, and other private individuals working in educational and cultural policy.

That picture—one of informal structures and heterogeneous motivations—dominated cultural diplomacy well into the twentieth century: prior to World War I, cultural diplomacy remained an informal effort. Nineteenth-century cultural expansionism in Europe involved, above all, a vast array of private and NGO interest groups. There were no centralized bureaucracies, no organizations such as USIS or the Goethe Institute that would have offered themselves as a tool for cultural diplomacy. Most politicians agreed that the presentation of culture abroad should remain confined to individual interest groups and entrepreneurs, and most administrators in the foreign offices in Paris, London, and Berlin were convinced that the active dissemination of culture was important, but none of their business. Their job consisted in monitoring and funding whatever musical production, exhibition, or show they felt might improve their nation's image in the world.

The initial offices and institutions created for the purpose of exporting culture reflected governments' unease with any direct and official involvement in cultural affairs. Many authors have pointed to France as the first nation to develop an official organ of cultural diplomacy in order to improve its image abroad.[19] The Alliance Française, created in 1883, originated in the philosophy that instruction in the French language would inspire other people to develop an affinity for France. The alliance itself, however, was formally a nongovernmental institution.[20] Likewise in Italy, in a collective effort that remained explicitly apolitical, a coalition of laymen and Catholics, monarchists and republicans, conservatives and progressives founded the Dante Alighieri Society in 1889, designed to promote Italian culture and language around the world, especially among the expatriate Italian community. When the United Kingdom entered the circle of cultural diplomats in 1934, its central institution, the British Council, constituted an independent organization funded, however, by the Treasury. Its goal was to "make British life and thought more widely known abroad, to encourage the study of the English language, and to render available abroad current British contributions to literature, science, or the fine arts."[21]

Even in the twentieth century and the cold war, the conceptual and structural approaches allow us to perceive the enormous breadth of motivations and organizations in the field. Unlike the United States, which aimed to correct what it perceived as a false image, many countries in the twentieth century set out to establish an image abroad for the first time. Motivations ranged from prospects of improved economic exports to cultural and political recognition around the world; often, both converged in one and the same country. Canada, for example, established an arm of cultural diplomacy in the early years of the cold war when the Royal Commission on National Development in the Arts, Letters and Sciences published a report in 1951 that called for "the promotion abroad of a knowledge of Canada" and the buildup of "cultural defences" against the "vast and disproportionate amount of material coming from a single alien source." Since European perceptions of Canada (as a subchapter of the United States) worried officials, Canadian cultural diplomacy up to the mid 1970s focused on France, Belgium, West Germany, and Britain.[22]

Other nations have sought to establish friendly liaisons with neighboring countries, with whom they may share economic and political interests but also mutual cultural ignorance. Since the 1970s the Australian government, for example, has sought to avoid the image of the "farthest outpost of Anglo-Saxon civilization" and instead emphasize Australia's distinctiveness and develop friendly ties with Oceanic and Asian nations.[23] Similarly, postcolonial African countries are struggling to project a variety of images that distinguish them from preconceived European and American biases. They celebrate the African contribution to world civilization and, at the same time, seek to stress national cultural peculiarities. For example, Nigeria has moved into the limelight of cultural diplomacy.[24] In 1977, 10,000 visitors attended the celebration "Festac 1977" in Lagos, designed to express the common cultural heritage of Africa and show the continent's contributions to world civilization. This event is often seen as the mental kickoff for Nigerian cultural diplomacy, but it also marks the dilemma of many nations on the continent: like citizens of other African nations, Nigerians worry that non-Africans see them as merely "African"—as underdeveloped and uncivilized. They wish to improve Arab-African relations, as they harbor the feeling that Arabs tend to treat people of West African origin as inferior. In order to correct this politically and economically harmful impression, the country's cultural diplomacy focuses on reminding the world that Nigeria is in Africa but not just African, and thereby distinguishing themselves from their neighbors.[25] Furthermore, much of Nigeria's cultural diplomacy attempts to protect Nigerian cultural artifacts by blocking the large-scale removal and exportation of them that endangers precisely the projection of cultural distinctiveness the country pursues.[26]

Even in crises areas of the cold war, cultural diplomacy took unpredictable turns that refute the vision of cultural diplomacy policy as subordinate to the foreign policy making process. Indeed, cultural diplomacy has occasionally replaced or counteracted formal diplomacy in cases of relations going sour. Beginning in 1949, for example, China developed a forceful program of cultural diplomacy, including a viable exchange program designed to foster the country's standing as a stronghold in the communist world. Chinese delegates partook in international athletic meetings, festivals, musical tournaments, and expositions, while thousands of visitors came to China. Curiously, the targets of Chinese cultural diplomacy often included nations with whom China had hostile diplomatic relations or none at all, such as noncommunist Japan. During the early period of the cold war, Japan had closer cultural relations with China than any other country in the world, with the exception of the Soviet Union. In 1956, 2,000 out of a total of 5,200 visitors to China from 75 different countries came from Japan.[27]

While the conceptual approach to the study of global cultural diplomacy offers numerous deviations from the "American model," the structural analysis yields just as many varieties. Here, the central questions concern the setup and inner organization of cultural diplomacy. Who is in charge? Who pays for it? And how do agents and funds relate to the state? Much of the existing research has portrayed American cultural diplomacy as a state-run affair, assigning a subordinate role to NGOs, foundations, and private individuals. If anything, scholars have criticized the US government and the CIA for manipulating dummy foundations in order to clandestinely channel funds to the most favored target groups. When compared with other nations' endeavors during the same time, this picture changes dramatically.

In a brilliant comparative essay, Freeman M. Tovell has juxtaposed the cultural policies and institutional organizations of several nations. For all the similarities in approach (artistic exchanges, visual arts, an emphasis on radio, television, and film, exchange of persons, scholarships, cultural centers, exhibitions, sports, etc.) Tovell finds significant differences: the French and the Germans continuously emphasize language, the British focus on education, the Russians focus on equal reciprocity, and the Canadians concentrate on exhibiting the diversity of their cultural development. Equally revealing is how these nations organize cultural diplomacy. The French assign their *mission civilisatrice* to the state. Britain keeps cultural diplomacy at arm's length by endowing the independent British Council with this task. The council is technically private but works closely with the government (e.g., the government chooses the countries where the British Council operates). Germany, due to its federal system, employs a mixture of both. It combines a government-run Cultural Affairs Directorate (which can set the policy and allocates the funds) with private agencies such as the DAAD (German Academic Exchange Service), the Institute for International Relations in Stuttgart, and the Goethe Institute, all of which implement and carry out state directives as they see fit; cultural relations have the same status as political and economic relations. Tovell also finds significant differences in the implementation of these programs, the interaction between the private and the public sectors, the relations within the government, and the decision about who, exactly, is in charge of cultural diplomacy.[28]

The consideration of conceptual and structural variables in the performance and organization of cultural diplomacy is, thus, vital to our understanding of the multifarious functions, actions, visions, and interpretations of what exactly cultural diplomacy is supposed to achieve and how it is to accomplish this task.

The Future of Cultural Diplomacy

All authors grappling with the history of global cultural diplomacy eventually perceive the relevance of their topics in the context of contemporary challenges faced by cultural diplomats around the world. The key questions for the reader of this volume and any other dedicated to the function of cultural diplomacy remain the same. What do these historical analyses mean for future endeavors in this field? Who are the best-suited agents of cultural diplomacy, and what methods should they use in the current circumstances around the globe? As we have seen, the "science" of cultural diplomacy describes the exchange of ideas, information, values, systems, traditions, and beliefs in all aspects of our societies—such as art, sports, science, literature, and music—with the intention of fostering mutual understanding. The case studies show that cultural diplomacy was traditionally defined in large part by national governments as a prime example of "soft power," or the ability to persuade through culture, value, and ideas, as opposed to "hard power," which traditionally conquers or coerces through military, political, or economic might. The key differences between the case studies are the agents themselves (state and/or nonstate) and the structures of cultural diplomacy that they use. These two components have remained at the forefront in the debates about cultural diplomacy in the public and private sectors today.

Historically, we can retrace a transition from the centuries of informal "ambassadors" traveling the world up until the nineteenth century (travelers, pioneers, conquerors, mediators, artists, etc.) to the twentieth century, when the global community witnessed the birth of new forms of diplomacy in which not only the identity but also the methods and tools of the ambassadors changed. The structure of official "independent institutions" that are financed by governments and, more often than not, operate in tandem with governmental policies is not uncommon, as exhibited in Britain, France, Italy, Germany, and later Spain, where such an institution's stated mission was to support its own country's image abroad.

The missing link in cultural diplomacy during the twentieth century has been a neutral bridge over which sustained two-way cultural dialogue and exchange can take place. Neutral in this case means a bridge not linked officially to a partisan policy, government, or private sector interest. Though pure and absolute neutrality is impossible, distance from governments and private-sector agendas seems advisable because it appeals to audiences. Governmental agencies—whose existence is grounded in a need to safeguard the rights of the citizens of the country—often find it difficult to "listen" to what other countries of the world have to say, rather than simply "telling" their own story abroad. In many cases, governmental agencies' individual national policy agendas limit them too strictly to sustain bilateral and multilateral relationships of true understanding, both of which are essential for intercultural and international dialogue. Even the representatives of civil society within these nations—NGOs, religious organizations, trade unions, or professional associations—do not seem to be perfectly suited to carry out this task since they also have their own specific missions and goals.

Alongside the development of governmental cultural diplomacy during the twentieth century came a proliferation of civil societies. Made up of a myriad of NGOs, charities, and institutions, many of them are dedicated to doing the very work that governments today are challenged to complete alone. To "succeed" here is to establish a sustainable relationship based on dialogue, understanding and trust between the civil societies of different nations. Where governments alone have been unable to create sustainable relationships of this nature, civil society organizations have proven capable of building and maintaining these relationships. Where state bureaucracy has hindered governmental officials from realizing their well-intended initiatives, civil societies have often had more freedom to pursue their own mission statements, at times idealistic, at others pragmatic. The legitimacy of governments carrying out active cultural diplomacy fluctuates at times when ill-suited individuals exercised control over an otherwise capable government; meanwhile, legitimacy remains with civil society institutions that have slowly and organically grown from the bottom up, rooted naturally and with integrity in the people they are designed to serve.[29] Without campaigning for a purely civil-society approach or a purely governmental approach, it seems clear from the essays presented in this book that cooperative efforts between the two should be recommended for the long-term success of cultural diplomacy.

If this is true, we may well ask what directions state and nonstate actors will take now, and what observations can be made about the current best practices worldwide. Two main theses can be identified. First, the more distance there is between the agent of a cultural diplomacy program and a political or economic agenda, the more likely the program is to succeed. Second, the more interactive (meaning that dialogue and exchange move in both directions between the agent and recipient of the cultural diplomacy program) the structure of the cultural diplomacy program, the more likely it is to be sustainable and therefore successful.

These two theses on the effectiveness of cultural diplomacy programs and the long-term deepening and strengthening of international relations have the potential for immense impact, if applied to current and future cultural diplomacy methodologies. As individual case studies reveal, the closer the programs are linked to governments and/or governmental agendas, the less legitimacy the programs have among their target audiences. In general, citizens of any country tend to dislike messages distributed by foreign governments, and very often people will associate government programs with propaganda. When cultural programs are run by civil societies, they seem independent and less compromised by policy concerns, even if their aims are in fact controversial.

National governments today are becoming aware of the significant restraints of their traditional models for cultural diplomacy. People around the world question the neutrality of their initiatives and their legitimacy. In some cases it is difficult to determine whether these governmental initiatives represent efforts to build dialogue, understanding, and trust, or are rather a means of promoting a national agenda. Take, for example, Germany's current bilateral relationship with Romania. In 2006 the president of Romania, Traian Băsescu, initiated a completely new intensive program of cultural diplomacy in an effort to directly improve his country's image in Germany and therefore throughout Europe, where Romania, as the EU's least affluent member, suffers from a huge image problem. Băsescu's first step was to hire a German private-sector advertising company to assist with a large-scale advertising campaign that attempted to present Romania as a young, dynamic nation with a strong and talented next generation coming to power in every field.[30] His second step was to increase the budget of the Romanian Cultural Institute by immense proportions.

The strategy attempts to send an intensive wave of communication from Romania into Germany in the form of advertising and cultural programs showing off the strengths of Romanian culture and tradition. The expected result is to create a greater awareness of Romania in Germany and to change the way in which people perceive Romanian identity. However, this strategy is shortsighted. The advertising campaign and the strengthened cultural program of the Romanian Cultural Institute, which has only a small number of branches in Germany, may succeed in providing a fresh presentation of Romania to the German public. But they will not change the long-range perceptions of the country in the EU. Romania desires long-term results, based on the methodology that with increased dialogue between not only small or elite groups, but between the civil societies of the two countries, increased understanding will come. The ultimate goal is to build mutual trust, strengthen trade and investment between Germany and Romania, and to enhance tourism as a pillar of Romania's development strategy. In short, timing, strategy and goals are not in tune.

The essence of cultural diplomacy across time and space can be summarized by two observations that may also be taken as recommendations for future cultural diplomacy strategies. First, the success of a cultural diplomacy program hinges in part on the extent to which the agent is separate from a political or economic agenda. Second, an interactive structure increases the likelihood of a cultural diplomacy program's sustainability and therefore success.[31]

There are, of course, risks involved. NGOs do not necessarily act in the interest of the state but have their own fish to fry and are difficult to control. Even though the current enthusiasm for PPPs (Public Private Partnerships) stresses a happy union between civil organizations and the state, often the two may regard each other as adversaries. Furthermore, the history before World War I has much to say about nonstate and often patriotic individuals and organizations who felt that they understood foreign relations much better than diplomats, ambassadors, and foreign officers and did terrible damage to the international dialogue. These risks need to be addressed in the future as well.

Nonetheless, in the post-9/11 world, nations and states realize—perhaps more fully than previously—that a lack of cultural understanding can inspire global conflict to an extent far less controllable than the superpower conflict during the cold war. Even with the best airport security measures and visa regulations imaginable, one can never replace the strength that comes from a sustainable dialogue and understanding between cultures or "civilizations." Cultural diplomacy is an enormous opportunity to avoid or minimize such clashes, albeit an opportunity that has not yet been fully understood or perfectly applied.

There is great potential for governments to work together with civil society and private organizations, companies, and individuals to create joint strategies in partnership with each other. This leads to greater neutrality, better reception by the foreign audiences, and more effective participation by these audiences in the programs and initiatives created. The state should not and cannot disappear from cultural diplomacy programs. Instead, it fills an important role by ensuring that the private agendas of civil society groups work in tandem with the national policy priorities and challenges. By applying a methodology using a diversity of different vehicles of cultural diplomacy, short-term and long-term strategic goals will be easier to fulfill, and bilateral and multilateral relations will be strengthened.

Endnotes

1. Anthony Haigh, *Cultural Diplomacy in Europe* (Strasbourg: Council of Europe, 1974), 21.
2. *Cultural Diplomacy* (International Educational Exchange Service, Bureau of International Cultural Relations, U.S. Department of State, 1959), iv.
3. Frederick Charles Barghoorn, *The Soviet Cultural Offensive: The Role of Cultural Diplomacy in Soviet Foreign Policy* (Westport, CT: Greenwood Press, 1976), 10, 11.
4. Richard Arndt, *The First Resort of Kings: American Cultural Diplomacy in the Twentieth Century* (Washington, D.C.: Potomac Books, 2005), xviii.
5. Cited in Sue Curry Jansen, "Foreign Policy, Public Diplomacy, and Public Relations: Selling America to the World," in *Bring 'em on: Media and Politics in the Iraq War,* ed. Lee Artz and Yahya R. Kamalipour (Lanham, MD: Rowman & Littlefield, 2005), 51–66.

6. Nicholas J. Cull, "Public Diplomacy: Lessons for the Past," unpublished paper (Annenberg School for Communication, University of Southern California, April 2007).
7. Manuela Aguilar, *Cultural Diplomacy and Foreign Policy: German-American Relations, 1955–1968* (New York: Peter Lang, 1996), 10–11.
8. Manuel Espinosa, *Inter-American Beginnings of U.S. Cultural Diplomacy, 1936–1948: Cultural Relations Programs of the U.S. Department of State* (Washington, D.C.: Bureau of Educational and Cultural Affairs, U.S. Department of State, 1976).
9. Intricate numbers and statistics are available for this region. We know, for example, that as early as 1956 the United States had sent some 14,000 people to Germany, while 12,000 Germans had visited the United States on such programs. Countless European and American researchers would visit scientific laboratories on the other side of the Atlantic Ocean for periods ranging from a month to a year. Karl-Heinz Füssl, "Between Elitism and Educational Reform: German-American Exchange Programs, 1945–1970," in *The United States and Germany in the Era of the Cold War, 1945–1990,* vol. 1, ed. Detlef Junker (New York: Cambridge University Press, 2004), 409–416; Michell G. Ash, "Science and Scientific Exchange in the German-American Relationship," ibid., 417–424.
10. David Caute, *The Dancer Defects: The Struggle for Cultural Diplomacy during the Cold War* (Oxford and New York: Oxford University Press, 2003).
11. David Pike, *The Politics of Culture in Soviet-Occupied Germany* (Stanford: Stanford University Press, 1992); Norman Naimark, *The Russians in Germany: A History of the Soviet Zone of Occupation, 1945–1949* (Cambridge, MA: Belknap Press of Harvard University, 1997).
12. For example, bureaucracy: USIA was created in August 1953. Four years later, the agency had ballooned to 12,000 people, 7,500 of whom were non-Americans. Richard L. Walker, "The Developing Role of Cultural Diplomacy in Asia," in *Issues and Conflicts: Studies in Twentieth Century American Diplomacy,* ed. George L. Anderson (Lawrence: University of Kansas Press, 1959), 43–62, here 48.
13. Kenneth Osgood, *Total Cold War: Eisenhower's Secret Propaganda Battle at Home and Abroad* (Lawrence: University of Kansas Press, 2006), 3.
14. Arndt, *First Resort of Kings,* 1–23.
15. Ibid., 7.
16. Ibid., 9–10.
17. David Potter, "The Private Face of Anglo-French Relations in the Sixteenth Century: The Lisles and their French Friends," in *The English Experience in France c. 1450–1558: War, Diplomacy and Cultural Exchange,* ed. David Grummit (London: Ashgate, 2002), 200–222.
18. Michael J. Levin, *Agents of Empire: Spanish Ambassadors in Sixteenth-Century Italy* (Ithaca, NY, and London: Cornell University Press, 2005), 183–99.
19. These efforts accelerated in the interwar period, when France faced international competition with Nazi Germany. The Nazis themselves had developed a highly visible and successful exchange program for students and academics, also soliciting the support of Germans living abroad. Eckard Michels, *Von der Deutschen Akademie zum Goethe-Institut: Sprach- und auswärtige Kulturpolitik, 1923–1960* (Munich: Oldenbourg, 2005).
20. Barghoorn, *Soviet Cultural Offensive,* 3.
21. Barghoorn, *Soviet Cultural Offensive,* 4. Spain has had a long history of informal exchanges. In 1991, Spain joined the European circle of cultural institutes with the Instituto Cervantes. In 2005, along with the Alliance Française, the Società Dante Alighieri, the British Council, the Goethe-Institut, and the Instituto Camões, the Instituto Cervantes was awarded the Prince of Asturias Award for

outstanding achievements in communications and the humanities. Wolfgang Bader and Igancio Olmos, eds., *Die deutsch-spanischen Kulturbeziehungen im europäischen Kontext: Bestandsaufnahme, Probleme, Perspektiven* (Frankfurt am Main: Vervuert, 2004).

22. Since private philanthropists seemed unable to live up to the demands of the job, the Canadian state—already a patron of the arts—carved out a new niche for its activities at home and abroad. At the same time, domestic tensions between francophone Quebec and Ottawa continually challenged the representation of a unified Canadian culture abroad. Cited in Andrew Fenton Cooper, "Canadian Cultural Diplomacy: An Introduction," in *Canadian Culture: International Dimensions,* ed. Andrew Fenton Cooper (Waterloo: Centre of Foreign Policy and Federalism, University of Waterloo/Wilfried Laurier University, 1985), 3–26; quotes p. 6. As the case of Canada shows, regional and domestic competition often inspires individual provinces to establish their own cultural diplomacy, as in the case of Quebec's permanent delegation to Paris and, successively, its establishment of offices in cities the world over. Claude Ryan, "The Origins of Quebec's Cultural Diplomacy," ibid., 59–68.
23. Robert J. Williams, "International Cultural Programs: Canada and Australia Compared," ibid., 83–137.
24. G. O. Olusanya, "Cultural Diplomacy: A Neglected Aspect of Nigeria's Foreign Policy," in *Culture and Decision Making in Nigeria,* ed. Sule Bello (Lagos: National Council for Arts and Culture, 1991), 135–141.
25. S. J. Timothy-Asobele, *Nigerian Cultural Diplomacy in the 20th Century* (Lagos: Promocomms, 2002); E. J. Alagoa, "'Antiquity' and 'Future' as Cultural Perspectives," in *Culture and Decision Making in Nigeria,* ed. Sule Bello (Proceedings of the 1st National Workshop on "National Cultural Parameters in Decision Making for Cultural Executive Promoters and Policy Makers," NIPSS, 1990), 93–102, here 99.
26. Ade Obayemi, "Management of Artifacts and Institutions," in Bello, *Culture and Decision Making in Nigeria,* 90.
27. Herbert Passin, *China's Cultural Diplomacy* (New York: Praeger, 1963), 2–10, 41, 107. In 1956 alone, 5,200 foreign visitors from 75 countries came to China. At the same time, China sent more than 1,300 cultural representatives to some 39 countries. Passin notes that while the Chinese were open to short-term ceremonial and political visits and exchanges, long-term study and research stints in the tradition of Fulbright and the Marshall Fund remained rare. While not recommending against visiting China, Passin concluded it was difficult to deviate or break away from an officially organized tour in order to establish direct contacts with people or experience an environment for which a visitor may have a particular affinity or research interest.
28. Freeman M. Tovell, "A Comparison of Canadian, French, British, and German International Cultural Policies," in Cooper, *Canadian Culture,* 69–82. See also Haigh, *Cultural Diplomacy in Europe,* 63–132.
29. See for example: www.newtraditions.de
30. Scholz & Friends GmbH, Berlin & Hamburg.
31. One of the largest challenges of "selling cultural diplomacy" as a means of strengthening bilateral and multilateral relationships is that it is very difficult to quantify. How can one quantify increased cultural understanding or increased bilateral trust? National opinion polls are one measure, and statistics on the attendance of language courses and cultural events are another, but these measurement tools can provide only a vague signal and are quite imprecise at properly measuring the rate of influence of the cultural diplomacy programs.

Bibliography

Aguilar, Manuela. *Cultural Diplomacy and Foreign Policy: German-American Relations, 1955–1968.* New York: Peter Lang, 1996.

Alagoa, E. J. "'Antiquity' and 'Future' as Cultural Perspectives." In *Culture and Decision Making in Nigeria,* ed. Sule Bello. Proceedings of the 1st National Workshop on "National Cultural Parameters in Decision Making for for Cultural Executive Promoters and Policy Makers," NIPSS, 1990.

Arndt, Richard. *The First Resort of Kings: American Cultural Diplomacy in the Twentieth Century.* Washington, D.C.: Potomac Books, 2005.

Ash, Michell G. "Science and Scientific Exchange in the German-American Relationship." In *The United States and Germany in the Era of the Cold War: 1945–1990,* vol. 1, ed. Detlev Junker. New York: Cambridge University Press, 2004.

Bader, Wolfgang, and Igancio Olmos, eds. *Die deutsch-spanischen Kulturbeziehungen im europäischen Kontext: Bestandsaufnahme, Probleme, Perspektiven.* Frankfurt am Main: Vervuert, 2004.

Barghoorn, Frederick Charles. *The Soviet Cultural Offensive: The Role of Cultural Diplomacy in Soviet Foreign Policy.* Westport, CT: Greenwood Press, 1976.

Caute, David. *The Dancer Defects: The Struggle for Cultural Diplomacy during the Cold War.* Oxford and New York: Oxford University Press, 2003.

Cooper, Andrew Fenton. "Canadian Cultural Diplomacy: An Introduction." In *Canadian Culture: International Dimensions,* ed. Andrew Fenton Cooper. Waterloo: Centre of Foreign Policy and Federalism, University of Waterloo/Wilfried Laurier University, 1985.

Cull, Nicholas J. "Public Diplomacy: Lessons for the Past." Unpublished paper, Annenberg School for Communication, University of Southern California, April 2007.

Cultural Diplomacy. Washington, D.C.: International Educational Exchange Service, Bureau of International Cultural Relations, U.S. Department of State, 1959.

Espinosa, Manuel. *Inter-American Beginnings of U.S. Cultural Diplomacy, 1936–1948: Cultural Relations Programs of the U.S. Department of State.* Washington, D.C.: Bureau of Educational and Cultural Affairs, U.S. Department of State, 1976.

Füssl, Karl-Heinz. "Between Elitism and Educational Reform: German-American Exchange Programs, 1945–1970." In *The United States and Germany in the Era of the Cold War, 1945–1990,* vol. 1, ed. Detlev Junker. New York: Cambridge University Press, 2004.

Haigh, Anthony. *Cultural Diplomacy in Europe.* Strasbourg: Council of Europe, 1974.

Jansen, Sue Curry. "Foreign Policy, Public Diplomacy, and Public Relations: Selling America to the World." In *Bring 'em on: Media and Politics in the*

Iraq War, ed. Lee Artz and Yahya R. Kamalipour. Lanham, MD: Rowman & Littlefield, 2005.

Levin, Michael J. *Agents of Empire: Spanish Ambassadors in Sixteenth-Century Italy.* Ithaca, NY, and London: Cornell University Press, 2005.

Michels, Eckard. *Von der Deutschen Akademie zum Goethe-Institut: Sprach- und auswärtige Kulturpolitik, 1923–1960.* Munich: Oldenbourg, 2005.

Naimark, Norman M. *The Russians in Germany: A History of the Soviet Zone of Occupation, 1945–1949.* Cambridge, MA: Belknap Press of Harvard University, 1997.

Obayemi, Ade. "Management of Artifacts and Institutions." In *Culture and Decision Making in Nigeria,* ed. Sule Bello. Proceedings of the 1st National Workshop on "National Cultural Parameters in Decision Making for Cultural Executive Promoters and Policy Makers," NIPSS, 1990.

Olusanya, G. O. "Cultural Diplomacy: A Neglected Aspect of Nigeria's Foreign Policy." In *Culture and Decision Making in Nigeria,* ed. Sule Bello. Lagos: National Council for Arts and Culture, 1991.

Osgood, Kenneth. *Total Cold War: Eisenhower's Secret Propaganda Battle at Home and Abroad.* Lawrence: University of Kansas Press, 2006.

Passin, Herbert. *China's Cultural Diplomacy.* New York: Praeger, 1963.

Pike, David. *The Politics of Culture in Soviet-Occupied Germany.* Stanford: Stanford University Press, 1992.

Potter, David. "The Private Face of Anglo-French Relations in the Sixteenth Century: The Lisles and their French Friends." In *The English Experience in France c. 1450–1558: War, Diplomacy and Cultural Exchange,* ed. David Grummit. London: Ashgate, 2002.

Ryan, Claude, "The Origins of Quebec's Cultural Diplomacy." In Cooper, *Canadian Culture.*

Timothy-Asobele, S. J. *Nigerian Cultural Diplomacy in the 20th Century.* Lagos: Promocomms, 2002.

Tovell, Freeman M. "A Comparison of Canadian, French, British, and German International Cultural Policies." In Cooper, *Canadian Culture.*

Walker, Richard L. "The Developing Role of Cultural Diplomacy in Asia." In *Issues and Conflicts: Studies in Twentieth Century American Diplomacy,* ed. George L. Anderson. Lawrence: University of Kansas Press, 1959.

Williams, Robert J. "International Cultural Programmes: Canada and Australia Compared." In Cooper, *Canadian Culture.*

Part I

CULTURAL RELATIONS AND THE SOVIET UNION

Chapter 1

VOKS

The Third Dimension of Soviet Foreign Policy

Jean-François Fayet

Beginning in the early 1920s, the Soviet Union adopted classic instruments of foreign policy—diplomatic and consular systems—and founded an international network of political parties, namely the Communist International. In addition, however, an entire network of so-called "cultural" organizations was implemented. The purpose of this network was to attract members of intellectual professions and the progressive bourgeoisie from Western nation-states. Far from arousing revolutionary vocations, as was the role of political propaganda, this cultural diplomacy was aimed at the dissemination of a positive and controlled image of Soviet life. The goal of this mission was to allow the Soviet Union to emerge from its diplomatic isolation. In comparison to other countries, such as the United States, Soviet cultural diplomacy was different. Specifically, it was directed by the state and the party, even though the many associations that participated in this international network officially originated in civil society. In this context, the extremely complex links between cultural exchanges, propaganda, and networks of influence were an essential aspect of Soviet foreign policy.

Apart from its characterization as manipulative propaganda, Soviet cultural diplomacy was best known for its excellent protagonists and its cultural initiatives through avant-garde artists, writers, and scholars. Therefore, many important Western intellectuals, including Theodor Dreiser, G. B. Shaw, Henri Barbusse, Romain Rolland, Albert Marquet, Louis Aragon, Elsa Triolet, Victor Gallancz, and Lion

Notes for this section begin on page 46.

Feuchtwanger, acknowledged and supported these efforts. This diverse network of cultural organizations, which was initially intended to make up for the lack of normal diplomatic relations, gradually became one of the most effective instruments in the history of Soviet foreign policy.

The famous "double-edged politics" analyst E. H. Carr once referred to the All-Union Society for Cultural Relations with Foreign Countries (VOKS) as the "third dimension of Soviet foreign policy." Encompassing everything between "official" diplomacy, embodied in the People's Commissariat of Foreign Affairs (NKID), and the organization of world revolution via the Communist International (Comintern or CI), this third dimension of Soviet foreign policy in fact covered a multitude of Soviet organizations beyond VOKS that were often interwoven, and sometimes even competing, with one another. Even the smallest of Soviet organizations had a foreign affairs department within these "people's commissariats" that consisted of trade unions, sporting organizations, and particularly those policy-making organizations devoted to education and public health. Furthermore, the CI developed a multitude of supplementary organizations classified as "cultural" by the communists and belonging to the W. Münzenberg Galaxy.[1] From an organizational viewpoint, the aim of this new cultural network of institutions, which were supposed to be officially independent from the Communist Parties (CP), was that they were to reach beyond party-line communists to a wider public.

Besides this institutional criterion, it is appropriate to provide a definition to delineate the field of this third dimension of Soviet foreign policy. As one often refers to VOKS, or rather more generally to cultural exchanges with the USSR, one must also consider the term "culture" and the following three factors. Firstly, one must consider the civilization in which the term "culture" is being defined. The expression "Soviet culture" should be taken as broadly inclusive, incorporating even its most ambiguous meaning, since it is in this context (beyond specifically artistic or cultural domains) that the term covers all aspects of what could be called "Soviet civilization"[2] with a positive connotation of progress. This of course ranges from the beginnings of its organizational progress to the development of a national culture, from literacy campaigns to the emancipation of women.

The second factor to consider is the art of propaganda and the agitation it might involve. Here it must be noted at the outset that for Marxists, these two terms did not have the pejorative connotation they later acquired in everyday language. Communists did not question the distinction between propagandist and agitator drawn by Plekhanov in 1891, even if it was formulated in the midst of the debates between Menshevism and Bolshevism.[3] VOKS, in its development stages, used basic propaganda that was intended to be understood as a way of breaking what Lenin called the "conspiracy of silence" by developing a series of specific themes for each targeted audience in an appropriate format. The task was to gradually develop a network, for disseminating the same idea of the Soviet ideal regardless of the agitated reactions of the actual public.

Finally, the third factor that merits consideration is the network of influence. Historians often understand this to be an organized social structure that responds to a targeted and logical agenda—in essence, a national political strategy in foreign affairs. It is evident that in all three of these factors influencing the development of a national "culture," the Soviet Union displayed great ingenuity.

As we have established, the principle, yet not exclusive, instrument of Soviet foreign policy was VOKS. From the beginning, this cultural network intrigued anti-communist organizations and personalities, bringing specific attention to the "*Bolshevism drawing room*," "*intellectual Communism*," and even "*Bolshevist snobbishness*." To be sure, this was nothing new. VOKS was directly connected to one of the main anti-communist organizations between the two world wars, the International Alliance against the Third International, better known in the 1930s under the name International Anti-Communist Alliance (EIA), which was founded by the Genevan lawyer Théodore Aubert in 1924. There was no doubt that

> [t]he Comintern has given orders to its agents abroad to promote the constitution in different countries of Societies for studying the new Russia. The activities of these societies should be led by devoted friends of the Soviets, but must not officially be of a Bolshevik nature. They should attract elements that are more or less neutral within these societies, which will serve as a screen for their real aims. These individuals may be easily manipulated by the real conspirators in the organization.[4]

An item in the December 1926 issue of *The Anti-Communist Journal* stated that VOKS's aim was to bring Western intellectuals into the network under the influence of the Comintern, most likely by incorporating scientific, literary, and artistic spheres into its programs. It was therefore noted that VOKS committee stayed in close contact with the propaganda section of the Moscow Executive and the State Political Directorate (GPU). In essence, the article proclaimed VOKS to be nothing more than an auxiliary propaganda organization. To the extent that this was true, VOKS was thus also a special section of the Cheka, which was responsible for keeping watch over Russian academics.

> This methodical and continuous action, continued the same article, is not without fruit. The Bolshevist spirit is insinuating itself in certain international institutions and in certain university circles which seem, like those of the United States, to be the most resistant. Without being Communist in the strict sense of the word, they allow themselves to be injected with the Communist virus and encourage its propagation.[5]

In 1927, the EIA created a specifically anti-VOKS program in order to "warn the university world." This move confirms that contemporaries well understood the role of VOKS, and more importantly, the central issues in Soviet cultural diplomacy.

Even though researchers rarely gained unimpeded access to the archives during the cold war, several authors have worked on this specific aspect of Soviet foreign policy. These intellectuals include Swiss public law specialist Carl Doka,[6] US political scientist Frederick C. Barghoorn (press agent for the American Ambassador in Moscow from 1943 until 1947),[7] Slavist Wolfgang Kasack,[8] and more recently, German historians Edgar Lersch[9] and Rolf Elias.[10] Among others, Soviet and GDR historians such as M. S. Kuzmin and A. E. Ioffe have analyzed the situation from a purely cultural perspective, ignoring the political and diplomatic issues involved.[11]

As these former Soviet archives are now available to the public, the entire history of this propagandist endeavor, including its dependence on Soviet institutions and its international networks, is no longer top secret. Moscow's strategies for building these networks can be found in collection 5283 of VOKS, held in the State Archives of the Russian Federation (GARF) in Moscow.[12] Access to this collection allows us to understand the reasons behind the emergence of cultural diplomacy in Soviet foreign policy, and the ways it was used as an instrument between the two world wars. When analyzing the records of this internal organization, the impact of the problems associated with the developmental process of VOKS become quite apparent. They were not only complementary to the Soviet culture initiative, but also competitive and very complex.

As stated, the development of this cultural dimension in Soviet foreign policy dates back to 1921, when the communists had just won the civil war and the country lay in ruins. The economy was at its lowest point, the transport systems were in complete disarray, and famine became a national concern. Soviet Russia needed to rebuild its economy and reestablish its diplomatic credibility, so the Soviet government encouraged the creation of hybrid institutions.

These mass organizations (leagues or fronts) were more or less politically neutral. Their task consisted of infiltrating the noncommunist masses and the members of the "petit-bourgeois intelligentsia." An important example of this new type of organization, which was to act as a "transmission belt"[13] between the noncommunist masses and the Soviet government, was the International Workers' Aid (IWA or Mezhrabpom). Founded by W. Münzenberg in Berlin in September of 1921,[14] Mezhrabpom supplemented the international appeal that was originally launched by Gorky to eliminate famine and restore and develop the Soviet economy. Mezhrabpom was the first to use "culture" in a propagandist context. For instance, it distributed informational material, organized tours by Soviet artists and scholars, and arranged conferences attended by foreigners as part of the humanitarian mission in Russia, much like that of Fritjof Nansen, the Norwegian explorer. It also appointed well-known artists and intellectuals to national support committees, recognizing such individuals as Albert Einstein, Georg Grosz, and Käthe Kollwitz. Furthermore, it created its own film studio (*Mezhrabpom-Film*), opened publishing houses, such as the *Neuer Deutscher Verlag,* and published a weekly newspaper, namely the *Arbeiter Illustrierte Zeitung,* with a circulation of 200,000 copies.

After it was created, Mezhrabpom initially appeared to evolve without real long-term prospects. However, the more likely world revolution came to seem as a possible development over the long term, the more effective a mass or nonparty organization became for Soviet leaders while strategizing their foreign policy agenda.[15] On 8 August 1925, the Council of People's Commissars adopted a decree that officially declared Mezhrabpom's national "culture" initiatives. Developing in practice into an increasingly influential political branch, it formed a network of intellectual professionals as its members; this network in turn was named the All-Union Society for Cultural Relations with Foreign Countries (VOKS).

VOKS also began as an extension of the office of the OBI (the Joint Information Bureau), a subdepartment of the Commission on Foreign Aid to Russia that was attached to the Central Executive Committee (TsIK). Founded in September of 1923 to coordinate information relating to foreign relief for Russia, OBI was then directed by Olga D. Kameneva, first chair of VOKS, and a number of other collaborators, including R. S. Weller. The information distributed by the OBI was indicative of a new dimension of policy: cultural propaganda. In line with Mezhrabpom practices, the OBI organized tours by artists and scholars, and curated Soviet exhibitions outside of

Russia.[16] It also welcomed many foreign journalists and representatives of international humanitarian organizations to Russia. In fact, as Kameneva wrote in a report in 1924, it kept them from being "plucked like pigeons."[17]

The OBI's "humanitarian" diplomacy from 1921 to 1924 and the "cultural" diplomacy of VOKS in subsequent years were a communicative, complex network. In numerous countries (e.g., the United States, England, and Switzerland), the first representatives of VOKS were in fact the former representatives of the OBI. Before officially introducing themselves as OBI representatives, they often arrived in countries as representatives of the Soviet Red Cross, the first, and perhaps for many years the only, Soviet institution able to work officially in countries that did not recognize Soviet Russia.[18] The first Soviet exhibitions to take place outside of Russia were dedicated to child protection. Organized under the auspices of the Soviet Red Cross, they included numerous references to the "new Soviet culture," such as its free health care, legalization of abortion, sanatoriums, and company creches.

Unlike the Mezhrabpom, which constituted its proletarian counterpart, the OBI acted mainly in nonproletarian circles. Typically, VOKS recruited members from the liberal professions and the progressive bourgeoisie in order to "penetrate the circles and institutions that remained outside the working area of the Comintern and the NKID."[19] The aim of VOKS consisted in "helping foreign countries to get to know Soviet culture and informing the USSR of the main foreign cultural events." Initially, VOKS made an effort to renew connections with cultural institutions—museums, scientific journals, academies, learned societies—that had been broken by seven years of war. In spite of its diplomatic isolation, Soviet Russia managed contacts with many international organizations, such as the League of Nations Institute of Intellectual Cooperation, the Epidemical Commission of the League, the International Labor Organization (ILO), the International Relief Union for Children, the International Education Office, the International Women's League, and countless international student associations.

However, an internal report from its chair in 1931 revealed that VOKS also had other ambitions:

> While, in its political aims and objectives, our work is not distinguished in any way from that of the Comintern and the Profintern, it is considerably more complex in form ... Without giving itself illusions on the long-term prospects, or on the political soundness of the fragile and unstable classes that are the members of the petit-bourgeois intel-

> ligentsia, the task of VOKS is to neutralize the most harmful campaigns against us in these masses, through good propaganda about the Soviet socialist fabric.[20]

This work was part of the broader aim of the preparation and dissemination of a positive and controlled image of the USSR abroad, in order to help the country reestablish its diplomatic credibility and rebuild its economy. According to O. D. Kameneva, this "cultural" policy did not, however, possess anything typically Soviet. As she stated explicitly to the Alliance Française:

> In all bourgeois States, a lot of importance is given to this type of work. One can judge this by the fact that these States spend a lot of money on cultural propaganda and rapprochement. Even in small States, such as Czechoslovakia, for example, within the Ministry of Foreign Affairs there is an informal bureau for foreigners, for editing newspapers in foreign languages and travel guides. Thanks to excursion facilities, the exchange of students and professors has undergone a lot of development abroad. Through this, the bourgeoisie is not only aiming to reestablish relations that were broken down by the war, but also to give off a pacifist smokescreen likely to prevent other wars in the future. This situation appears clearly in the programs and lectures of international organizations such as the League of Nations and the Institute of Intellectual Cooperation ... It is interesting, however, to note that, rather than pacifist chitter-chatter, the efforts at cultural rapprochement from countries such as England and France are always oriented towards a perspective of political (and military) alliance, of vassals to the dominant powers and to each other, as is revealed by the example of relations between France-Czechoslovakia-Poland-Rumania.[21]

Certainly, cultural relations played a major role in political and military relations between the Soviet Union and allied countries.

The dual ambition of VOKS—to promote cultural and political propaganda—also appeared in the organizational skills of its personnel, which reflected both a cultural façade and, more traditionally, the underlying communist structure. The chairmen and executives of VOKS guaranteed the cultural vocation of the institution, typically by appearing in public and signing all official documents. Those responsible for contacting foreigners, such as the presidents and plenipotentiary representatives, had a specific sociological profile in VOKS. Also, the proportion of women members was often higher than in other Soviet institutions, with numerous representatives of the former intelligentsia among them. Their foreign language skills proved very valuable, enabling them to reach a targeted public for VOKS.

Its successive leaders[22] and those responsible for foreign contacts had little in the way of political background. Rather, they were often trained in emigration, held a university degree, and spoke several languages. Before becoming the director of the association until 1929, Olga D. Kameneva, Trotsky's sister and Kamenev's first wife, managed the theater section of the People's Commissariat for Public Education and coordinated several positions in the government. Her successor, Professor Fedor N. Petrov, had been trained in the diplomatic service of the tsar. The director of the Department of Science in the People's Commissariat for Education of the RSFSR, he also worked as editor-in-chief for the *Great Soviet Encyclopaedia.* In 1933 he was replaced by Alexandre Y. Arossiev, a writer and cofounder of the Krug Publishing House with Babel, Gorky, and Pasternak, who had also previously been involved in various diplomatic duties in France, Sweden, and Lithuania. Arossiev was held in high esteem by Western intellectuals like Romain Rolland. During and after World War II, VOKS was first directed by the art critic V. S. Kemenov, then the lawyer A. I. Denissov, and finally Ms. N. V. Popova, who had previously directed the Committee of Anti-Fascist Women.

A key pattern in the placement of VOKS plenipotentiary representatives was evident in their profiles. Their skills corresponded directly with the main characteristics of the country they represented. For example, the representative of VOKS in Switzerland was Dr. S. Y. Bagotsky, who had first arrived as a representative of the Soviet Red Cross and then participated in the organization of the Commissariat of Public Health.[23] This was even reflected in the management positions of VOKS. Examples may include important political figures in Soviet culture, such as Anatole V. Lunacharsky and Andreï S. Bubnov of the People's Commissariat for Education, Nicolas A. Semachko representing the public health sector, and representatives of various scientific and cultural institutions (museums, academies, and universities), state publications, and Soviet photographic and cinematographic trusts. Notably, the important Soviet political figures coordinating VOKS tended to attempt to gain positive international reputations and recognition for their cultural activities. If possible, they wanted to expand their networks even further, making contacts with those who lacked any official link to the CP. Two examples of these reputable people were Romain Rolland, author of *Above the Battle,* and the famous bibliographer N. A. Rubakin. Rubakin's library on the shores of Lake Geneva, which was established in 1906 served as a cultural endorsement of VOKS activities since 1925 along with a few other international organizations, and was strongly associated with what was known as the "spirit of Geneva."[24]

However, like all Soviet institutions VOKS was a "social organism" and was therefore subjected to the control of the state and the party. That the CP funded VOKS and appointed its section and bureau directors explains why they were closely aligned with the communist world. Rather than being only "cultural" diplomats, these party members were often specialists in agitation and propaganda. The State Central Directorate of Censorship (Glavlit) assigned these particular positions.[25]

Ultimately, VOKS collaborated with the NKID. Their representatives outside the USSR acted as intermediaries for journalists from the Soviet Rosta and the Tass press agency, and for the political police (the GPU and the NKVD). The NKVD directed the recruitment of guides, closely observed foreigners, and provided supervision for Soviet cultural figures during their stays abroad to prevent aspiring defectors from leaving the country. Fully dependent on other institutions, VOKS was also a highly structured organization. It was divided into scientific and technical departments in fields such as agriculture, legal science, education, higher education, foreign languages, medicine, public health, and ethnography. VOKS also had a fine arts department for music, theater, cinematography, photography, graphic arts, literature, sculpture, choreography, architecture and museography. The VOKS endowment was continuously accumulating an impressive structural network. Its principal organ was its Secretariat, which coordinated the different departments, sections, and bureaus of VOKS with other Soviet institutions. Above all, the Secretariat communicated with foreign correspondents, individuals, and institutions, including associations for study and cultural relations, and "Friends with the New Russia" societies, which were set up in most countries.[26] Under the Secretariat was the Central Bureau, with divisions like the Bureau for Exchange of Publications, the Press Bureau, the Exhibitions Bureau, and finally, the Bureau for Welcoming Foreigners, to which nonproletarian visitors to the USSR were directed by Soviet authorities.

In 1926 VOKS guided 3, 211 foreign visitors through the country, among them the American mission led by Sherwood Eddy. Visitors were provided with the materials necessary to organize lectures and exhibitions that extolled the success of the new Soviet society since the soldiers had returned to their home countries. The USSR concert management division invited foreign musicians to take part in the musical section of VOKS. Luminaries such as the young and already very famous composer Arthur Honegger and the Italian dramatic actor Sandro Moissi participated in VOKS events. At the same time, the USSR sent artists on tour abroad. The artist V. E. Meyerhold, the filmmaker Eisenstein, academics such as the historian M. N. Pokrovski, and "heroes"—including Professor Samoïlovitch and his apprentice, who saved the members of the Italian force during their polar expedition of the icebreaker *Krassin* in the Great North Exploration, and the aviator Tchouknovsky—took advantage of this VOKS network. Foreign locations of organized VOKS concerts were based upon a region's rapprochement with the Soviet Union and often were dedicated to works by Soviet composers like Shostakovich.

Each bureau was subdivided into 11 regional sections based on linguistic criteria—Anglo-American, Oriental, Latin, Central European, and Slavonic countries. In order to adapt the work to a specific location, cultural features of the society had to be analyzed. This complex organizational structure enabled VOKS to supply other countries with statistics, photos, films, translated articles, exhibition artefacts, and educational and scientific materials. The exchange of these details helped distribute a favorable and controlled image of the building of a new Soviet civilization.[27] In other words, VOKS acted as an intermediary between the Soviet government institutions and the foreign public that feared contact with communist organizations and Soviet foreign policy.

VOKS was quickly confronted with the emergence of supplementary, but also competitive institutions, which clouded its mission. The fundamental turning point is symbolized by the celebrations of the tenth anniversary of the October Revolution in 1927. This event marked the first Friends of the Soviet Union (FSU) Congress, attended by 947 delegates from forty-three countries. Contrary to reports published in the Soviet and communist press, there was nothing spontaneous about this congress. Instead, it was part of a vast plan, proposed by W. Münzenberg in December 1926, for the organization of a "great wave of world affinity with the USSR." Aiming to make maximum use of the tenth anniversary celebrations, the plan required the highest level of Soviet organization in September 1927.[28] The Soviets selected their guests, set the agenda for the first congress, and prepared the draft resolution. At this time, FSU national societies were not yet official since they were only created after the Moscow FSU Congress.[29]

The International Association of Friends of the Soviet Union, founded in May 1928 in Cologne, was little more than an umbrella organization. Many of the participants in the Moscow FSU Congress were correspondents of VOKS. There were also members of rapprochement and study societies as well as other groups, such as Esperantists and Free Thinkers, the Mezhrabpom, sports organizations (Sportintern), and the Department of International Relations in the Soviet Executive Council of Trade Unions. All of these groups were renamed "Friends of the USSR" for the occasion. Even though VOKS was originally not a part of the Friends of the Soviet Union, it played an important role in the preparation of the FSU Congress. It gave the organizational committee a network of contacts, providing addresses, translators for editing brochures, and guides for crossing borders or preparing for excursions and shows. But while the activities of VOKS and the FSU were complementary in the USSR, the latter did not host foreign visitors. For this reason, the two agencies succeeded in working together on common projects. For example, they published the first Soviet travel guide, which was co-edited by VOKS and the *Neuer Deutscher Verlag* by Münzenberg.[30]

However, outside the USSR their relations quickly devolved into conflict. Like VOKS, the FSU aimed to disseminate a favorable image of the USSR. This meant publishing specific journals[31] and establishing contacts between societies from Western countries and the USSR, without officially being an intermediary for the Communist Party. In theory, the target audience for both organizations was relatively distinct. The FSU focused on the nonparty proletarian classes, and VOKS on the societies for study and relations, which by contrast concentrated on the intellectual professions, teachers, students, and nonparty bourgeoisie.

However, in reality this network of mass communication was more complex than anticipated. On 2 November 1928, Erich Baron, chairman of the German Society of Friends of the New Russia, wrote to the chair of VOKS, Olga Kameneva, to discuss relations between VOKS and the FSU.[32] There were in fact two societies in Germany whose names were almost identical—the Gesellschaft der Freude des neuen Russlands (founded in 1923) and the Bund der Freunde der Sowjet Union (1928)—which, he stated, "[led] to a lot of confusion and serious misunderstandings not only in the circles of the society, but also in public opinion." Baron specifically mentioned the reaction of the Berlin police, with whom he had had no problems until this time. But since the beginning stages of the new society, the FSU policemen had harassed him continually, seeking connections between the two societies. Baron was also irritated that the FSU in no way limited its activities to the proletarian classes, and that it had even taken away some of his most prestigious members. Since this ambiguity existed in most countries, Olga Kameneva sent these complaints to the directorate of the CPSU, insisting on "the problems for its clientele, the bourgeois intelligentsia, with the AUS, and the need to deal clearly with the question of the respective activities of the two societies."[33] Yet the problem was never resolved.

In the hope of reducing this confusion, VOKS and the Society of Friends of the New Russia began to disseminate their message in a much more apolitical style than the FSU. They carefully avoided using terms such as "Revolution," "Bolshevik," and, even more so, "Communist," instead concentrating on the more traditional aspects of Russian culture. However, in each country disputes occurred regularly between the Society of Friends of the New Russia and the Friends of the Soviet Union over the distribution of each new film show, and the ambiguity concerned not only the targeted audience but also the product that was to be distributed. An article published in *Pravda* on 16 August 1930 criticized VOKS, which it accused "of not having understood its task, which consists of showing and explaining the new Russia (and not ancient Russia)." The essay further confirmed the permanence of the identity crisis confronted by VOKS. In 1932, the reporter for the Latin sector of VOKS was therefore also able to write about Switzerland in a report that seems equally true for other countries as well. He stated:

> In Switzerland, there is no specific difference between the AUS Society and the society for cultural rapprochement with the USSR, there is permanent confusion in the work of these societies. Some of their members work simultaneously for both societies, which means that the intelligentsia has no specific representation of the different areas of intervention of these two societies.[34]

Meanwhile, the organizational skills of W. Münzenberg worked to win "fellow-travelers" of intellectual professions for the League against Imperialism and Colonial Oppression (1927), the World Anti-War Committee, better known as the Amsterdam-Pleyel Committee (1932), the Association of Revolutionary Writers and Artists, and soon afterwards the Universal Peace Rally (1935). Here, VOKS continued to restrict positions and control the remaining available spaces.

At the same time, VOKS adapted the Department of Tourism in the USSR. Until 1929, VOKS had a quasi-monopoly on noncommunist bourgeois and intellectuals travelling to the USSR. The state-owned stock company therefore created Intourist for tourism. The purpose was to restrict its activities to noncommunist figures who carried a significant amount of prestige, such as the architect Le Corbusier. In spite of the agreement signed between the two institutions,[35] relations between VOKS and Intourist were just like those of VOKS with the FSU—a source of permanent misunderstanding and conflict. In a manner typical of Stalinist Russia, the uniform image that they aimed for became only more defined as these organizations successfully disseminated a positive image of the USSR abroad.

Officially, VOKS was not eliminated from the Soviet foreign policy agenda until 1957. It was then replaced by the Union of Soviet Societies for Friendship and Cultural Exchanges with Foreign Countries, whose foreign correspondents would be known as "France-USSR," "Switzerland-USSR," etc. However, from 1934 up to the signature of the Nazi-Soviet Pact, the intensification of the Stalinist terror and violence affected many VOKS employees' profiles. Finally, the political polarization caused by the Spanish Civil War limited any possibility of cultural work encouraging Soviet reality in the global political plans of the communists.

As the results of VOKS's work demonstrate, a number of factors governed the impact of the cultural propagandist endeavor on a targeted country culture. Was it a question of the artificial transplantation of a foreign doctrine or rather a "culture" onto the social body of another country concerned? Was there already a tradition in the recipient country that would explain why a particular culture might or might not take root? Specific criteria could be identified in considering a favorable host environment. First, a tradition of cultural relations with Russia was symbolized by the teaching of the Russian language in a given country. For example, this was very important in the case of German-Russian relations. Second, the extent to which the Russian revolution was interpreted in light of its own history made a difference. In France, the historical memory of the 1789 revolution encouraged a tolerant attitude toward the new regime originating in the October Revolution, which could not be the case with Great Britain.

A third factor was the nature of diplomatic relations. In countries that refused to recognize the USSR until 1933, such as Switzerland and the United States, the activities of VOKS were used as a screen for other, more political activities. Other countries, such as Germany, maintained official diplomatic relations with the USSR as of the early 1920s and developed bilateral structures specifically dedicated to cultural and technical exchanges. A fourth favorable factor was the existence of cultural forums for workers, such as the Maisons du Peuple, or, in more general terms, "alternative spaces" where Soviet cultural products such as films, concerts, and conferences could be presented. Finally, and not surprisingly, Soviet cultural diplomacy was better received in societies that actually showed an interest in cultural and artistic avant-garde exchange. These different factors enable historians to discuss the shift from the Soviet Union's political history of culture and its manipulation in the service of diplomatic objectives to a social history of culture, its actors, and its acceptance.

Endnotes

1. Babette Gross, *Willi Münzenberg: Eine politische Biographie* (Stuttgart: Deutsche Verlags-Anstalt, 1967); Rolf Surmann, *Die Münzenberg-Legende: Zur Publizistik der revolutionären deutschen Arbeiterbewegung 1921–1933* (Cologne: Prometheus, 1983); E. H. Carr, *The Twilight of the Comintern, 1930–1935* (London: Macmillan, 1983), 385–399; *Willi Münzenberg, un homme contre: actes, colloque international, 26–29 mars, Aix-en-Provence* (Aix-en-Provence: La Bibliothèque, 1993); José Gotovitch and Anne Morelli, eds., *Les solidarités internationales: Histoire et perspectives* (Brussels: Labor Editions, 2003), 17–21; Sean Mc Meekin, *The Red Millionaire: A Political Biography of W. Münzenberg, Moscow's Secret Propaganda Tsar in the West* (New Haven: Yale University Press, 2003).
2. Beatrice and Sidney Webb, *Soviet Communism: A New Civilization?* (London: Longmans, Green and Co., 1935).
3. "The propagandist presents a lot of ideas to one individual or a few individuals. The agitator presents one single idea or a few ideas but to a whole mass of people", V. Plekhanov, *The Work of the Socialists in the Struggle against Famine in Russia* (1891), quoted in *Dictionnaire critique du marxisme,* ed. Georges Labica and Gérard Bensussan, 2nd ed. (Paris: Presses universitaires de France, 1985), 15.
4. "La IIIe Internationale et la VOKS," Offcut from the Permanent Bureau (BP) 1927. EIA Archives. Department of Manuscripts of the Public University Library (BPU), Geneva.
5. "Le bolchevisme contre la science: La VOKS," *Revue Anticommuniste,* 1926, Carton du BP. 1926. Archives EIA. BPU.
6. Carl Doka, *Kulturelle Aussenpolitik* (Zürich: Stiftung Pro Helvetia, Berichthaus, 1956).
7. Frederick C. Barghoorn, *The Soviet Cultural Offensive: The Role of Cultural Diplomacy in Soviet Foreign Policy* (Princeton: Princeton University Press, 1960) and *Soviet Foreign Propaganda* (Princeton: Princeton University Press, 1964).
8. Wolfgang Kasack, "Kulturelle Aussenpolitik," in *Kulturpolitik der Sowjetunion,* ed. Oskar Anweiler and Karl-Heinz Ruffmann (Stuttgart: Kröner, 1973), 345–390.
9. Edgar Lersch, *Die Auswärtige Kulturpolitik der Sowjetunion in ihren Auswirkungen auf Deutschland 1921–1929* (Frankfurt am Main et al.: Peter Lang, 1979).
10. Rolf Elias, *Die Gesellschaft der Freude des neuen Russlands: Mit vollständigem Inhaltsverzeichnis aller Jahrgänge der Zeitschrift «Das Neue Russland», 1923–1932* (Cologne: Pahl-Rugenstein, 1985).
11. Erhard Pachaly, Günter Rosenfeld, and Horst Schützler, "Die kulturellen Beziehungen zwischen Deutschland und der Sowjetunion," in *Die große sozialistische Oktoberrevolution und Deutschland,* vol. 1, ed. Alfred Anderle (Berlin: Dietz, 1967), 443–514.
12. Among recent works produced on these archives are Michael David-Fox, "The Fellow Travelers Revisited: The 'Cultured West' through Soviet Eyes," in *The Journal of Modern History,* no. 75 (June 2003): 300–335; Jean-François Fayet, "La

VOKS: la société pour les échanges culturels entre l'URSS et l'étranger" in *Relations internationales,* nos. 114/115 (2003): 411–423; Rachel Mazuy, *Croire plutôt que voir? Les voyages en Russie soviétique, 1919–1939* (Paris: Odile Jacob, 2002); Ludmila Stern, "The All-Union Society for Cultural Relations with Foreign Countries and French Intellectuals, 1925–1929," *Australian Journal of Politics and History* 45, no.1 (1999): 99–109; Sophie Coeuré, *La Grande lueur à l'Est: Les Français et l'Union soviétique 1917–1939* (Paris: Seuil, 1999).

13. José Gotovitch, "Les organisations de masse," in *Centenaire Jules Humbert-Droz: actes, Colloque sur l'Internationale communiste, La Chaux-de-Fonds, 25–28 septembre 1991* (La Chaux-de-Fonds: Fondation Jules Humbert-Droz, 1992), 95.
14. Gotovitch, "Les organisations de masse," 90.
15. M. Dreyfus, "Willi Münzenberg et les organisations de masse proches du Komintern 1923–1935," in *Willi Münzenberg, un homme contre: actes, colloque international,* 107–118.
16. Edgar Lersch, "Hungerhilfe und Osteuropakunde: Die Freunde des neuen Russlands in Deutschland," in *Deutschland und die Russische Revolution,* ed. Gerd Koenen and Lew Kopelew (Munich: W. Fink, 1998), 617–645.
17. O. D. Kameneva to Moloto, 8.10.1924, F.495/99/95, doc.139, Russian State Archive of Socio-Political History (RGASPI), Moscow.
18. Report from O. D. Kameneva on the OBI, 26.5.1924, F.495/99/95, doc.119. RGASPI.
19. O. D. Kameneva to Molotov. 8.10.1924, F.495/99/95. doc.134. RGASPI.
20. Forecast assessment of VOKS. F. N. Petrov. 4.2.1931. F.495/99/26. doc. 11–20. RGASPI.
21. O. D. Kameneva to Molotov. 8.10.1924, F.495/99/95. doc.132. RGASPI.
22. O. D. Kameneva: 1925–1929, F. N. Petrov: 1929–1932, E. O. Lerner: 1933, A. Y. Arossiev: 1934–1940. V. S. Kemenov: 1941–1948. A. I. Denissov: 1948–1955. V. G. Iakovlev: 1956. N. V. Popova: 1957.
23. Jean-François Fayet and Peter Huber, "La mission Wehrlin en Union soviétique," *Revue internationale de la Croix-Rouge,* no. 85 (March 2003), 95–117.
24. Alfred E. Senn, *Nicholas Rubakin: A Life for Books* (Newtonville, MA: Oriental Research Partners, 1977); Jean-François Fayet, "N. A. Roubakine (1862–1946): un militant 'culturo-révolutionnaire'," *Cahiers d'histoire du mouvement ouvrier,* no. 19 (2003): 71–87.
25. List of founder members of VOKS. F. 5283/1/4. doc.13. GARF.
26. For Germany there was the Gesellschaft der Freunde des neuen Russlands, founded in June 1923; for the United States, the American Society for Cultural Relations with Russia; for Belgium, the Cercle des relations intellectuelles russo-belges; for France, the Nouvelles Amitiés franco-russes, created in March 1924, then the Comité des relations scientifiques avec l'URSS, founded in 1925, and from May 1927 on, the Association des Amis de la Russie nouvelle; for Switzerland, the Société d'Etudes documentaires sur la Russie contemporaine (1924), then the Société culturelle de rapprochement avec l'URSS (1930).
27. The VOKS bulletin was edited in Moscow in Russian, German, French, and English: Bulletin d'information de la Société panunioniste pour les relations culturelles avec l'étranger, hebdomadaire (1924–1925), Bulletin d'information de la Société pour les échanges culturels entre l'URSS et l'étranger (1926–1927), Bulletin d'information. Organe de la Société pour les relations culturelles entre l'URSS et l'étranger, 1927–1929, 52 n°/year, V.O.K.S. Organe de la Société pour les relations culturelles entre l'URSS et l'étranger (1930–33), monthly 1930–31, bimonthly 1932–33, Recueil Illustré du VOKS, 1934–1938, V.O.K.S. (1938–1939).
28. Resolution dated 17.0.1927, F.495/60/98: point 1, RGASPI.

29. Hans Münch, "Der Bund der FSU," *Beiträge zur Geschichte der deutschen Arbeiterbewegung,* no. 31 (1989): 200–206; Rachel Mazuy, *La section française des Amis de l'Union soviétique, 1927–1939,* PhD diss., Université Paris-X Nanterre, 1988.
30. A. Rado, *Guide à travers l'Union soviétique* (Berlin: Neuer Deutscher Verlag, 1929). Officially Münzenberg himself did not have a connection with VOKS, but some of the employees of the NDV collaborated with VOKS.
31. At the international level, the first issue of the Information Bulletin from the International Committee of the AUS Federation, edited in Berlin by Otto Kühne, did not appear until July 1929. Thereafter, like VOKS, the International Association of the AUS published a bulletin in several languages, *Vérité sur l'Union soviétique,* which in 1932 became *Des faits sur l'URSS.* Several national sections of the AUS edited their own journals: *L'Appel des Soviets* (which in 1933 became *Russie d'aujourd'hui*), *Russian Today, Freund der Sowjets* (later *Der Drohende Krieg*).
32. F.495/99/26. doc.138–141. RGASPI.
33. Quoted by Sophie Coeuré, *La Grande lueur à l'Est: Les Français et l'Union soviétique 1917–1939.* (Paris: Seuil, 1999), 144.
34. Latin sector reporter. F 5283/2/7198. doc. 9. GARF.
35. Agreement between VOKS and Intourist. 1931. F. 5283/1/16. doc.1–2. GARF.

Bibliography

Barghoorn, Frederick C. *Soviet Foreign Propaganda.* Princeton: Princeton University Press, 1964.

———. *The Soviet Cultural Offensive: The Role of Cultural Diplomacy in Soviet Foreign Policy.* Princeton: Princeton University Press, 1960.

Carr, E. H. *The Twilight of the Comintern, 1930–1935.* London: Macmillan, 1983.

Coeuré, Sophie. *La Grande lueur à l'Est: Les Français et l'Union soviétique 1917–1939.* Paris: Seuil, 1999.

David-Fox, Michael. "The Fellow Travelers Revisited: The 'Cultured West' through Soviet Eyes." *The Journal of Modern History,* no. 75 (June 2003): 300–335.

Doka, Carl. *Kulturelle Aussenpolitik.* Zürich: Stiftung Pro Helvetia, Berichthaus, 1956.

Elias, Rolf. *Die Gesellschaft der Freude des neuen Russlands: Mit vollständigem Inhaltsverzeichnis aller Jahrgänge der Zeitschrift «Das Neue Russland» 1923–1932.* Cologne: Pahl-Rugenstein, 1985.

Fayet, Jean-François. "La VOKS: la société pour les échanges culturels entre l'URSS et l'étranger." *Relations Internationales,* nos.114/115 (2003): 411–423.

———. "N. A. Roubakine (1862–1946): un militant 'culturo-révolutionnaire.'" *Cahiers d'histoire du mouvement ouvrier,* no. 19 (2003): 71–87.

Fayet, Jean-François, and Peter Huber. "La mission Wehrlin en Union soviétique." *Revue internationale de la Croix-Rouge,* no. 85 (March 2003): 95–117.

Gotovitch, José, and Anne Morelli, eds. *Les solidarités internationales: Histoire et perspectives.* Brussels: Labor Editions, 2003.

Gotovitch, José. "Les organisations de masse," in *Centenaire Jules Humbert-Droz: actes, Colloque sur l'Internationale communiste, La Chaux-de-Fonds, 25–28 septembre 1991.* La Chaux-de-Fonds: Fondation Jules Humbert-Droz, 1992.

Gross, Babette. *Willi Münzenberg: Eine politische Biographie.* Stuttgart: Deutsche Verlags-Anstalt, 1967.

Kasack, Wolfgang. "Kulturelle Aussenpolitik." In *Kulturpolitik der Sowjetunion,* ed. Oskar Anweiler and Karl-Heinz Ruffmann. Stuttgart: Kröner, 1973.

Labica, Georges, and Gérard Bensussan, eds. *Dictionnaire critique du marxisme.* 2nd ed. Paris: Presses universitaires de France, 1985.

Lersch, Edgar. "Hungerhilfe und Osteuropakunde: Die Freunde des neuen Russlands in Deutschland." In *Deutschland und die russische Revolution,* ed. Gerd Koenen and Lew Kopelew. Munich: W. Fink, 1998.

———. *Die auswärtige Kulturpolitik der Sowjetunion in ihren Auswirkungen auf Deutschland 1921–1929.* Frankfurt am Main et al.: Peter Lang, 1979.

Mazuy, Rachel. *Croire plutôt que voir? Les voyages en Russie soviétique, 1919–1939.* Paris: Odile Jacob, 2002.

———. *La section française des Amis de l'Union soviétique (1927–1939)* PhD dissertation, Université Paris-X Nanterre, 1988.

McMeekin, Sean. *The Red Millionaire: A Political Biography of W. Münzenberg, Moscow's Secret Propaganda Tsar in the West.* New Haven: Yale University Press, 2003.

Münch, Hans. "Der Bund der FSU." *Beiträge zur Geschichte der deutschen Arbeiterbewegung,* no. 31 (1989): 200–206.

Pachaly, Erhard, Günter Rosenfeld, and Horst Schützler. "Die kulturellen Beziehungen zwischen Deutschland und der Sowjetunion." In *Die große sozialistische Oktoberrevolution und Deutschland,* vol. 1, ed. Alfred Anderle. Berlin: Dietz, 1967.

Rado, A. *Guide à travers l'Union soviétique.* Berlin: Neuer Deutscher Verlag, 1929.

Senn, Alfred E. *Nicholas Rubakin: A Life for Books.* Newtonville, MA: Oriental Research Partners, 1977.

Stern, Ludmila. "The All-Union Society for Cultural Relations with Foreign Countries and French Intellectuals, 1925–1929." *Australian Journal of Politics and History* 45, no. 1 (1999): 99–109.

Surmann, Rolf. *Die Münzenberg-Legende: Zur Publizistik der revolutionären deutschen Arbeiterbewegung 1921–1933.* Cologne: Prometheus, 1983.

Webb, Beatrice, and Sidney Webb. *Soviet Communism: A New Civilization?* London: Longmans, Green and Co., 1935.

Willi Münzenberg, un homme contre: actes, colloque international, 26–29 mars, Aix-en Provence / organisé par la Bibliothèque Méanes, l'Institut de l'image, Aix-en-Provence. Aix-en-Provence: La Bibliothèque, 1993.

Chapter 2

Mission Impossible?

Selling Soviet Socialism to Americans, 1955–1958

Rósa Magnúsdóttir

In 1955, two years after Stalin's death, the Soviet All-Union Society for Cultural Relations with Foreign Countries (VOKS) stated that the year had "marked the revival of Soviet-American cultural exchanges."[1] Indeed, 1955 saw several mutual exchanges of delegations and a growing number of American tourists in the Soviet Union—who "in many cases were useful in spreading true information about our country in the United States." The Soviet side was pleased to note the "steadily rising interest of American society in the life and culture of the Soviet people" and mainly credited this growing interest to the recent success of Soviet cultural organizations and their work with individual American citizens.[2] This process of "revival" led to the slow realization that conventional Soviet propaganda strategies, which in the postwar period relied much on anti-Americanism, were not working in the United States. In the American context, the Soviet state thus had to rely less on propaganda and more on cultural diplomacy. The process of reviving and rethinking Soviet cultural relations with Americans is the topic of this essay.

The high point in Soviet-American cultural relations was the signing of an official cultural agreement between the two governments in January 1958. However, the process of rethinking previous Soviet propaganda strategies continued well beyond that time. This essay highlights some of the challenges the Soviet cultural delegates faced in the United States. The difficulties they encountered show how the

---

Notes for this section begin on page 68.

Soviet Union, often labeled "the propaganda state," was losing the Soviet-American propaganda war as early as the mid 1950s. Soviet propaganda efforts in the United States present a case that is both problematic and enlightening: problematic because anti-communist propaganda in the United States made it extremely difficult for a Soviet information campaign to function on American soil, and enlightening because Soviet experiences in America proved educational for Soviet agitators, who in the 1950s adapted their propaganda strategy to an approach resembling that of traditional cultural diplomacy.

Although the differentiation between propaganda and cultural diplomacy can be ambiguous, in the case of the Soviet Union it is an important distinction to consider. In the United States, governmental control of cultural and information diplomacy was openly debated before and during World War II.[3] However, the Soviet Union tried to disguise its informational and propaganda campaigns as spontaneous movements organized by the public itself. Since the 1920s and 1930s, the Soviet propaganda machine had relied on these so-called front organizations.[4] Their efforts were dictated by the Agitprop Commission of the Communist Party of the Soviet Union (CPSU) and then implemented by several state organizations masked as public ones that not only reported to, but were also controlled by the CPSU.[5] Most well known, perhaps, was the Communist International or Comintern, a supposedly independent organization which organized like-minded political parties and groups around the world. While some changes were notable during and after World War II, such as the dissolving of Comintern in 1943, it was only in the 1950s that the Soviet state actually realized that the front organizations had become an obsolete propaganda strategy.

Therefore, the use of the term "propaganda" in the Soviet context applies to the preferred way of spreading the socialist mission through mass organizations such as the peace movement or left-wing trade unions.[6] Despite victory in World War II, Soviet authorities had to face the fact that immediately after the war, foreign support for the Soviet project decreased. Only through the revival and rethinking process of the 1950s did Soviet authorities realize that their preferred propaganda methods were no longer working. In the postwar context—especially in the United States, where the Soviet Union's access to front organizations had always been limited—some form of cultural diplomacy became necessary, simply because it was the Soviet state's only means to get the American public's attention. Cultural diplomacy thus was not only a matter of cooperation and equal exchanges for the purpose of improving overall political relations.

Even if it meant exposing Soviet people more to the United States, its values and way of life, and inviting more Americans to the Soviet Union, cultural diplomacy seemed like the only way for the Soviet Union to even attempt to gain followers for the socialist project in the United States.

In examining how the Soviet Union pursued its mission of "telling the truth" about socialism at home and abroad, its propaganda strategy for the United States, a country that started to organize cultural diplomacy activities only during World War II, seems completely out of character. Immediately after the war, the Soviet Union seemed to be winning the propaganda war in Europe, where anti-Americanism was one of its main strategies. However, with the increased appeal of consumerism and the increased weight of American propaganda, Soviet authorities found themselves on the defensive, especially when it came to promoting the Soviet Union to Americans themselves. Emerging from the relative isolation of the immediate postwar years, the Soviet propaganda mission had to adapt to the increasingly aggressive and appealing American propaganda.

Literature analyzing Soviet knowledge about the United States in the 1920s and 1930s, including the fascination with American culture in the Soviet Union during World War II, is easy to find. Unfortunately, little or no attention has been devoted to the issue I raise here: newly available Soviet archival sources show how several Soviet cultural officials concluded that the mission of promoting the Soviet Union and socialism to Americans needed to be completely redesigned and rethought. Not only was the structure of Soviet propaganda failing, but it also became clear that during the relative isolation of the late Stalin years, Soviet officials had not been able to keep up with the rapid social changes in the United States during and immediately after World War II. Thus, America in the 1950s was relatively unknown to them.

The early Khrushchev period allowed for some recognition of the fact that the Soviet strategy of promoting the Soviet socialist state and its values were not working as it should. The front organizations were preaching to the converted and there was not enough appropriate information and materials about the Soviet Union. According to Soviet officials, general demand for Soviet materials increased in the United States as the McCarthy era came to an end. In view of changes in foreign policy under Khrushchev, the CPSU seemed more invested in conducting a cultural diplomacy mission to the United States.

This story of how Soviet propaganda started the process of reinventing itself as a cultural diplomacy mission relies on several sources. For one, it uses the analyses of the developments and problems of Soviet-American relations made by VOKS officials and Soviet embassy officials in the United States. For example, VOKS contributed the 1955 revival of Soviet-American cultural exchanges mainly to several high-profile delegations.[7] A Soviet agricultural delegation visited the United States in midsummer, and in late fall a delegation of journalists traveled "from coast to coast" in the United States. The choice to send an agricultural delegation indicated that the US was once more a model for industrial and agricultural technologies. As for the prominent Moscow journalists selected for the delegation, they were able to familiarize themselves with all aspects of US media, including print, radio, and television, in rural settings as well as urban areas. In addition to presenting developments in their respective professional fields, both delegations were charged with the task of spreading "true information about the Soviet Union" among Americans.[8]

To build on the estimates by VOKS and Soviet embassy officials, the report submitted to the Central Committee by the head of the 1955 Soviet journalistic delegation, Boris Polevoi, is extremely useful. The report was surprisingly critical in its evaluations of Soviet impression management and very revealing of the problems facing the Soviet propaganda campaign. Polevoi, a Soviet writer and journalist, spent World War II on the front, and his writings about the war were well known in the Soviet Union. Not unfamiliar with Americans, Polevoi was present at the famous meeting between Soviet and American soldiers on the Elbe River in Germany in April 1945. After his 1955 journey to the United States, Polevoi also wrote and published a book called *American Diaries*.[9] However, his sixteen-page report about the delegation's experience in the United States is much more interesting. He concluded that the Soviet cultural diplomats realized in the course of this cultural exchange that their knowledge about the United States was no longer current. His viewpoint was that Soviet delegations would have to be better informed about the enemy's social and cultural issues if they were to represent their own country and its politics successfully.[10] It was no longer possible to unilaterally spread Soviet propaganda with the help of friendly circles, least of all in the United States: the time had come for the Soviet people to interact with Americans and exchange information.

The Revival of Soviet-American Cultural Exchanges

The Soviet delegates received strict directives from the Soviet Communist Party on how to present Soviet socialism abroad. Overall, the Soviet authorities were "pleased with the positive treatment" and the media coverage the delegations received in the United States.[11] VOKS representatives attributed the positive treatment of the Soviet guests both to increased interaction with Americans and to improvements in the informational materials about the Soviet Union available to Americans.[12] According to VOKS, the American people met the agricultural delegation with "warmth and hospitality," and the delegates "found great sympathy among 'ordinary Americans' towards the Soviet country and the Soviet people."[13] American networks aired footage about the Soviet journalists' trip through the US. They were recognized and greeted on the streets, where ordinary people "stopped the cars of the Soviet journalists in order to shake their hands and invite them to their homes."[14] Both the Soviet and the American media allotted considerable coverage to the visits, and the tangible optimism on all levels bore witness to the rekindled energy of Soviet-American cultural relations.

While fulfilling their busy agenda of meetings with representatives of various US media and visiting journalism faculties at prestigious universities, the Soviet journalists enjoyed great hospitality everywhere they went. Important people took time to meet with them—owners and editors-in-chief of newspapers and television networks, departmental chairs, university professors. Everyone they met approved of the "renewal and strengthening of cultural relations, the exchange of know-how, mutual contacts and the growing exchange of delegations." The journalists also familiarized themselves with the "cultural treasures of America," visiting museums and art galleries and attending concerts. They devoted time to observing factories, mines, and farms as well, and were happy to report that these visits received much attention in the print media.[15]

But more important than sightseeing and "in line with the directive" was that the delegation strove at all times to "explain the Soviet point of view," to clarify the Soviet way of life and its policies of coexistence and peace.[16] In order to do so, the journalists held press conferences and appeared on radio and television programs to reach a broad audience: "It was typical at these meetings for those present to almost always support the Soviet journalists, even showing sympathy to the Soviet speakers."[17] The delegates had also been ordered to give interviews to "reactionary" media, so they spoke to *U.S. News and World Report,* "which normally took an anti-Soviet stand on foreign issues," and seemed pleased with the results. However, Polevoi did note that not all communications with the media had gone smoothly. *Time* magazine, he wrote, distorted the answers that Soviet delegates gave during a press conference and never published the letter that the journalists sent to contradict the original printed article.[18] Polevoi reported that "in all conversations with Americans, during radio speeches, television broadcasts and during all interviews we gave to the press, in accordance with the directive, we constantly maintained a humble and friendly tone." The journalists were impressed that they were forced to change their positive tone only once, in response to Senator Joseph C. O'Mahoney's (D-Wyoming) "abusive attack on the Soviet press." Answering his criticism of the Soviet press and his "ignorant assessment of the Soviet constitution," the journalists gave him "an angry and sound rebuttal, which the next day, much to our surprise, was objectively noted in the Washington press."[19]

The US State Department planned the itinerary of the delegation, and it was closely followed. The one exception was that their meetings in Chicago were canceled and they went to Salt Lake City instead. Foreseeing a big anti-Soviet demonstration in Chicago, the US government wanted to spare the delegates the embarrassment. Although generally pleased with the schedule, the delegates did complain to their escort from the State Department that no interaction with ordinary Americans was planned. This was clearly an important part of their mandate, because the delegates firmly pressed the issue, with the result that they were allowed to meet with ordinary American families almost every night. They were divided into two, and sometimes into three groups, which, according to Polevoi, gave them "the most valuable material about the life and mood of real America."[20]

Their hosts were from all walks of life: from simple artisans and office workers to millionaires. They met with many editors and publishers, but also insurance agents, dairy farmers, prosperous ranchers, business executives, and representatives of commerce. They were even invited to visit a group of Mormons, who "usually do not accept foreigners." In Hollywood they were feted by "bigwigs and bosses" as well as ordinary artists. Everyone was pleasant, and the Soviet journalists felt that the informal meetings were a source of much learning about Americans and their perception of the Soviet Union. They found that Americans loathed the cold war as much as the Soviet people did, and noted their fear of the Soviet Union and its "cunning intentions."[21] Mutual trust had to be built, and although Polevoi claimed that the people they met with had been instructed by State Department representatives to emphasize this need for greater cultural relations, he, too, seemed to be saying that better "cultural relations" were an important step towards easing tensions between the Soviet Union and the United States.

Overall, the journalists praised these encounters, saying they were much more impressive and informative than meetings with officials, but there was another important factor to consider. As Polevoi wrote:

> We are certain that we were hurt by poor knowledge of American life. The superficial, vulgar illumination of processes going on in the country, and especially our superficial knowledge about the economy prevents the establishment of good relations. We are constantly harping on the dark side of American life, conducted in the same spirit of endlessly repeating one or the other outdated themes.[22]

This must have been a matter of some concern for the Soviet authorities. It did not get any better when a friend of the Soviet Union, African-American singer, actor, and activist, Paul Robeson, offered the delegation the following advice: "In the name of God, do not advocate for the Negroes with the methods of Beecher Stowe ... The Negro Question is more complicated than that."[23] Polevoi wrote that they had accepted Robeson's advice. He also advocated for the need to update Soviet knowledge about the position of African-Americans, and of black people all over the world. His viewpoint was that Soviet cultural delegates should speak on behalf of "all cultured humankind," look beyond the dichotomy of black and white, and take into account the substantial social progress of African-Americans. Polevoi claimed that taking a position with "Negroes" as a whole against white people would only disadvantage the Soviet Union, causing people to reject its cause.[24]

As was expected of them, all of the journalists wrote accounts of their trip for their respective publications. Additionally, Polevoi and Gribachev published books that recounted their experiences. The delegates were instructed that their writings were to adhere strictly to the "spirit of Geneva," focusing only on what had already been achieved in Soviet-American relations. Yet the journalists argued that it was possible to publish enlightening information about American life without "*deviating from our principal ideological position.*"[25] As Polevoi wrote, they wanted to "objectively shed light on the life and on the most interesting achievements of the American people."[26]

The delegates' reflections on their experiences abroad were published in newspapers, weekly journals, and travelogues, which was one of the Soviet authorities' preferred ways of "helping" ordinary people to understand the West. The writings of this delegation are held to have marked a noteworthy change in the presentation of the American image to the Soviet people. At the time, Frederick C. Barghoorn heard from "an American in Moscow" that Vladimir Berezhkov of *Novoe vremia* (*New Times*) claimed that the trip had marked a "rediscovery of America." Barghoorn concluded that in spite of the ideological language and the precautions about American life, the accounts conveyed "the teeming activity, material prosperity, and glittering gadgetry of America"[27] to the Soviet reader. The journalists apparently succeeded in writing acceptable accounts of America because they simultaneously emphasized the Soviet "ideological position" and "shed light" on American life. Polevoi's *American Diaries* presented its readers with a more attractive image of America than any other Soviet account of the postwar era had done,[28] and even the Central Committee was pleased. A 1958 evaluation of "false portrayals of bourgeois realities in contemporary Soviet art and literature" complimented Polevoi and Gribachev[29] on their publications. The report praised their "especially successful" accounts of foreign travel in that they "exposed the reactionary politics ruling in the bourgeois world, revealed the inhumanity of bourgeois society and the difficult position of workers."[30]

Generally, Soviet authorities were torn between reconciling the public to increased relations with the West, and reducing the risk of too much contamination by Western influences. Such concerns became even more pressing as they attempted to control the experiences and reporting of people who had traveled to the United States. Furthermore, the Soviet side had an interest in learning from the Americans on how to successfully conduct propaganda in the United States. In this regard, however, they still had a lot to learn. Polevoi not only pointed out the lack of knowledge about American society, but also offered opinions on how best to proceed with the cultural exchanges without embarrassing Soviet officials. Polevoi stated: "We think that we should completely rethink the system of propaganda about American topics. We should reject in every way possible provocative publications and concentrate in depth on the main points while clearly illuminating the problems of American life."[31]

Unlike Stalin, Khrushchev realized that sending Soviet delegations abroad could prove to be helpful. He relied on Soviet delegates to gather facts, and he, at least sometimes, carefully studied the facts and information they brought back.[32] Since delegation reports were sent to the Central Committee, it is likely that Khrushchev saw many of them. In any case, the advice of Soviet delegates, and sometimes of well-meaning Americans, reached high officials in the Communist Party hierarchy and may have contributed to the rapid change in perceptions of Soviet cultural relations with the West, allowing bilateral cultural agreements to improve foreign relations and increased openness.

Rethinking Soviet Propaganda for Americans

The perceived success of 1955 was considerable and slowly, some kind of "rethinking the system of propaganda about American topics" was taking place in the Soviet Union. In Moscow, VOKS agents reported that the possibilities of creating exchanges in the international community had been "insufficiently taken advantage of." Nevertheless, they noted that things were looking up in Soviet-American cultural relations. The "serious obstacles" presented by the American government, i.e. McCarthyism, were becoming less of an issue, and they sensed an increasing interest in the Soviet Union. They were pleased to report that during the first ten months in 1955, they received 350 letters from Americans looking to correspond with Soviet organizations and individuals, as opposed to only 260 letters in 1954.[33]

The same report applauded United Press Agency reporter Henry Shapiro's recent coverage of the situation in Moscow. Shapiro had just returned to Moscow after a two-year absence and found the Soviet Union completely changed. Before, he had been unable to do much interesting work as Soviet people used to "run away from foreigners." Now, he claimed, the atmosphere was different: he was met with "unusual politeness and friendliness," and people actually sought conversations with him. Also, he observed that people were better dressed and that stores sold better products. This kind of reporting obviously pleased the Soviet authorities, as it was precisely the kind of "propaganda" that they themselves wanted to disseminate. It escaped them, however, that Shapiro's observations emphasized change, thus indicating that only two years earlier, the Soviet people had not felt free to talk or display friendliness to American journalists.[34]

Well-dressed people shopping in well-stocked stores were of course ideal images for propaganda, and according to Elizabeth

Moos at the National Council for American-Soviet Friendship, these images were best conveyed to Americans on film. In her words, "Correct conclusions will be drawn from good pictures, *showing works better than telling for our audiences.*"[35] She continued:

> Documentary films on the daily life of the Soviet people are urgently needed. They should not run more than a half hour each and have a minimum of commentary. In fact, the pictures with music and captions would be most useful, the person showing the film could then make commentary. Such pictures should show family life, an ordinary working day, industry, agriculture, recreation, trade union centers, an average holiday in the park, in the houses of culture; children in school, nursery and kindergarten.

Moos observed that because the documentaries the Soviets sent featured special celebrations and congresses of the Communist Party, they did not create interest in the Soviet way of life.

> While these are beautiful, they are not as effective as educational material because they do not depict ordinary, everyday, life. In considering documentaries for the USA the producer should start from the assumption that the average person in our audience has utterly preconceived ideas that are false about life and work in the Soviet Union, particularly about the family and trade unions. Pictures of the wonderful new projects and great buildings do not affect this false concept. Pictures of children and parents at home, people at the market, people enjoying themselves in the parks, libraries, etc., are helpful.[36]

As we have seen with Paul Robeson and his blunt discussion of the "Negro Question," Elizabeth Moos was not the only American fellow traveler who offered advice on how the Soviet Union should present itself to Americans. In the same vein, Soviet cultural officials asked their American friends for advice on how to best appeal to American audiences.

In 1944, the Soviet Union and the United States started printing and distributing glossy magazines to introduce their countries and societies to one another. The American magazine *Amerika Illustrated* proved to be very popular: too popular according to Soviet authorities, who restricted the availability of the journal in the Soviet Union. This eventually resulted in the State Department's decision to cancel the publication of *Amerika Illustrated* in 1952.[37] In 1956, following the 1955 Geneva summit, the agreement was renewed and both countries resumed publishing these magazines. The Soviet journal *Information Bulletin* was then renamed *USSR*. Never as popular in the United States as *Amerika Illustrated* was in the Soviet Union, the Soviet side struggled with what to publish in *USSR*. The editors decided that general stories about the life of Soviet people as well as shorter pieces about famous Soviet writers, art, and music would interest American readers. They also decided to dedicate an issue of *USSR* to Marshall Georgy Zhukov, the most famous Red Army Commander during World War II, "whose name is popular in the USA," and focus on photographic material.[38] For unknown reasons, these plans were never realized.

On 12 April 1957 the editor of *USSR*, Comrade Mamedov, met with a group of twenty Americans identified as "American readers of *USSR*." They shared their take on the journal, critiqued it, and offered their opinions on how to develop future issues of *USSR*.[39] One of the Americans, Marcus Goldman, a PhD in geology, had visited the Soviet Union in the 1930s and had "a progressive mood." He advised the editor not to write so much about machines and technical issues, stating that a recent article on a mechanic had been both shallow and uninteresting to many Americans. Goldman suggested they publish more stories and poems and go more deeply and more professionally into cultural and scientific issues. He specifically criticized an article about popular Soviet scientific films that he thought was both superficial and poorly illustrated. An African-American mechanic, Clarens Martins, who was especially interested in articles about science and technology, also said that the articles were superficial and did not explain Soviet issues in detail. He admitted that his perception might differ from that of other readers who had less knowledge of technological issues, but he claimed that "more depth" would increase interest in the journal because "middle Americans have an adequate grasp of technology."[40]

Several reviewers also commented on how difficult it was to find the journal in the United States, and remarked that the English translations were poor.[41] These opinions, assembled with the help of the Soviet ambassador in Washington, D.C., were remarkably similar to those of focus groups organized by professional marketing firms in order to evaluate services and test new products or ideas. However, relying on their American friends for support was a common method of Soviet propaganda masters, one that they did not necessarily have to reevaluate, seeing that they were getting honest advice from their fellow-travelers. They might actually have improved their mission, had they fully heeded the advice they received.

The most important part of a delegation's mission was to get Soviet propaganda across to Americans. The journalists in 1955 had not been altogether pleased with their preparation and subsequent lack of success. In fact, they concluded that it was necessary for the

Soviet Union to change its strategy toward Americans and offered a long list of advice explaining their views. On behalf of the delegation, Polevoi related some advice on how to best spread the truth about the Soviet Union in the United States while at the same time representing Khrushchev's social, economic, and political accomplishments to Americans. They all repeatedly emphasized how helpful it was to meet with Americans in their homes and how they genuinely enjoyed these meetings, which were always pleasant because they showed that Americans actually wanted to maintain friendly relations with the Soviet Union.

Polevoi reported that Americans respected the sufferings and achievements of the Soviet Union during World War II. This feeling of empathy, he stated, could be utilized in the Soviet propaganda that emphasized the "reconstruction of mutual understanding and trust between our two nations."[42] He thought that reminding Americans of their wartime alliance would surely be an effective strategy—after all, World War II had ended only ten years earlier. As a veteran of the meeting of Soviet and American soldiers on the Elbe River, there was no doubt that this subject was close to Polevoi's heart.[43] In his *American Diaries,* Polevoi searches for a man named John Smith, whom he had met on the Elbe River in 1945. Then, skipping to ten years later, he claimed to be unable to find "a 'real American'" such as Smith[44] suggesting to the Soviet reader that while the wartime alliance was worthy of remembrance, the average John Doe of 1955 America was uncultured and corrupt compared to the average Soviet man. This is a good example of how Polevoi balanced his view of Americans in his public writing while privately criticizing Soviet abilities to judge American life and behavior. Incidentally, Polevoi's next trip to the United States was in 1958, when he attended a reunion of Soviet-American veterans, the first of its kind to be celebrated in the US.

Polevoi claimed, on behalf of Soviet journalists, "that we have finally learned how to actually propagandize the advancements of Soviet politics and the Soviet way of life in the United States." He continued, "it is not achieving anything to rely only on our very limited and isolated group of friends of the Soviet Union." Such people were already convinced of the superiority of the Soviet way of life, he said.[45] All in all, they had been preaching to the converted. Polevoi illustrated how Western ambassadors, embassy workers, and journalists used every opportunity to give public talks anywhere they could find an audience: at prominent universities, on the radio, and on television. Soviet diplomats and journalists in New York and Washington, D.C., had never taken advantage of these opportunities and had acquired a reputation as "hermits" among foreign journalists in these cities. Yet when Soviet delegates inquired about the roots of this inactivity of their compatriots abroad, they were told that they were not supposed to deviate from the prepared text "from above." The journalists were very concerned to discover that their diplomats and journalists had lost the ability to trust their own judgment. Had they forgotten the work of Soviet diplomats and journalists in the 1930s and during World War II? As good representatives of the Soviet way of life, they had advocated for the establishment of mutual understanding and trust between nations. This was a serious problem to consider: "We really need to do something and we need to do it now, because we have this problem not only in the United States, but also in other capitalist countries, and we have much to lose and [our behavior] indulges anti-Soviet lore."[46]

In his suggestions on behalf of the journalists, Polevoi recounted several facts that might be nourishing stereotypes of the Soviet Union and its people as uncivilized and uncultured. Soviet cultural organizations, for example, were notorious for letting requests from abroad go completely unanswered.[47] Also, no Soviet cities—not even Moscow—had any information available to tourists and visitors. This was in vivid contrast to the US, where even the smallest city had "colorful brochures" loaded with photographs and information about the city and its sights as well as a map with an index of hotels, theaters, museums, and restaurants. Given the growing number of tourists and increasing rate of cultural exchanges to the Soviet Union, this situation needed to be quickly improved; the expenses could be justified because they were in line with the government's aim to introduce Soviet achievements to foreigners.[48]

As stated, the journalists were very impressed with the welcome Americans gave them. All host cities had put together a welcoming committee staffed with local intellectuals or eminent citizens who invited the Soviet guests into their homes and escorted them to the theater or to other cultural events. It was noted that "[s]uch a committee would help create warmer contacts with the guests and would remove the outward appearance of state organizations involved in control that always have a bad effect upon representatives of foreign countries."[49] This advice appears to have been well heeded by the government. At the 1957 World Youth Festival in Moscow, the organizers emphasized the need for local receiving committees in all small cities and towns en route to Moscow.[50] From then on, local welcoming committees arranged by the Soviet Communist Party became a constant factor in all cultural activities involving foreign visitors in the Soviet Union.

Although important, a welcoming committee would still not be the "gateway to the country." That honor went to the Aeroflot airline, the first Soviet experience a foreigner traveling into the Soviet Union would have. The American farmer John Jacobs, "a man favorable to the Soviet Union,"[51] advised the journalistic delegation that "as a 'gateway to the country,' it served no purpose. If the gateway is bad, nothing good can be expected to follow." Of course, Jacobs said, he himself thought the Soviet gateweay not to be very important; he was very satisfied with Soviet achievements in science and technology. It was just for the sake of other people flying to the Soviet Union, that he mentioned that a foreigner stepping onto an Aeroflot carrier in Prague or Helsinki would immediately notice a difference in service. Polevoi also wrote that "our ILY[52] lag behind the airplanes of the capitalist countries, but what we are talking about here is service, which normally is understood as 'servis.'" The Russian word for service clearly did not begin to grasp what the American term entailed.

Polevoi described the flight delays as outrageous and the crew of flight attendants as completely incompetent: "They do not know languages, do not offer newspapers or magazines, and do not pay any attention to the passengers."[53] Furthermore, "breakfast was served without napkins, straight from a box. The food was cold, two days old, had been prepared and brought in from Moscow and was dried up." It got worse; passengers who wanted an extra cup of tea were told by the "misses" (*devushki*) that they would have to pay for the extra sugar and tea themselves because only "*two pieces of sugar per passenger*" were allotted by headquarters.[54] "This is odd," Polevoi wrote, "but it is a fact." Apparently, the issue of service on Aeroflot flights was not new. Noting the increasing numbers of tourists visiting the Soviet Union, Polevoi warned that the lack of service had the potential to cause the Soviet image "serious, even political damage."[55]

As America recovered from the damage inflicted by the Communist witch hunts upon its popular moods and opinions toward "communism" in general, Soviet authorities still had to work against strong anti-Soviet currents to get ordinary Americans interested in their country. The Soviet Union remained deeply concerned about this widespread lack of interest in their country. According to Soviet diplomats, young Americans were convinced that the American style of democracy was superior and repeatedly pointed to the lack of democracy in the Soviet Union, exemplified by, for example, restricted freedom of speech and freedom of the press. As for emphasizing heavy industry at the expense of consumer products, they noted that people in the United States generally thought that Soviet people were "poorly dressed, badly nourished, and live in bad apartments ... They keep saying that unemployed people in the United States live better than workers in the Soviet Union."[56] The American press and population certainly admired the Soviet Union's success in technology and in rebuilding the economy, but used the shortages of consumer goods to belittle their accomplishments: "American satellites may be only the size of an orange and Soviet citizens may have more satellites, but the American people have enough oranges and other fruits in abundance."[57] Khrushchev had used the metaphor of comparing satellites to fruits in order to ridicule American accomplishments in outer space, but as this passage shows, the American press found a way to turn it against him.

In 1958, the general effort of Soviet propaganda in the United States was to be directed at the "exposure of false arguments." However, the means and methods of fighting the American propaganda machine on its home territory were limited. Soviet radio broadcasts were aired only on restricted waves in the United States, and few American listeners tuned in or even received the broadcasts. Instead, the reality was that thirty-nine million television sets in the United States, and countless radio stations, were constantly broadcasting anti-Soviet materials via the "methods of American advertising." Also, Soviet embassy workers judged that repetition was a very effective strategy for getting the anti-Soviet message through to ordinary Americans.[58]

In the summer of 1958, it was reported that the number one book on the *New York Times* bestseller list was John Gunther's *Inside Russia Today,* and second on the list was J. Edgar Hoover's tale of American communists, *Masters of Deceit: The Story of Communism in America and How to Fight It.* Milovan Djilas's *The New Class* was also well advertised, and according to the report, many other "anti-Soviet books" on topics such as the Gulag were given plenty of space in American bookstores.[59] Embassy officials argued that their rebuttals of anti-Soviet books such as *Inside Russia Today* were not printed quickly enough. They also suggested publishing many more books in foreign languages, reasoning that "it would be most effective if we were to publish a book called *Inside America Today,* illuminating all the questions raised by Gunther in his book, but applying them to American realities."[60] Indeed, the American anti-Soviet literature market gave Soviet authorities ideas on how to produce their own anti-American propaganda.

The embassy praised the propaganda efforts of Soviet delegations. However, they recommended that exchanges between delegations could be more effective.[61] Officials urged Soviet artists to accept all invitations to perform in the United States because they knew that these events generally got much attention among the American public. They also speculated that it would be beneficial to include "a Jewish number" in their ensembles, as "many Jews live in America and often they hold influential positions." This, they claimed, would be seen positively in the United States, as American propaganda "often states that anti-Semitism prevails in the USSR."[62]

In spite of the general success in exchanging delegations, the Soviets needed to be better prepared for questions they would encounter in the United States. Apparently, "very often Americans pose provocative questions ... their own propaganda makes fools of them and they do not think in terms outside of this propaganda." As specific examples of sensitive questions that needed to be clarified in advance, the report mentioned the "era of Stalinism," the freedom of expression in the USSR, and the invasion of Hungary in 1956. The journalists noted that "[a]voiding answering such questions leaves a very bad impression and can be used to the advantage of American propaganda."[63] This was always a difficult issue, as Soviet delegates often felt their hosts were rude to ask questions that challenged the nature of the Soviet system. Their ultimate realization that avoiding sensitive topics was damaging to the Soviet image represented an important step forward in communication.

"Correct Conclusions" about the Soviet Union

Soviet delegations and cultural officials slowly realized the difficulty of the mission of selling socialism to Americans. It was evident that Soviet knowledge about the United States, the country and its people, was not only superficial but also often outdated. This, in turn, fed into one of the Soviet state's main fears, namely that Soviet citizens who came in touch with American popular culture and values were easily converted. The Soviet authorities discouraged any infatuation with the West on behalf of Soviet citizens and were slow in realizing that it was difficult for the delegates to balance their information gathering about US industrial supremacy while simultaneously expecting them to criticize the American social system and praise all things Soviet. Officials involved in cultural relations with the United States had to tread a narrow path between learning useful things about American society and searching for negative aspects at the same time. Although their accounts of the United States were heavily influenced by the expectations of the Soviet government, these cultural exchanges often left a long-lasting impression on the Soviet participants.

Attempting to spread Soviet socialism while simultaneously fearing the conversion of the delegates became a major problem for the Soviet leadership. Soviet authorities seemed on the defensive in almost all aspects of the cultural cold war. Poor service and lack of well-trained staff were serious problems, but they were by no means the only worries plaguing government officials. Soviet propaganda in America was out of date, and American visitors repeatedly denounced the poor knowledge that Soviet people had of the United States. Ultimately, Soviet accomplishments at home were not impressive enough to convince skeptical capitalist visitors of the nation's strength and superiority.

The Soviet Communist Party was always determined to "control intellectual life"[64] but found it difficult to balance updating the appearances of Soviet cultural delegations while controlling their experiences. As Soviet visitors realized that their knowledge about the United States was superficial and outdated, they tried to convince the authorities that they needed to prepare their delegates better and modernize the Soviet image. As they had less access to friendly circles abroad, Soviet delegates concluded that the lack of "correct" informational materials, both in the United States and at home, hurt their mission of telling the truth about the Soviet Union. By 1955 it was becoming clear that the Soviet Union lagged behind the West in the quality of its service and the general availability of consumer goods. This was a definite threat to the Soviet image abroad. The Soviet leadership had to adapt to a changing world by rethinking its propaganda strategy, especially in the United States. However, they remained far behind in their foreign policy because the Americans had already long understood that cultural diplomacy was an important factor in their foreign-policy making strategies.

Still, the admission that the Soviet Union lagged behind was an important one. Rallying Soviet people around the future goal of overtaking and surpassing America, as Khrushchev did in 1957, was in line with suggestions from various Soviet participants recounted here about what they could learn from the United States and how to improve the Soviet mission. While the political atmosphere underwent dramatic changes in the mid-1950s, there were certain continuities in the way Soviet authorities perceived their success in representing themselves in the US as well as in the Soviet Union. Throughout the years, the feeling of not reaching enough people became more pressing and lack of means to publicize the mission increased, especially once McCarthyism was no longer an obstacle in the United States. But the struggle to reconcile more exposure to American values with the strict ideological mission of the Soviet state also grew sharper.

The language that Soviet cultural officials and their American sympathizers used in discussing ways of depicting the Soviet Union shows the somewhat naïve belief that, with the correct methods, they would be able to convert Americans to the socialist cause. Soviet cultural officials were willing to help Americans reach "correct conclusions"[65] about the Soviet Union and correct "false ideas" about socialism. They seemed convinced that "telling the truth" about the Soviet Union would surely convert "unprejudiced" people to the Soviet cause. Thus, the Soviet state continued, to little or no avail, their mission of trying to convince Americans of the good in socialism.

Interestingly enough, Soviet delegations, or fact-finding missions, the American focus groups organized by the Soviet Embassy in Washington, D.C., and farmers such as John Jacobs all identified the problem Soviet authorities were facing in terms of managing impressions: they did not know how to package Soviet modernity and progress so that it was appealing and competitive to capitalist, i.e. American audiences. Even the very first Soviet experience a foreigner most likely would have, the Aeroflot flight from Helsinki or Vienna, was embarrassingly inadequate, and Soviet efforts to impress Americans in the 1950s were mostly in vain.

This was an ongoing struggle within all Soviet organizations and government departments, involved in cultural and personal exchange with the United States. The struggle to control the experience and perceptions deriving from increased travel, openness, and flow of information—so that they would not have people recount their experiences in a "spirit of servility"[66]—always went hand in hand with the mission of telling the "truth" about the Soviet Union and its accomplishments. However, lacking in resources, tools, and qualified people, the Soviet state found itself on the defensive in this battle. In these debates, its position was that the "superficial" nature of the exchanges was the major cause of its problems, and that Soviet people needed better training to see behind the façade of what they were being shown in America.

The problem of reconciling the various goals of the Soviet cultural mission was an ever-present one. Polevoi's conclusion, that the Soviet strategy of relying on friendly circles abroad, i.e. front organizations, was bankrupt started to hit home in the mid to late 1950s. Following the moderate success of 1955, Soviet authorities concluded that their cultural policies needed to be updated and modernized. Thus, the organizational structure of Soviet cultural relations within foreign countries was revolutionized between 1957 and 1958. Soviet authorities aimed to modernize the mission of promoting a new image of the Soviet Union, while helping foreigners reach "correct" conclusions about socialism while also controlling the Soviet people's perceptions of the West. As they slowly learned how to apply the more acceptable policy of cultural diplomacy, Soviet authorities adapted their propaganda to increase exchange and cooperation, even if this meant updating and improving their knowledge about the American enemy.

Endnotes

1. Gosudarstvennyi Arkhiv Rossiiskoi Federatsii (hereafter GARF), f. 5283, op. 14, d. 577, l. 169.
2. GARF, f. 5283, op. 14, d. 577, ll. 169–71.
3. Emily S. Rosenberg, *Spreading the American Dream: American Economic and Cultural Expansion, 1890–1945* (New York: Hill and Wang, 1982), 212. The Soviet part has mostly been ignored in the cultural cold war research on propaganda campaigns waged by the Soviet state and Communist Party in the United States, and Soviet reactions to American propaganda in the Soviet Union. See also Amanda Wood Aucoin, *Deconstructing the American Way of Life: Soviet Responses to Cultural Exchange.* PhD diss., University of Arkansas, 2001; David Caute, *The Dancer Defects: The Struggle for Cultural Supremacy During the Cold War* (Oxford and New York: Oxford University Press, 2003); Walter L. Hixson, *Parting the Curtain: Propaganda, Culture, and the Cold War, 1945–1961* (New York: St. Martin's Press, 1997); Robert Francis Byrnes, *Soviet-American Academic Exchanges, 1958–1975* (Bloomington: Indiana University Press, 1976); J. D. Parks, *Culture, Conflict, and Coexistence: American-Soviet Cultural Relations, 1917–1958* (London: McFarland, 1983); Yale Richmond, *Cultural Exchange and the Cold War: Raising the Iron Curtain* (University Park, PA.: Pennsylvania State University Press, 2003); Yale Richmond, *U.S.-Soviet Cultural Exchanges, 1958–1986: Who Wins?* (Boulder, CO: Westview, 1987); Yale Richmond, *Soviet-American Cultural Exchanges: Ripoff or Payoff?* (Washington, D.C.: Kennan Institute for Advanced Russian Studies, 1984).
4. The Soviet Union became known throughout the world for its propaganda techniques, and Soviet methods of mass mobilization have been studied in depth. See Jeffrey Brooks, *Thank you, Comrade Stalin! Soviet Public Culture from Revolution to Cold War* (Princeton: Princeton University Press, 2000); David L. Hoffmann, *Stalinist Values: The Cultural Norms of Soviet Modernity, 1917–1941* (Ithaca, NY: Cornell University Press, 2003); Peter Kenez, *The Birth of the Propaganda*

State: Soviet Methods of Mass Mobilization, 1917–1929 (Cambridge and New York: Cambridge University Press, 1985); Clive Rose, *The Soviet Propaganda Network: A Directory of Organisations serving Soviet Foreign Policy* (London: Pinter, 1988; New York: St. Martin's Press, 1988); Frederick C. Barghoorn, *The Soviet Cultural Offensive: The Role of Cultural Diplomacy in Soviet Foreign Policy* (Princeton: Princeton University Press, 1960).

5. Barghoorn, *The Soviet Cultural Offensive,* 158.
6. Nigel Gould-Davies, "The Logic of Soviet Cultural Diplomacy," *Diplomatic History* 27, no. 2 (2003): 193–214, here 204.
7. GARF, f. 5283, op. 14, d. 577, l. 169.
8. J. D. Parks also notes that the year 1955 was "pivotal" in American-Soviet cultural relations because it saw a growing number of Americans traveling to Moscow. See Parks, *Culture, Conflict, and Coexistence,* 139.
9. Polevoi's book was originally published in 30,000 copies in 1956. In 1957, it was published again in a series for middle school children called "Shkolnaia biblioteka" (School Library). This edition was printed in 50,000 copies.
10. Rossiiskii gosudarstvennyi arkhiv noveishei istorii (RGANI), f. 5, op. 16, d. 734, ll. 131–145. "Otchet o poezdke delegatsii sovetskikh zhurnalistov po SShA." An American journalistic delegation also visited the Soviet Union in February of 1955. See RGANI, f. 5, op. 30, d. 119, ll. 51–54.
11. GARF, f. 5283, op. 14, d. 577, l. 169.
12. GARF, f. 5283, op. 14, d. 577, ll. 169–171.
13. V. Matskevich, *Chto my videli v SShA i Kanade* (Moscow: Gosudarstvennoe izdatel'stvo politicheskoi literatury, 1956), 3. This book was published in 200,000 copies.
14. GARF, f. 5283, op. 14, d. 577, l. 169.
15. RGANI, f. 5, op. 15, d. 734, ll. 131–132.
16. RGANI, f. 5, op. 15, d. 734, l. 132.
17. RGANI, f. 5, op. 15, d. 734, ll. 132–133.
18. RGANI, f. 5, op. 15, d. 734, l. 133.
19. RGANI, f. 5, op. 15, d. 734, l. 137.
20. RGANI. f. 5, op. 15, d. 734, ll. 133–134. Quote l. 134.
21. RGANI, f. 5, op. 15, d. 734, l. 134 and 137.
22. Ibid.
23. RGANI, f. 5, op. 15, d. 734, l. 135.
24. Ibid.
25. RGANI, f. 5, op. 15, d. 734, l. 137. Emphasis in original.
26. Ibid.
27. Barghoorn, *The Soviet Cultural Offensive,* 298–299.
28. Ibid., 298.
29. Nikolai M. Gribachev, *Avgustovskie zvezdy* (Moscow: Sovetskii pisatel', 1958). This is cited in the editor's footnotes to refer to this published document, but I think it is more likely that the original report was referring to Gribachev's nonfictional account of the delegations' travels in the United States. See: *Semero v Amerika; Zapiski korrespondenta "Literaturnoi gazety" o poezdke v SShAgruppy sovetskikh zhurnalistov v oktiabre-noiabre 1955g* (Moscow: Sovetskii pisatel', 1956). The theme of America seems to have continued to occupy Gribachev, who also published a poem about the United States in 1961. See: *Amerika, Amerika … poema* (Moscow. Sovetskii pisatel', 1961).
30. E. S. Afanas'eva and V. Iu. Afiani, eds., *Ideologicheskie komissii TsK KPSS 1958–1964: Dokumenty* (Moscow: Rosspen, 1998), 127.
31. Ibid.

32. On 4 October 1955 Khrushchev personally met with the delegation, asking several questions about what they had seen in America. He was interested in anything from detailed descriptions of American facilities and tractors to information about American strategies for growing corn, and the delegates answered all his questions in detail. See RGAN I, f. 5, op. 30, d. 107, ll. 1–45.
33. GARF, f. 5283, op. 14, d. 577, l. 170.
34. GARF, f. 5283, op. 14, d. 577, l. 170.
35. GARF, f. 5283, op. 14, d. 577, l. 7. Emphasis in original.
36. Ibid.
37. See for example Rossiiskii gosudarstvennyi arkhiv sotsial'no-politicheskoi istorii (hereafter RGASPI), f. 82. op. 2, d. 982, ll. 27–29, 32–35, and 49–52. Also see *Foreign Relations of the United States* (hereafter *FRUS*) 4 (1950): 1119–1120 and *FRUS* 4 (1950): 1103–1104.
38. RGANI, f. 5, op. 30, d. 20, ll. 16–17.
39. GARF, f. 9518, op. 1, d. 346, ll. 8–12.
40. GARF, f. 9518, op. 1, d. 346, ll. 8–12.
41. GARF, f. 9518, op. 1, d. 346, ll. 8–12.
42. RGANI, f. 5, op. 15, d. 734, l. 134.
43. Barghooorn, *The Soviet Cultural Offensive,* 298.
44. Boris Polevoi, *Amerikanskie dnevniki* (Moscow: Sovetskii pisatel', 1956), 65, 80, and 169. Also discussed in Barghoorn, *The Soviet Cultural Offensive,* 298.
45. RGANI, f. 5, op. 15, d. 734, l. 138.
46. RGANI, f. 5, op. 15, d. 734, l. 138. The delegates were also shocked to find out that the staff of the New York TASS agency had very poor English skills and little knowledge about American life.
47. RGANI, f. 5, op. 15, d. 734, ll. 140–141.
48. RGANI, f. 5, op. 15, d. 734, l. 143.
49. RGANI, f. 5, op. 15, d. 734, l. 144.
50. RGASPI, f. m-3, op. 15, d. 186, ll. 1–11.
51. According to the report, John Jacobs had been to the Soviet Union and written a few reports and about ten articles that all stressed the spirit of friendship and mutual understanding. RGANI, f. 5, op. 15, d. 734, l. 142.
52. This refers to the airline designed by the famous Soviet aircraft designer, Sergei Vladimirovich Iliushin, who designed attack aircrafts before and during the war and passenger planes after the war ended.
53. RGANI, f. 5, op. 15, d. 734, ll. 142–143.
54. Ibid. Emphasis in original.
55. RGANI, f. 5, op. 15, d. 734, ll. 142–143.
56. GARF, f. 9518, op. 1, d. 347, l. 137.
57. Ibid. This was apparently from the *New York Times.*
58. GARF, f. 9518, op. 1, d. 347, ll. 144–147. The power of film as propaganda is discussed repeatedly in Soviet sources. In 1955 Polevoi proposed having an American film festival in the Soviet Union and a Soviet one in the US. See RGANI, f. 5, op. 15, d. 734, l. 140.
59. GARF, f. 9518, op. 1, d. 347, l. 148.
60. GARF, f. 9518, op. 1, d. 347, l. 151. Polevoi stated that there was great shortage of Soviet books in the United States. He also mentioned the issue of royalties and suggested that the government pay several progressive authors their royalties. Also see RGANI, f. 5, op. 15, d. 734, ll. 131–145. The issue of royalties was repeatedly discussed when rethinking and improving Soviet-American cultural relations, and it was a sensitive point for the Soviet authorities, who ignored international treaties on copyrights and royalties.

61. GARF, f. 9518, op. 1, d. 347, ll. 144–147. Polevoi also recommended increasing exchanges of journalists after visiting the journalism faculty at Columbia University. Also see RGANI, f. 5, op. 15, d. 734, l. 141.
62. GARF, f. 9518, op. 1, d. 347, l. 152.
63. GARF, f. 9518, op. 1, d. 347, l. 151.
64. William Taubman, *Khrushchev: The Man and His Era* (New York: W. W. Norton & Company, 2003), 306.
65. GARF, f. 5283, op. 14, d. 577, l. 7. The wording is also used in GARF, f. 5283, op. 22s, d. 581, l. 28.
66. Afanas'eva and Afiani, *Ideologicheskie komissii TsK KPSS,* 128.

Bibliography

Afanas'eva, E. S., and V. Iu. Afiani, eds. *Ideologicheskie komissii TsK KPSS 1958–1964: Dokumenty.* Moscow: Rosspen, 1998.

Aucoin, Amanda Wood. *Deconstructing the American Way of Life: Soviet Responses to Cultural Exchange.* PhD diss., University of Arkansas, 2001.

Barghoorn, Frederick C. *The Soviet Cultural Offensive: The Role of Cultural Diplomacy in Soviet Foreign Policy.* Princeton: Princeton University Press, 1960.

Behrends, Jan C. *Die erfundene Freundschaft: Propaganda für die Sowjetunion in Polen und in der DDR.* Cologne: Böhlau, 2006.

Brooks, Jeffrey. *Thank you, Comrade Stalin! Soviet Public Culture from Revolution to Cold War.* Princeton: Princeton University Press, 2000)

Byrnes, Robert Francis. *Soviet-American Academic Exchanges, 1958–1975.* Bloomington: Indiana University Press, 1976.

Caute, David. *The Dancer Defects: The Struggle for Cultural Supremacy during the Cold War.* Oxford and New York: Oxford University Press, 2003.

Gould-Davies, Nigel. "The Logic of Soviet Cultural Diplomacy." *Diplomatic History* 27, no. 2 (2003): 193–214.

Gribachev, Nikolai M. *Avgustovskie zvezdy.* Moscow: Sovetskii pisatel', 1958.

Hixson, Walter L. *Parting the Curtain: Propaganda, Culture, and the Cold War, 1945–1961.* New York: St. Martin's Press, 1997.

Hoffmann, David L. *Stalinist Values: The Cultural Norms of Soviet Modernity, 1917–1941.* Ithaca, NY: Cornell University Press, 2003.

Kenez, Peter. *The Birth of the Propaganda State: Soviet Methods of Mass Mobilization, 1917–1929.* Cambridge and New York: Cambridge University Press, 1985.

Matskevich, V. *Chto my videli v SShA i Kanade.* Moscow: Gosudarstvennoe izdatel'stvo politicheskoi literatury, 1956.

Parks, J. D. *Culture, Conflict, and Coexistence: American-Soviet Cultural Relations, 1917–1958.* London: McFarland, 1983.

Polevoi, Boris. *Amerikanskie dnevniki.* Moscow: Sovetskii pisatel', 1956.

Richmond, Yale. *Cultural Exchange and the Cold War: Raising the Iron Curtain.* University Park, PA: Pennsylvania State University Press, 2003.

———. *U.S.-Soviet Cultural Exchanges, 1958–1986: Who Wins?* Boulder, CO: Westview, 1987.

———. *Soviet-American Cultural Exchanges: Ripoff or Payoff?* Washington D.C.: Kennan Institute for Advanced Russian Studies, 1984.

Rose, Clive. *The Soviet Propaganda Network: A Directory of Organisations Serving Soviet Foreign Policy.* London: Pinter, 1998; New York: St. Martin's Press, 1988.

Rosenberg, Emily S. *Spreading the American Dream: American Economic and Cultural Expansion, 1890–1945.* New York: Hill and Wang, 1982.

Semero v Amerike: Zapiski korrespondenta "Literaturnoi gazety" o poezdke v SShA gruppy sovetskikh zhurnalistov v oktiabre-noiabre 1955g. Moscow: Sovetskii pisatel', 1956.

Taubman, William. *Khrushchev: The Man and His Era.* New York: W. W. Norton, 2003.

Part II

CULTURAL DIPLOMACY IN CENTRAL EUROPE

Chapter 3

Hungarian Cultural Diplomacy, 1957–1963

Echoes of Western Cultural Activity in a Communist Country

Anikó Macher

This essay discusses Hungarian cultural diplomacy during the era of the consolidation of the regime that followed the Hungarian revolution of 1956 and ended with three events of major importance for the country: the last great wave of de-Stalinization of 1962–63, the second amnesty of imprisoned revolutionaries, and the end of debate on the so-called "Hungarian question" at the United Nations.

Historians working on post-1956 Hungarian foreign policy tend to underscore its ambiguous nature: how did the Hungarian communist leadership, in spite of its unquestioning loyalty to the USSR, have enough room for maneuver to serve its national interests? They unanimously regard János Kádár's pragmatism as the primary factor shaping the Hungarian model.[1] Yet the subject of Hungary's cultural diplomacy as a USSR satellite state in the cold war is still ignored and even repudiated. Meanwhile, an increasing amount of published work focuses on Hungarian cultural diplomacy and its role in the country's foreign policy in the 1920s, 1930s, and 1940s.[2] This essay, based on extensive archive research, questions the existence of any form of cultural diplomacy during the 1956–63 period.

As a member of the Warsaw Pact, Hungary was a single-party dictatorship adhering to the Soviet model of cultural diplomacy. Historians have noted how Soviet cultural diplomacy was used to foster

Notes for this section begin on page 97.

a rapprochement with the West, in line with the policy of détente; while on the other hand it was an instrument enabling the party to exercise the control it thought necessary to prevent the breakup of the empire and of ideological unity.[3] But the truth of the matter in European people's democracies like Hungary was rather more complex. Given that they shared a long-standing cultural heritage with countries of the West, reviving bilateral relations with Western European countries, during the cold war period until 1989, generally tended to stimulate the rediscovery of not only their European but also their national identities.[4] So their cultural diplomacy evolved according to the dual logic of the ideological warfare inherent to the cold war and the process of "de-satellization." Their newly recovered European and national identity highlighted the fact that the Eastern bloc was not monolithic.

This chapter cannot hope to be exhaustive, and some questions are bound to remain open: to what extent, for instance, were the people's democracies exploited by the USSR and used as extensions to, or even substitutes for, Soviet diplomacy; or, conversely, to what extent were they developing hidden policies designed to promote their own national interests?[5]

That said, the first aim here will be to see how Hungary used "culture" as a foreign-policy tool, with Hungarian cultural diplomacy seeking to revive the country's international standing after the suppression of the 1956 revolution and during a period of transition otherwise known as "de-Stalinization." Next will come a description of the background to that diplomacy, i.e., its infrastructure and the decision-making processes involved in international cultural relations. The complexity of the latter will bring us, in turn, to the matter of the separation of Soviet-inspired ideology from cultural activities. The fine line between the converging concepts of culture and propaganda[6] becomes more discernible when one is talking about the indirect, underlying message in Hungarian cultural diplomacy and the direct—even aggressive—propaganda used to promote communist ideology.[7] But it is an important distinction to draw here because Hungary targeted Western states, especially France, that had a tradition of guarding against ideological interference in all things cultural.[8]

Finally, it is important to stress how Hungary enjoyed the advantages of significant assets inherited from the pre–World War II period. Two institutions—the Hungarian institutes in Paris (Párizsi Magyar Intézet) and in Rome (Római Magyar Akadémia)—found themselves in the unique position of being the only cultural bodies of any people's democracy to remain open on the other side of the Iron Curtain during the cold war. France and Italy, for their part, had their own institutions in Hungary acting as showcases for Western cultures (Institut Français de Budapest and Instituto Italiano di Cultura).

East-West Cultural Contacts and Hungarian Cultural Diplomacy Before the Revolution of 1956: Background

As of 1953, Soviet cultural diplomacy was aimed primarily at arranging scientific and technological exchange programs with Western democracies in the hope of learning about their technological and scientific developments. In reaction to this policy, the institutional framework of Western cultural policy and diplomacy at the time changed radically at both the national and international levels. In 1953, for example, NATO's Committee on Information and Cultural Relations began holding regular meetings to elaborate a common cultural affairs–based policy that would meet with the unanimous approval of its Member States;[9] in 1955 conferences held in Geneva began discussing "cultural relations";[10] and in October of that year, the French Ministry of Foreign Affairs, for instance, decided to establish a Department of East-West Relations.

NATO countries wanted to ensure the gradual liberalization of Eastern European satellite countries, using careful tactics without overtly expressing their intentions. They also tried to start a process of self-determination and self-liberalization in the European people's democracies by indirect nonmilitary means, concentrating on propaganda. Hungary constituted a promising territory because the communist regime did not have as long a tradition there as in the USSR, and Western diplomats interpreted the strong sentiments in Hungarian society of belonging to a nation as a potential threat to that regime. Older intellectuals were nostalgic for Western culture while the youth were unhappy with Soviet culture, which they saw as an imposition from outside.[11]

The 20th Congress of the Soviet Communist Party in February 1956 gave new impetus to the development of East-West cultural relations. Cultural exchanges played a major role in the USSR's peaceful coexistence politics, and Hungary joined other people's democracies in following Soviet directives. But even before it was recognized in theory that socialist development had taken different forms (as seen in the 1955 Soviet-Yugoslav declaration), Hungarian Prime Minister Imre Nagy, who had taken over from Mátyás Rákosi in 1953, had introduced a series of experimental new policies that launched a process of de-Stalinization.[12] Mátyás Rákosi, on his return to power in 1955, had to keep some elements of that reform despite his attempts to partially re-Stalinize the country. Hungary's international cultural policies therefore changed with each successive regime. The dictatorship sought to soften its stance, proposing to develop cultural relations with the Western bloc as part of a policy of opening up to them. The first Western country targeted was France, which was seeking at the time to maintain its cultural influence and prestige in Central and Eastern Europe.[13]

After the 20th Congress, NATO countries decided to follow the above-mentioned concerted yet prudent policy of gradually disuniting the Eastern bloc and encouraging each country's autonomy. That said, while France, for example, negotiated a cultural exchange program with Hungary, others, such as the United Kingdom, supported bilateral relations only at nongovernmental levels.[14] Nevertheless, all NATO states agreed on a common goal: just one week before the Hungarian revolution in October 1956, they were still hoping slowly to transform the East through propaganda emphasizing the traditional Western roots of Soviet satellite countries' cultures as opposed to the alien cultural norms imposed by the USSR. The revolution came as a surprise to most Western observers and disrupted not only the Western cultural policy toward Hungary and Eastern Europe but also Hungary's cultural policy, both at home and abroad.

Absence of a Hungarian International Cultural Policy: Survival of Cultural Diplomacy, 1957–1958

The puppet government of Hungary and the newly renamed Hungarian Socialist Workers Party (HSWP) did not promulgate an international cultural policy until 1960. There were several interrelated reasons for this. First, the Soviet suppression of the revolution in November 1956 and the subsequent wave of repression in Hungary resulted in the country's isolation in international politics, and its foreign relations were paralyzed by the prolonged discussion of the so-called "Hungarian question" at the United Nations.[15] In February 1957, the United Nations suspended the mandate of the Hungarian delegation, thus wrecking attempts by János Kádár's government to gain the recognition of the Western bloc.

Second, Hungarian internal affairs were ridden with contradictions due to the slow pace of de-Stalinization in the USSR. In 1957 the struggle between Khrushchev and the Stalinists in Moscow induced the Hungarian communist leaders to adopt a policy of "wait and see." The question everybody was asking was whether the process of de-Stalinization would continue or not. But in 1957–58 it was no longer possible to return to Stalinism or to restore a monolithic communist bloc in Eastern and Central Europe. János Kádár's relatively moderate policies were hampered by the Stalinist faction of his party, and he managed to consolidate his position only in November 1959 on the occasion of Khrushchev's visit to Budapest.

Third, it took time for the post-revolution government to develop its ideology in terms of national and international cultural policy. Following the Hungarian intelligentsia's active involvement in the revolution, the communist world identified "revisionism" as the greatest ideological threat. The Hungarian leadership reacted in July 1958 by publishing, after a long period of preparation, a party document entitled "The Directives of Cultural Policy," which became the preeminent reference paper in matters of Hungarian cultural policy.[16] The document condemned both revisionism and Stalinism, an attitude that party jargon termed a "fight on both fronts." In the early days, the Kádár regime believed that the need to address the "mistakes of the past"—i.e., right-wing excesses and dogmatism—called for action both to combat and repress the intelligentsia, which had played a major role before and during the revolution, and to replace the cultural concepts of the Rákosi dictatorship. In practice, for instance, the party would tolerate artistic styles other than socialist realism. It would determine cultural policy, but would cease being directly responsible for its implementation, a role delegated to the state cultural institutions.

This guaranteed the party's control over cultural life and rendered its power less visible. At the diplomacy level, this principle made it easier for Western diplomats to keep contact with the Hungarian cultural elite. In addition, it expanded the international scope of state-run institutions like Hungarian Radio and Television, the Hungarian Academy of Sciences, the Office of International Concerts, and Hungarofilm. The "Directives of Cultural Policy" document was unambiguously anti-Stalinist yet still pro-Soviet. But it did not define the outlines and aims of international cultural policy, which mainly took the form of ad hoc relations between Hungarian state-run cultural institutions and Western cultural institutions and intelligentsia.[17] Hungary's amorphous external cultural actions in the 1957–58 period were determined by political propaganda as the party leadership sought to revive the country's international standing through long-standing institutions belonging to the traditional machinery of its cultural diplomacy.

Hungarian Cultural Actions in the West

After the 1956 revolution, the Soviet leadership set out to strengthen the unity of the Eastern bloc and to control the communist parties in power. Soviet propaganda organs hailed the "unity of all communist parties led by the Soviet Union" in the name of "international communism," declaring that all communists around the world had a "common front." The execution of Imre Nagy and his comrades in June 1958 constituted a warning to countries in the Eastern bloc whose politicians or officials dared to experiment with national communism.

Hungarian propaganda faithfully followed the Soviet model. It was formulated by the International Liaisons Department of the HSWP Central Committee, whose officials primarily set out to justify the legitimacy of Kádár's puppet government and to underpin their arguments with the myth of having stopped a "counterrevolution" in 1956. At the same time, they tried to enhance the image of the country as a counterpoint to the post-revolution repression and executions. It was particularly important to neutralize the counter-propaganda of Western intelligentsia protesting against the imprisonment of Hungarian writers, and also to regain the support of the Western communist intelligentsia.[18]

In December 1957 the party strongly condemned the Hungarian Ministry of Foreign Affairs for having failed to produce effective propaganda to justify the suppression of the 1956 "counterrevolution",[19] and for having paid too little attention to "imperialist attacks." Hungarian propaganda was paradoxical in that it attacked NATO countries while upholding the doctrine of peaceful coexistence. Its hidden agenda was to normalize and repair bilateral relations, and to put an end to discussion of the "Hungarian question" at the United Nations.[20] In order to normalize Hungary's relations with the NATO countries, the party's political committee issued a decision in January 1958 aimed at improving economic and cultural relations, establishing foreign press departments, sending press attachés to the Western democracies, harmonizing the work of Hungarian missions abroad, and publishing a journal in foreign languages (e.g., *The New Hungarian Quarterly*).[21] The decision therefore emphasized that the Ministry of Foreign Affairs needed to improve its activities concerning information and propaganda. Consequently, the ministry devised elaborate and detailed tactics "to avoid a renewed discussion of the

Hungarian question in international organizations" and "to change its defensive propaganda." This more ambitious plan now contained specific diplomatic steps to be taken and devised a way to introduce higher standards in diplomacy.

Information services (foreign-language journals) were launched immediately, but improvements concerning diplomacy took more time and preparation.[22] One of the main reasons for this was that the Hungarian officials sent to represent the country in Western capitals in 1958 were only chargés d'affaires rather than accredited, plenipotentiary ministers. They faced a difficult task in that Western politicians refused to maintain regular contacts with them, receiving diplomats from Hungarian legations only rarely. Contacts with Western intelligentsia were also irregular because many, even the communists, were reluctant to enter into sustained relations with Hungarian communists.[23] The Hungarian cultural institutes in Rome (Római Magyar Akadémia) and Paris (Párizsi Magyar Intézet) were considered more approachable because they were not officially part of Hungarian diplomatic missions, which enabled easier and more direct contact with local ministries of foreign affairs and intelligentsia.

In early 1958, the Hungarian party leadership decided to reorganize the work of Hungarian cultural institutes abroad based on the belief that they represented a framework of traditional, Hungarian cultural diplomacy that was no more than a means of optimizing foreign propaganda operations. Having been managed by Hungarian immigrants after the revolution, control of the Hungarian institute in Rome once again fell into the hands of the Kádár regime in 1957. A new director, who was also the cultural attaché, was appointed in 1959. In September of that year, the new director of the institute in Paris found himself having to regain the trust and appreciation of the "progressive" French intelligentsia, including Louis Aragon and Tristan Tzara of the Dada movement, and to counteract the influence of Hungarian immigrants hostile to the Kádár regime.[24] In the meantime, the government sent a Hungarian cultural attaché to Paris, but his role was mainly to check that the institute and the Hungarian legation acted in accordance with party policies.

The following October, when the party's political committee set about dealing with the problem of how to produce well-organized and consistent propaganda, it began to admit the shortcomings of previous years.[25] Subsequent propaganda and international cultural plans continued to be dominated by the matter of the "Hungarian question" at the United Nations, and by the effort to combat the offensive tone of NATO countries. Henceforth, propaganda activities became intertwined with a new, offensive definition of international cultural policy designed to disseminate Hungary's "positive achievements."

Absence of A Western Cultural Policy Approach To Hungary

In the years following the 1956 revolution, Western-bloc countries did not officially recognize Kádár's puppet government. Indeed, the continuing repression and executions in Hungary made it impossible for them to support Hungary at all. Paradoxically, many countries did not close their legations in Budapest because they wanted to monitor developments in Hungary.[26] This contradiction reveals the dilemma of NATO and neutral countries. On the one hand, severing all diplomatic ties would imply that the Western countries were turning their back on Hungary. This was not a solution. On the other hand, even a temporary closure of foreign legations in Budapest would have meant the end of an important geopolitical vantage point that enabled Westerners to observe the development of Soviet internal and external policies. Such a loss was considered unacceptable by Western powers, especially in the post-revolution period, when the Soviet leadership was striving to restore stability to Hungarian political life.

NATO's Committee on Information and Cultural Relations decided on a cultural boycott of Hungary while waiting to see how the situation in that country evolved. Member states agreed to freeze all cultural actions for an unlimited period and to withdraw from all Hungarian events.[27] Nevertheless, French and Italian representatives kept their cultural institutes in Budapest in an effort to maintain their exceptional cultural position. Those institutes also served to monitor what was going on in Hungary at a time when policymakers in NATO capitals had no official contacts with Budapest. Instead their informal contacts with Hungarian intellectuals afforded them valuable insights into what was going on within the local opposition.

The Italian and French cultural institutes in Budapest (Institut Français de Budapest and Instituto Italiano di Cultura) acted as the representatives of Western European culture. Their presence in Hungary was based on reciprocity, and their directors enjoyed the special status of also being the cultural attachés of their respective countries. The importance of the French institute was greatly enhanced by its rich library and collection of periodicals. It organized language courses, lectures on art and literature, and concerts, and provided a film-lending service. The Italian institute's library was smaller due to damage suffered during the war, but it provided a range of services such as scholarships to study in Italy. The lack of well-planned, spectacular cultural activities did not necessarily imply that the West had withdrawn its cultural presence altogether.[28]

Diplomatic Life and Culture: Budapest, 1957–1959

In the years following the revolution, Hungarian internal propaganda argued that "the counterrevolution of 1956 was an attempt by Western imperialist powers and reactionary forces at home to tear Hungary away from the Eastern bloc. After this attempt failed, the imperialists launched a new attack—a slander campaign to isolate the country through a diplomatic and economic blockade." In other words, the political leadership had identified an "imperialist conspiracy to overthrow the Hungarian people's democracy" as one of the causes of the "counterrevolution." This propaganda, which was ultimately designed to legitimize the Kádár puppet government, included a media campaign against Western cultural institutes where cultural attachés from the West were described as exerting so much influence on the Hungarian intelligentsia that they could be considered responsible for the outbreak of the "counterrevolution."[29]

In January 1958, the Ministry of Foreign Affairs' Department of Propaganda prepared an overview of "the propaganda activities of [Western] legations in Budapest," which analyzed their methods of cultural action. It highlighted the threat posed by a thaw in relations with the West that had seen Western diplomats using their wide circle of personal contacts to influence the intelligentsia and the world of art. The Hungarian political leadership introduced a number of administrative rules through which they aimed to reduce actual and potential contacts between those diplomats and the Hungarian public. In the early summer of 1958, for example, courses and film loans were suspended, thus entailing a substantial reduction in the activities of the French institute.

The Italian and French cultural institutes in Budapest, together with other representatives of Western culture, became increasingly influential as Kádár sought to strengthen his position against Stalinist tendencies in Hungarian politics. In the spring of 1957, the Kádár leadership had already helped strengthen Western cultural presence with a series of concessions.[30] It even used the institutes as informal channels through which to approach Western powers. Meanwhile, the police, which had remained Stalinist, were also making their presence felt by harassing foreign diplomats. Stalinists could not accept "decadent Western culture," which was regarded as an ideological threat. During this period of double standards, however, Western cultural institutes were gaining momentum on the political scene in Hungary.

Hungary's Stalinist police force launched their most significant attack on the presence of Western culture in December 1957 with the arrest of Marianne Halkó, secretary of the French institute. She was imprisoned for one year and interrogated about the relationship between French diplomats and Hungarian intellectuals.[31] The so-called Halkó case soon gained an international dimension. Likewise, during a so-called war of visas, several Hungarian personalities and artistic groups found themselves unable to obtain permission to travel to France.

Marianne Halkó had been taken into custody because of her alleged secret intelligence activities. But her ordeal was deemed necessary from the Stalinist point of view because it both sent out a warning to the director of the French institute, Guy Turbet-Delof, and sabotaged any rapprochement by the Kádár regime with the West.[32] The police and the Stalinist faction of the leadership deliberately targeted Western cultural institutes with their campaign of violence. In Kádár's view, France was responsible for Hungary's vulnerability to Western cultural influences. The authorities around Kádár understood that culture occupied a far more important position in French diplomacy than in that of most other European countries, where economic, commercial, and political considerations prevailed.

The Halkó affair did not prevent the Kádár leadership from pursuing its policy and attempting to draw up French-Hungarian cultural conventions in the course of semi-official diplomatic discussions, even after the start of the Halkó affair. In January 1958, for instance, they made an unofficial tentative to approach to Turbet-Delof.[33] Bilateral agreements between the two countries would provide an opportunity to move closer to France and, hence, to normalize foreign relations. The French response was rather slow and ultimately negative. The "Hungarian question" did not yet allow for talks of such importance.

Members of the Hungarian intelligentsia in important cultural positions had already contributed to the preparation of the proposed conventions. Some Hungarian intellectuals were employed as government officials by the communist regime on account of their contacts and networks in Italy and France. Often, they were asked to negotiate with diplomats from Western legations and cultural institutes, and frequently they came to represent Hungary abroad, thus serving the Kádár government in more ways than one. Gyula Ortutay, rector of the University of Budapest, provided a large room at the university for various events organized by the French institute and the growing numbers of people they attracted.[34] This arrangement was suspended in 1958 under pressure from the Stalinist faction. As early as 1956, Béla Köpeczi, director of the Department of Publishing at the Ministry of Culture (Népművelési Minisztérium), had begun leading talks on a French-Hungarian book exhibition and had guaranteed the continuous publication and translation of Western literature into Hungarian.[35] A year later, István Sőtér, head of the Institute of Literary Studies at the Hungarian Academy of Sciences, started preparing a trip to Paris, but it did not take place until the beginning of 1959. The main aim of the trip was to create contacts with French intellectual circles and to enter into talks with the French Ministry of Foreign Affairs.[36]

All in all, despite upholding the principle of reciprocity, NATO country legations in Hungary and Hungarian legations abroad could have very different ways of operating and suffered from quite different forms of restrictions. Hungarian cultural institutes and legations had a rather limited system of contacts, relying mainly on members of local communist parties and intellectuals with communist leanings. This substantially reduced the scope of Hungarian foreign policy. Nevertheless, the active nature of diplomatic life in Budapest compensated for the loss, with representatives of the Hungarian intelligentsia and the world of art being invited to receptions organized by Western missions or officials from the Hungarian Ministry of Foreign Affairs. This in turn provided a perfect forum for initiating bilateral relations and obtaining information, in spite of the restrictive actions taken by the Stalinist faction of the ruling party and the police in 1958. Given the lack of dialogue at the state level, these diplomatic steps were necessary to mend relations between Hungary and the member states of NATO.

After the 1956 crisis, and as a result of the policy of peaceful coexistence, Marxist ideology experienced a major decline in the Eastern bloc. Communist leaders were forced to revise their ideological positions, and Hungary was no exception. Instead of the aggressive and accusatory tone previously used in regard to the Western bloc, Hungarian propaganda gradually started emphasizing the excesses of the Stalinist regime. From 1959 on, once the Kádár leadership had consolidated its autonomy and succeeded in the process of de-Stalinization, the regime became more and more tolerant of open manifestations of Western culture in order to satisfy Hungarian public opinion.

Turning Point in the History of Hungarian Cultural Diplomacy (1959): International Cultural Events as Part of Hungarian Cultural Diplomacy

In a series of musical events, concerts, lectures on musicology, and exhibitions launched in 1959, Budapest began receiving international artists from neutral countries and those of NATO, among others. This form of revival of Hungarian cultural diplomacy was, in a way, reminiscent of the years 1945–49. The events started with a celebration of the Haydn bicentenary in autumn 1959.[37] While highlighting Hungarian ties with the Austrian composer, the celebration also sought to achieve a symbolic improvement in Austro-Hungarian relations.[38] The festivities continued with the commemoration of famous Hungarian composers such as Ferenc Erkel in 1960 and Ferenc Liszt and Béla Bartók in 1961.[39] The Hungarian leadership approved of music as a vector for international understanding, since music was less directly ideological than most other art forms. Consequently, the festivities did not disturb the USSR or the Hungarian Stalinists.

More important results were achieved by a French book show in Budapest and a Hungarian book show in Paris in the autumn of 1959. Because communist leaders feared that works of literature conveying Western values would influence huge masses of people and turn them against communist ideology, literature and publishing tended to be the most closed and strictly controlled areas of culture in people's democracies. However, the Hungarian intelligentsia, like that of Poland, had mounted an especially vehement resistance to Soviet influence. As early as June 1956, Béla Köpeczi, then head of the Department of Publishing at the Ministry of Culture (Népművelési Minisztérium), had requested that propaganda-based literature be eliminated from Hungarian publishing activities. The movement grew in strength and continued in the wake of the revolution, when Soviet literature lost its dominant status. The varied range of foreign works published in Hungary included scientific books as well as fiction by Dante, Agatha Christie, Colette, Jean Cocteau, André Gide, Julien Green, and Françoise Sagan, to name but a few.

Plans to organize prestigious book shows had been proposed as early as 1956, once the 20th Congress of the Soviet party had allowed for such events, in the hope of producing occasions as successful as those of 1946–48. On 9 April 1959, after years of preparatory talks, the Hungarian Ministry of Culture (Művelődésügyi Minisztérium) signed a cooperation agreement with the organizing committee of the *Exposition française des livres et des graphiques.*[40]

This was only possible thanks to the favorable political conditions fostered through the channels of communication that President de Gaulle had opened up with Eastern European countries within the framework of French cultural foreign policy.[41] The first six months of 1959 saw a sharp increase in meetings between officials from the Hungarian legation and the French Ministry of Foreign Affairs official in charge of relations with Hungary.[42] The most significant result was that the Eastern European section of the French Ministry of Foreign Affairs began receiving Hungarians who requested a meeting. In May 1959, in spite of anti-Hungarian policies in international organizations like the United Nations, France approved the appointment of a new representative of the Hungarian government as minister plenipotentiary in Paris. The fact that France found it easier to protect its dominant cultural position in Budapest with the help of well-maintained diplomatic contacts allowed for the normalization of bilateral French-Hungarian relations.

The two book shows in Budapest and Paris in autumn 1959 stood out in the context of Hungarian cultural diplomacy: for the first time in twenty-five years, an event highlighting Hungarian literature had been held in a major Western capital. Unsurprisingly, Pál Rácz, chargé d'affaires of the Hungarian legation in Paris, declared in his speech at the opening of the Paris show that it was a stepping stone for a further broadening of cultural relations. The books on Hungary that were displayed at the two events smacked less of political propaganda than in the past. Most were foreign-language publications that were more objective and less ideological. The Hungarian authorities had made this choice to avoid political problems. In fact, they had decided that no book by János Kádár or any living politician should be exhibited. So in contrast to past affairs, the Paris show—housed at the Sorbonne and opened by the university's rector and Jean Baillou, vice-director of the Department of Cultural Relations at the French Ministry of Foreign Affairs—was not a propaganda event organized by and for communist parties. The guest list included representatives of prestigious institutions such as the Bibliothèque Nationale, the Collège de France, and the Archives Nationales. Even though the Hungarian political leadership was dissatisfied with the media coverage of the event, they judged the attitude of official French foreign policy to be fair because France had helped to organize it.

The Kádár regime clearly demonstrated, by the wide selection of French works translated into Hungarian, a desire not to limit the range of books to those by communist authors. Meanwhile, it was the first time that Hungarian literature had been presented in such a manner to the French public. Furthermore, it provided an opportunity for Hungarian diplomats to meet the rector of the Sorbonne and to raise the question of creating a department of Hungarian linguistics and literature at his university, a topic that had been mooted since 1947. Ultimately, the Hungarians considered the book show a success because it signaled the beginning of a series of contacts with French literary circles and intelligentsia.[43]

As for the French show in Budapest, which attracted almost forty thousand visitors over a two-week period, it was probably the most successful cultural event of the period in Hungary. French diplomats and the Hungarian leadership organized receptions and official lunches that provided numerous opportunities for socializing and made it possible for the French delegation to meet Hungarian publishers, writers, and artists.[44] Dictatorships have never underestimated the value of books as a means of propaganda. But in Hungary one can also clearly see a gradual loosening of ideological rigidity that paved the way for the semblance of cultural liberalism that was to emerge in the years to come.

The First Hungarian International Cultural Policy Directives

Starting in April 1958, the Hungarian Ministry of Foreign Affairs took steps to improve the country's relations with NATO. Reports drawn up on the links between international relations and culture were submitted to the political committee for approval, with copies sent to inform the Ministry of Culture. One especially detailed report published in February 1959 formed the basis of an international cultural relations debate in the political committee the following April. Pro-Western party leaders agreed that culture must play a prominent role in Hungarian foreign policy toward the NATO countries.[45] In 1960 the Ministry of Foreign Affairs produced a document that for the first time explicitly adopted an active approach to international cultural relations with those countries.[46]

This directive came during a short period of reduced tension in international politics stemming from Khrushchev's visit to the United States in September 1959 and the signing of an agreement in Geneva on the establishment of a body to oversee bilateral disarmament. Hungarian society had high hopes that the country could perhaps become neutral and that the political regime could change. However, it had failed to take into account an obvious parallel of quite frightening proportions for political leaders: the democratic movements following the first rapprochement between East and West after the 1955 Geneva conferences, which culminated in the Hungarian revolution of 1956. The leadership, on the other hand, was only too aware of this, and its propaganda interpreting global events sought to present such activities less as an effort to reduce tension on the international scene than as an attempt at "cultural penetration" designed to separate Hungary from the rest of the Eastern bloc. From an ideological viewpoint, an agreement with the "capitalist world" seemed impossible.

Hence two factors in particular aroused the suspicions of the Hungarian leadership and influenced its definition and implementation of international cultural policy. First, since 1959 Hungary had in fact been explicitly singled out by Western governments as one of the Eastern-bloc countries to be targeted for cultural actions. Second, the West was striving to harmonize a common cultural strategy. NATO archives, especially records of the regular meetings of NATO's Committee on Information and Cultural Relations, clearly show a change in cultural policy toward Hungary.[47] Budapest was well aware of this, as evidenced at the first special meeting of Hungarian plenipotentiary diplomats accredited to NATO countries, held in December 1959, where Deputy Foreign Affairs Minister Károly Szarka drew attention to the new cultural strategy launched by the West against Hungary. Diplomats serving in London and Paris presented analyses of British and French cultural activities concerning Hungary,[48] and the following year cultural policy was made the main focus of the second special meeting.[49]

Khrushchev's trip to Paris in the spring of 1960 signaled that the people's democracies could develop bilateral relations with Western democracies.[50] For Hungary, it implied that new talks could begin on bilateral cultural exchange programs. Hungarian scientists and artists could now obtain passports more easily, students could travel to France on scholarships even before the exchange programs had been signed, and more and more Hungarian secondary schools could offer courses in English, French, and German as a second foreign language (the first always being Russian). American culture was, of course, still banned, but the British legation set up a small reading room and a lending library in its building in Budapest, where Western press and documentaries were made available. The awkwardness of the situation can be well illustrated by the fact that the British Council, which had been accused of spying and forced to close in 1950, was still not allowed to reopen. The legation's services remained modest in scale, and because the police monitored anybody who dared approach the building, it was unable to organize new language courses. At the same time, as of 1960 the Kádár leadership tolerated invitations to the United Kingdom for Hungarian writers and granted travel permits (though it was lesser-known authors, not the chief luminaries, who were the first allowed to go, with the exception of Áron Tamási and Géza Ottlik).[51]

Notwithstanding a general tendency of improving cultural relations in the people's democracies, which raised the public's hopes of liberalization, the Soviet leadership tried to counterbalance this by insisting on ideological strictness. In February 1960, it organized a consultation meeting of the Warsaw Pact in Moscow at which it stressed the need for the Eastern bloc to maintain its unity and cohesion, and underscored the importance of its propaganda. From the 1960s on, Hungarian cultural diplomacy therefore found itself having to answer the big questions arising from the political, diplomatic, and ideological context of 1959. How could Hungary continue improving its cultural relations with NATO countries while avoiding any conflict with the new line of Soviet propaganda—aimed at preventing Western cultural infiltration and, at the same time, at strengthening the cohesion of the Eastern bloc? How could Western culture be made available to the Hungarian public without inviting criticism from Soviet policymakers? The difficulty of this task is amply demonstrated by the ways in which Hungarian institutions dealing with international cultural policy were reorganized and restructured, and by the self-contradictory nature of the cultural exchange programs signed.

Hungarian Cultural Diplomacy 1960–1963: A Room for Maneuver

Hungarian International Cultural Policy Institutions

Since 1957, Hungary's political leadership had kept on its agenda the task of coordinating the various Hungarian institutions dealing with international cultural relations. Its aim was to eliminate overlapping functions within these bodies, and in 1958 it sought to bring all such organizations under the aegis of a single umbrella body modeled on the Soviet institutional structure. A series of exchanges between the Hungarian and Soviet delegations led to the implementation of two key institutional reforms in 1960 and 1962. The fact that neither was an exact copy of the Soviet model suggests that Hungarian foreign policy had some measure of freedom in spite of Soviet control.[52]

In March 1960, the party decided to set up the Committee of Information and Culture (CIC) to provide the framework for supervising the numerous propaganda and cultural institutions dealing with international cultural policy.[53] It was supposed to coordinate and centralize the often self-contradictory activities of propaganda and cultural policies, but was already found to be falling short of expectations by the following year. From then on it was the Institute of Cultural Relations (ICR) that took the lead role in Hungarian international cultural relations in the context of Kádár's pragmatic de-Stalinization process.[54] In October 1961, the nomination of József Bognár as head of the ICR in Budapest marked a turning point in its functioning.[55]

In June 1962, after a decision taken by the party's political committee on 29 May 1962, two ministerial decrees were issued in an attempt to put the country's cultural affairs in order.[56] The centralized function of the CIC in overseeing international cultural relations and propaganda activities was reformed, and the committee itself was dissolved. The ICR became an autonomous organization directed by the Hungarian Council of Ministers and was placed in charge of preparing directives concerning international cultural relations with NATO countries. It also organized talks on international agreements and cultural exchange programs with other countries in the Western bloc and coordinated state and nongovernmental institutions in their work in the realm of international culture. This undoubtedly gave the party an opportunity to exercise control more easily over international relations. But the decentralization of cultural relations from the Ministry of Foreign Affairs was crucial in that it ensured a certain degree of autonomy for international cultural affairs.

From the Kádár leadership's point of view, well-prepared international cultural policy could help reestablish political and diplomatic ties with the West. Good cultural relations would inevitably pave the way for good relations in the fields of economics and foreign affairs, which would eventually strengthen Hungary's international standing.[57] Cultural relations do indeed provide an excellent means of establishing contacts even when the political climate does not permit any official exchanges. In Hungary, semi-official or informal cultural links preceded and heralded centralized official state relationships. This way of thinking about cultural policy helped Hungary normalize its relationships with Austria and the United States, among others, and resulted in flexible and fruitful cultural diplomacy.[58]

Cultural Exchange Programs With NATO Countries

The 21st Congress of the Soviet Communist Party in 1959 paid particular attention to cultural exchanges with capitalist countries. Although the USSR had cultural agreements with all the major capitalist countries, its policy was still dominated by the propaganda of "gaining ground for socialism in the ideological warfare between the two regimes" and "resisting capitalist attempts to sow the seeds of an ideology that would harm socialist culture." The Soviet leadership encouraged scientific and technological exchanges but opposed relationships in the fields of social studies, history, and philosophy.

In the early 1960s, Hungarian international cultural policy followed the Soviet model in promoting cultural exchange programs with NATO countries. Three major changes occurred. First, the cultural exchange programs renewed each year as of 1961 enabled Hungary's international cultural relations to achieve legally recognized status. Second, Hungary started to play an active role in foreign cultural relations, hosting international negotiations at various, ever-higher, diplomatic levels. Third, wide-ranging, detailed foreign cultural policy directives sought to capitalize on conflicts in the relationships between Western countries by developing good contacts with France, Italy, and Britain in order to isolate the United States.

In the course of a variety of talks, Hungary's cultural diplomacy set out to enforce the principle of reciprocity and to envisage fewer but more significant and higher-quality cultural events. A first one-year cultural exchange program signed with France in October 1961 was followed by yearly renewals and a two-year exchange program signed in December 1964, which led to a cultural agreement in 1966. Focusing specifically on De Gaulle's policy of "European Europe," Hungarian leaders hoped to learn about the discord among Western states from French policymaking and an analysis of French debate and views on European integration.[59] The leadership established very carefully prepared agreements with France that set out its position, but only after checking every detail with the scientific and cultural institutions concerned.[60] The main problem to arise from the talks revolved around the decision as to which administrative unit should select the students, professors, or researchers. This ultimately proved to be a spectacular example of containment policy on the part of the French. At the same time, it was a failure for the Hungarian leadership in that delegations of Hungarian writers were going every year to France yet the principle of reciprocal relations did not see any major French writers visiting Hungary in return.[61]

Bilateral relations with Italy typified the ways in which Hungary followed the Soviet directive stipulating that countries should make use of their traditions and "cultural values." In 1960 the Hungarian Risorgimento Committee was set up to organize the commemoration of the hundredth anniversary of unified Italy,[62] at a time when the cultural agreement signed under Mussolini in 1935 was still in force.[63] The Hungarian-British exchange program signed in October 1961 and renewed annually thereafter was similarly much more modest than its French equivalent. It did not comprise scholarships for students, exchanges of language assistants, invitations to theater companies or musicians, and so on. No major change occurred until the mid 1960s, although the organization of summer schools was begun and an exchange program was established between the Hungarian Academy of Sciences in Budapest and the Royal Society of the United Kingdom.[64]

The steps taken between 1960 and 1962–63 show Hungary to have been concentrating more on the establishment of cultural exchange programs with an increasing number of NATO and neutral countries. Over time these programs became greater in scope, better planned, and more consistent than ever before. Moreover, as the "Hungarian question" was slowly dropped from the international political agenda, more was done to prepare directives and coordination efforts concerning cultural relations. Soviet-based ideological terminology also changed as the declared aim of cultural exchange programs shifted to aiding development and increasing the visibility of Hungarian science and culture. Furthermore, the authorities organized two-year "updating" courses on cultural diplomacy for working diplomats. In addition to dealing with "questions of ideological warfare" these included a subject entitled "Hungarian culture in the stream of international culture."[65]

Beginning as early as 1960, the Hungarian institutes in Paris and Rome had turned their attention away from propaganda to focus on diffusing Hungarian science and culture—their original role in the 1920s. In order to enable the institutes to fulfill their task of implementing the cultural diplomacy policies initiated by the diplomatic missions, their activities had to be separated from those of the legations. This gave them far more possibilities and far greater scope in maintaining relations with the host country's cultural institutions. They also maintained relations with individuals who were important to that country's cultural or scientific life, and looked after Hungarian students arriving there on scholarships. In other words, the institutes were expected to bolster their prestige by increasing the quality of their diplomatic work and cultural relations. As the institutes became more academic and abandoned activities dedicated to mass culture, the Hungarian authorities felt the need to separate cultural diplomacy from propaganda.[66] Nevertheless, personal networks and cultural activities remained limited, and the institutes themselves were still isolated from the cultural life of Western democracies. As far as France was concerned, the only real change came about when the Hungarian institute in Paris volunteered to take part in the 1964 French-Hungarian cultural exchange program, at which point its contacts became more numerous and influential.[67]

In spite of these developments, the way in which Hungary maintained its cultural presence in Western democracies, and the presence of the latter's culture in Hungary, remained somewhat arbitrary. In order to win the hearts and minds of the Hungarian public, the leadership tolerated Western cultural activities, language courses, and other cultural activities to an ever-increasing degree in Hungary. But at the same time, the state and the party leadership tried to exercise control over strictly Hungarian cultural activities in the West. The growth of exchange programs did not mean that anybody could secure a scholarship or travel as member of a delegation. This produced a paradoxical situation in which Hungarian cultural institutes abroad had difficulties fulfilling their task of representing Hungarian culture. Meanwhile, a lack of coordination on the part of some cultural organizations led the Office of International Concerts, the state-run Hungarian Radio and Television Company, and other such bodies, in spite of party efforts, to become more and more autonomous in their foreign relations.

In the West, with cultural exchange programs on the increase, the cultural experts of certain Western democracies also began working in a more coordinated manner.[68] American, British, French, German, and Italian diplomats all agreed on the need to respect the principle of reciprocal exchange in order to contain communist propaganda, and to sign off on short-term, one-year programs that could always be curtailed at the drop of a hat. A meeting of Western politicians involved in cultural affairs in May 1962 in Rome highlighted a shift in opinion in Western cultural policies and stimulated considerable debate among the NATO countries. The point of contention was that unlike the United States, which was more reserved, France and the United Kingdom had set out to develop cultural relations with European people's democracies and not with the Soviet Union. They defended their position by pointing to their common cultural heritage with those countries. More importantly, however, they argued that developing cultural relations with the West could help the people's democracies combat the more dogmatic factions in their parties as they endeavored to carry out the process of de-Stalinization. Cultural exchange programs with Western democracies were a source of national pride for governments in the satellite countries, which in turn promoted the further enhancement of cultural relations. According to British observers, the attitude of people's democracies at this time was no longer based exclusively on Soviet principles.[69] Ideological differences and national sentiments led to disharmony and diverging approaches among Central and Eastern European countries.

This change became more and more obvious after 1962. Little did it matter that the 22nd Congress of the Soviet party had declared in 1961 that "cultural relations with capitalist countries will be fruitful only if they are based on the strengthening of existing cultural relations with other socialist countries, which can be achieved through cultural cooperation between socialist countries." The Eastern bloc did not have a common foreign cultural policy beyond forcing propaganda and the notion of ideological unity on its people. On the contrary, the countries in question competed with each other to establish themselves in relationships with Western states, which resulted in rivalry among them. It is beyond the scope of this study to analyze the policies of the various people's democracies, but the Hungarian example shows well those countries' room for maneuver *vis-à-vis* Soviet directives. Cultural actions were not always in sync with the will of the Soviet leadership. In 1962, for instance, while the latter grew more reserved in its cultural dealings—and reduced the number of exchange programs—with NATO countries, the Hungarian leadership worked on further improving such relations and on developing more exchange programs. Another example: while Khrushchev was issuing a warning about the ideological threat of "the bourgeois influence" in a speech to the Soviet writers' association in March 1963, the Hungarian leadership was moving away from the socialist realism style when selecting which literary works to export to the West.

Starting in 1963, when the "Hungarian question" was abandoned at the United Nations, many Western democracies raised the level of their diplomatic relations with Hungary and established embassies.[70] Cultural rewards also reached a higher level. In 1964, Jean Basdevant and Richard L. Speaight, senior officials at the French and British ministries of foreign affairs, took part in cultural exchange program negotiations with Hungary. Hence Hungarian international cultural policy gained a well-defined shape by 1963, remaining confined to the framework of the Eastern bloc but involving increasing cooperation with Western democracies hand in hand with a prudent endeavor to assert its national identity and uphold a semblance of sovereignty. Cultural exchange programs created a legal basis for such cooperation. But they could also be presented as forming part of Hungarian propaganda activities, and Hungary could refuse to accept certain Western initiatives. International cultural negotiations also served internal political aims—e.g., to satisfy Hungarian public opinion and to profit from the economic effects of better relationships. Through cultural diplomacy, Hungary had reached a point from which to start using foreign policy as a conventional means of paving the way to normal contacts at ambassadorial level between Hungarian diplomats and Western officials. This in turn led to visits and meetings between Hungarian and Western ministers at the state level.

Conclusion

Through analysis of the periods under discussion, this essay has sought to show that cultural diplomacy has continuously formed part of Hungarian foreign policy, albeit in a variety of different forms. Limited in scope after the 1956 revolution, it began to be better defined and more active in 1959–60, thus shifting from the informal and sporadic to the consistent and structured, legally underpinned by intergovernmental cultural exchange programs.

Post-revolutionary Hungary was unique on account of its diplomatic isolation and the fact that its capabilities were limited exclusively to soft power, i.e., to cultural diplomacy. The Kádár puppet government sought to regain its standing and legitimacy, in keeping with Soviet interests, by targeting Western countries and seeking to establish links with their state machinery. Normalizing intergovernmental relations became the overriding goal, over and above the upkeep of the para-communist umbrella organization networks. This raised the profile of the Hungarian state in international cultural relations, with the party apparently content to remain in the shadows. The Hungarian institutions dealing with cultural affairs then underwent restructuring, and the message to the West was changed to emphasize that the Stalinist period was over and Stalinism would never return. Next, with the Soviet-inspired rhetoric of peaceful coexistence falling short of the mark, the Hungarian state set about improving the country's image by promoting the universal values of its national culture, e.g., through the music of Béla Bartók. Drawing on extensive archive material, this essay has also sought to explore the Hungarian state's endeavors to turn its assets to its advantage by modernizing the framework of its cultural diplomacy (its cultural institutes), exploiting its Western-educated intelligentsia and mobilizing its members as cultural diplomats, and fostering the conditions for cultural diplomacy by investing in book shows and other such events.

The story of Hungarian cultural diplomacy shows that culture provides an excellent means of creating informal contacts. It is rich, colorful, and resilient, and it can deliver an indirect message without compromising ideological constraints. At the same time, culture commands far less attention than a political summit or political negotiations. Cultural activities did not help directly to resolve the Hungarian question at the United Nations, but cultural diplomacy did provide a means of establishing good bilateral contacts that often made up for the dearth of political contacts. So there are good grounds for asserting that during this period of transition, Hungarian cultural diplomacy successfully served as a first step toward opening the country up to Western Europe.

Endnotes

1. For more on Hungarian history during the cold war, see László Borhi, *Hungary in the Cold War, 1945–1956* (Budapest and New York: Central European University Press, 2004); and the bibliographies published on following websites: <www.isn.ethz.ch/php > (Parallel History Project on NATO and the Warsaw Pact, June 2010); <www.rev.hu> (1956 Institute, Budapest, June 2010). On Hungary's international relations after World War II, see Magdolna Baráth, "Magyarország a szovjet diplomáciai iratokban, 1957–1964" [Hungary in the Soviet Diplomatic Documents, 1957–1964], in *Múlt századi hétköznapok: Tanulmányok a Kádár rendszer kialakulásának időszakáról* [Everyday in the Last Century: Essays on the Period of the Formation of the Kádár Regime], ed. János M. Rainer (Budapest: 1956-os Intézet, 2003), 55–89; Csaba Békés, *Európából Európába: Magyarország konfliktusok kereszttüzében, 1945–1990* [From Europe to Europe: Hungary in the Crossfire of Conflicts, 1945–1990] (Budapest: Gondolat, 2004); Csaba Békés, "Titkos válságkezeléstől a politikai koordinációig: Politikai egyeztetési mechanizmus a Varsói Szerződésben, 1954–1967" [From Secret Crisis Management to Political Coordination: Political Coordinating Mechanism in the Warsaw Pact, 1954–1967], in Rainer, *Múlt századi hétköznapok,* 9–54; Gusztáv D. Kecskés, "Les caractéristiques de la politique étrangère de la Hongrie de 1945 à 1990," in *Culture et politique étrangère des démocraties populaires,* ed. Antoine Marès, Cultures et sociétés de l'Est, 45 (Paris: Institut d'études slaves, 2007), 147–165. On Hungarian internal politics, see János M. Rainer, *Ötvenhat után* [After Fifty-Six] (Budapest: 1956-os Intézet, 2003); János M. Rainer, ed., *"Hatvanas évek" Magyarországon* [The "Sixties" in Hungary] (Budapest, 1956-os Intézet, 2004).
2. One of the most important aims of Hungarian cultural policy after 1919 was to be seen as part of Western Europe. To further such aims, a new system of state scholarships was introduced and new Hungarian institutions (Collegium Hungaricum) were set up abroad (law no. XIII/1927 and decree no. 17.200/1936

of the Ministry of Culture for the setting up of the Hungarian institutions abroad in Berlin, Paris, Rome, Vienna, and Warsaw). Due to political conflicts between France and Hungary, the Hungarian Institute in Paris was rather late in beginning its work: it opened in 1928 and was more limited in its functioning than those in Berlin, Rome, and Vienna. On the history of these institutions, see, for example, Ignác Romsics, "Francia-magyar kulturális kapcsolatok és a párizsi 'Magyar Intézet' a két világháború között" [French-Hungarian Cultural Relations and the Hungarian Institute in Paris between the Two World Wars], *Magyarságkutatás* A Magyarságkutató Intézet évkönyve, 1989 (1989): 193–202. On the 1940s, see József N. Szabó, *Hungarian Culture—Universal Culture: Cultural Diplomatic Endeavours of Hungary, 1945–1948* (Budapest: Akadémiai Kiadó, 1999); Anikó Macher, "La diplomatie culturelle franco-hongroise, 1945–1950," in *La culture dans les relations internationales,* ed. François Roche (Rome: Editions de l'École française de Rome, 2003), 251–262; Antal Gönyei, ed., *Dokumentumok Magyarország nemzetközi kulturális kapcsolatainak történetéből, 1945–1948* [Documents on the History of Hungarian International Cultural Relations, 1945–1948] (Budapest: Téka, 1988). On the cold war period, see, for example, Ibolya Murber, "A bécsi Collegium Hungaricum újjászervezése (1963)" [The Re-organization of the Collegium Hungaricum in Vienna (1963)], *Levéltári Szemle,* no. 4 (2005): 26–40.

3. Thomas Gomart, *Double détente: Les relations franco-soviétiques de 1958 à 1964* (Paris: Publications de la Sorbonne, 2003); Victor Rosenberg, *Soviet-American Relations, 1953–1960: Diplomacy and Cultural Exchange during the Eisenhower Presidency* (Jefferson, NC : McFarland Publishers, 2005).
4. For example, see Mihály Fülöp, "Mémoires de guerre froide et identité européenne," in *Les identités européennes au XXe siècle,* ed. Robert Frank (Paris: Publications de la Sorbonne, 2004), 101–109.
5. For example, see Zoltán Garadnai, "La Hongrie de János Kádár et le processus d'Helsinki," in *Vers la réunification de l'Europe Apports et limites du processus d'Helsinki de 1975 à nos jours,* ed. Elisabeth du Réau and Christine Manigand (Paris: L'Harmattan, 2005), 123–139.
6. On the mechanism of Hungarian propaganda, see, for example, Gergő Bendegúz Cseh, Melinda Kalmár, and Edit Pór, eds., *Zárt, bizalmas, számozott: Tájékoztatáspolitika és cenzúra 1957–1963* [Secret, Confidential, Numbered: Policy of Information and Censure, 1957–1963] (Budapest: Osiris Kiadó, 1999).
7. Pierre du Bois, "Cold War, Culture and Propaganda, 1953 to 1975," in *The Making of Detente: Eastern and Western Europe in the Cold War, 1965–75,* ed. Wilfried Loth and Georges-Henri Soutou (London and New York: Routledge, 2008), 9–24; Walter L. Hixson, *Parting the Curtain: Propaganda, Culture and the Cold War 1945–1961* (New York: St. Martin's Press, 1997).
8. Marès, *Culture et politique étrangère des démocraties populaires.*
9. NATO Archives, Committee on Information and Cultural Relations, AC/52-D/53, Report of the Cultural Advisor to the Secretary-General on the strengthening of the cultural cooperation among NATO countries, 21 July 1954.
10. Archives du Ministère des Affaires Étrangères, France (hereafter AMAE), série Affaires culturelles, 1949–1960, Dossier 29 and Nigel Gould-Davies, "The Logic of Soviet Cultural Diplomacy," *Diplomatic History,* no. 27 (April 2003): 193–214. Heads of government and foreign ministers began discussing East-West relations at the 1955 Geneva conferences. At the Foreign Ministers' Conference (27 October—10 November 1955), France released a memorandum setting out the views of all three Western delegations and containing a program of 17 points for action in the field of cultural exchange: e.g., the introduction of a ban on the jam-

ming of radio broadcasts and on restrictions concerning diplomatic missions; the opening of information centres; the possibility of disseminating books and publications; the development of private tourism and so on.

11. Étienne Manac'h, Ministère des Affaires étrangères à la Légation de France à Budapest, 5 March 1956, Centre des Archives Diplomatiques de Nantes, France (hereafter cited as CADN), Archives de l'ambassade de France à Budapest, Box 64.
12. János M. Rainer, *Nagy Imre: Politikai életrajz 1896–1953* [Nagy Imre: Political Biography], vol. 1 (Budapest: 1956-os Intézet, 1996); János M. Rainer, *Nagy Imre: Politikai életrajz 1953–1958* [Nagy Imre: Political Biography], vol. 2 (Budapest: 1956-os Intézet, 1999).
13. On the renewal of negotiations on cultural agreements, see, for example Beszélgetés Christian Pineau francia külügyminiszterrel, Kutas Imre párizsi magyar követ jelentése [Discussion with the French Minister of Foreign Affairs, Christian Pineau, The Hungarian Minister Plenipotentiary in Paris, Imre Kutas to the Hungarian Minister of Foreign Affairs], 29 March 1956, Magyar Országos Levéltár (Hungarian National Archives, hereafter MOL), Külügyminisztérium (Ministry of Foreign Affairs, hereafter KÜM), XIX-J-1-k, Franciaország [France], 18/i, 003905/1956, 278/szig. titk./1956, Box 36.
14. NATO Archives, Committee on Information and Cultural Relations, AC/52-D/197/2, Particular Conditions Concerning the Contacts between NATO and Satellite Countries, Note of the United Kingdom's delegation, 17 October 1956.
15. On the so-called "Hungarian question," see Csaba Békés, "The Hungarian Question on the UN Agenda: Secret Negotiations by the Western Great Powers October 26th–November 4th 1956, British Foreign Office Documents," *Hungarian Quarterly*, no. 157 (2000): 103–122; John P. Glennon, Edward C. Keefer, Ronald D. Landa, and Stanley Shaloff, eds., *Foreign Relations of the United States, 1955–1957: Eastern Europe* (Washington: United States Government Printing Office, 1990); Gusztáv Kecskés, "Franciaország politikája az ENSZ-ben a 'magyar ügy' kapcsán, 1956–1963" [France's Policy on the "Hungarian Question" within the UN, 1956–1963], *Századok*, no. 5 (2000): 1171–1194.
16. On communist ideology in the early period of the Kádár era, see, for example, Melinda Kalmár, *Ennivaló és hozomány* [Nourishment and Dowry] (Budapest: Magvetö, 1998).
17. On the missions of Hungarian scientists abroad, see Alexits György beszámolója [Note of György Alexits], 25 July and 16 August 1957, MOL, KÜM, XIX-J-1-k, Franciaország [France], 18/b, 003546/1957, Box 25. György Alexits, a member of the Hungarian Academy, traveled at the invitation of the Sorbonne to Paris in 1957. The idea was that individual missions and personal relations with the scientific world could become precursors to establishing relations at the state level.
18. Éva Standeisky, *Az írók és a hatalom, 1956–1963* [Hungarian Writers and Government Power, 1956–1963] (Budapest: 1956-os Intézet, 1996); István Deák, "'On the Leash' review of *Az írók és a hatalom, 1956–1963* [Hungarian Writers and Government Power, 1956–1963] by Éva Standeisky," *The Hungarian Quarterly*, no. 156 (winter 1999). <www.hungarianquarterly.com/no156/054.shtml> (*The Hungarian Quarterly*, June 2010)
19. Feljegyzés a külügyi osztály munkájáról [Note on the Work of the Ministry of Foreign Affairs], 3 December 1957, MOL, MSZMP iratai [Documents of the Hungarian Socialist Workers' Party], M-Ks, 288. f. 32. cs. 1. őe. 1957.
20. Összefoglaló A. Gromiko külügyminiszter és E. Sík külügyminiszter a Magyar Külügyminisztériumban tartott megbeszéléséről [Summary of Talks between the Soviet and Hungarian Ministers of Foreign Affairs, Gromyko and Sík, at the

Hungarian Ministry of Foreign Affairs], 7 April 1958, MOL, KÜM, XIX-J-1-j, Szovjetunió [Soviet Union], 26/a, Box 6.

21. Az MSZMP Politikai Bizottságának 1958. január 15-i ülésén a Külügyminisztérium munkájáról hozott határozata [Decision of the Political Committee Concerning the Work of the Ministry of Foreign Affairs], 15 January 1958, MOL, KÜM, XIX-J-1-r, Külügyminisztérium titkársága (Secretariat of the Ministry of Foreign Affairs), sz.n./1958, Box 1.
22. Hungarian propaganda was produced mainly by the so-called Friendship Societies: nondiplomatic bilateral organizations (based on the Soviet model) supported by the communist government of Hungary that presented popular cultural events with the cooperation of Western communist parties.
23. Rácz Pál ügyvivő jelentése a magyar külügyminiszternek [Report of P. Rácz, Chargé d'Affaires in Paris to the Minister of Foreign Affairs], 8 August 1958, MOL, KÜM, XIX-J-1-j, Franciaország [France], 4/a 001919/3/1958, Box 3.
24. A Magyar Intézet ügye [The Situation of the Hungarian Institute], 10 March 1959, MOL, KÜM, XIX-J-1-j, Franciaország [France], 2/c, 00496/2, Box 2 and Párizsi tapasztalataim: Gereblyés László a Külügyminisztériumnak [My Experiences in Paris: L. Gereblyés to the Ministry of Foreign Affairs], [?] 1961, MOL, Kulturális Kapcsolatok Intézetének iratai [Documents of the Institute of Cultural Relations], XIX-A-33-b, 003/1961, Box 8.
25. Összefoglaló az MSZMP Politikai Bizottsága 1959. október 6-i döntéséről [Summary on decision of the Political Committee on 6 October 1959], 6 October 1959, MOL, KÜM, XIX-J-1-u, Miniszterek és miniszterhelyettesek iratai [Documents of Ministers and Vice-Ministers], Péter János iratai [Papers János Péter], szn., Box 49.
26. The following countries had foreign legations or embassies in Budapest: Austria, Belgium, France, Greece, Italy, Netherlands, Poland, Switzerland, and the United States of America. Diplomatic life continued in spite of such events as the execution of Imre Nagy in June 1958, which did not stop the French legation, for example, from holding a reception on 14 July 1958.
27. NATO Archives, Committee of Political Advisers, AC/119-WP/45, Recent Developments in the Communist World and their Implications for Western Policy, 27 May 1957; AC/119-WP/30, Report on the Satellite Countries, 11 March 1957; AC/119- WP/5 revised, Relationships with Kádár's Government, 18 February 1957; Committee on Information and Cultural Relations, AC/52-D/224/4, General Policy Adopted by the Italian Government Concerning Exchange Programmes with the Soviet Bloc Following the Recent Hungarian Events, 14 March 1957.
28. Dépêche d'Étienne Manac'h au directeur de l'Institut Français de Budapest, Guy Turbet-Delof, 2 May 1957, AMAE, série Europe 1944–1960, Hongrie, tg. no. 33, Dossier 106.
29. Az MSZMP Központi Biztottságának Külügyi Osztályának előterjesztése az MSZMP Politikai Bizottságához [Proposal of the Central Committee to the Political Committee], 10 January 1958, MOL, MSZMP iratai [Documents of the Hungarian Socialist Workers' Party], M-Ks, 288. f. 32. cs. 11. ő.e. 1958.
30. For example, by setting up an international library in Budapest starting in 1957.
31. Állambiztonsági Szolgálatok Történeti Levéltára [Historical Archives of the Hungarian State Security], Dossier Marianne Halkó, 1957–1958. V-144/22 and AMAE, série Europe 1944–1960, Hongrie, Dossier 107: "Affaire Halkó."
32. Dépêches de Guy Turbet-Delof au Ministère des Affaires étrangères, 1949–1958, CADN, Archives de l'ambassade de France à Budapest, Box 173. Guy Turbet-Delof, born in Bordeaux in 1922, graduated from the École Normale Supérieure

in Paris and arrived in Hungary in April 1947. He was the director of the French cultural institute in Budapest and cultural attaché of the French Legation in that city from 1949 to 1958. See: Guy Turbet-Delof, *La révolution hongroise de 1956, Journal d'un témoin* (Paris: Edition Ibolya Virág, 1996).

33. Note de l'attaché culturel, Guy Turbet-Delof, 25 January 1958, CADN, Archives de l'ambassade de France à Budapest, AC/4/58, Box 173; Note de l'attaché culturel, 22 January 1958, CADN, Archives de l'ambassade de France à Budapest, AC/3/58, Box 165; Suggestions pour une dépêche d'envoi, note de l'attaché culturel, 17 October 1957, CADN, Archives de l'ambassade de France à Budapest, s. n., Box 173.
34. As minister of culture between 1947 and 1950, Gyula Ortutay, ethnographer and historian of literature, was the promoter of the signature of a French-Hungarian cultural agreement, without success. He was the rector of the Budapest University Eötvös Loránd between 1957 and 1963.
35. Béla Köpeczi studied in Paris between 1946 and 1949. He was minister of culture from 1982 to 1988 and professor at the Budapest University Eötvös Loránd from 1965 to 1991. On Hungarian culture, see Béla Köpeczi, *Trente années de la culture hongroise: une révolution culturelle* (Budapest: Corvina, 1982). On publishing activity in Hungary during the cold war, see István Bart, *Világirodalom és könyvkiadás a Kádár-korszakban* [Literature and Book Publishing during the Kádár Regime] (Budapest: Osiris Kiadó, 2002).
36. István Sőtér had a scholarship in Paris at the École Normale Supérieure between 1935 and 1936. He was director of the Literary Section of the Hungarian Academy of Sciences from 1957 to 1984, president of the Hungarian PEN from 1960 to 1970, and rector of the Budapest University Eötvös Loránd from 1963 to 1966. On French-Hungarian cultural relations, see István Sőtér, *L'esprit français en Hongrie* (Budapest: Officina, 1944). On his visit to Paris from 12 to 30 January 1959, see Beszámoló a Magyar Külügyminisztériumnak [Report to the Ministry of Foreign Affairs], 7 February 1959, MOL, KÜM, XIX-J-1-k, Franciaország [France], 18/g, 001408/1959, Box 34.
37. Összefoglaló értékelő jelentés az 1959. évi Haydn ünnepségekről [Summary on the Haydn Festivities] 10 October 1959, MOL, MSZMP iratai [Documents of the Hungarian Socialist Workers' Party], M-Ks, 288. f. 33. cs. 8. őe. 1959.
38. Magyar-osztrák viszony 1957-ben [Relations between Hungary and Austria in 1957], [?] 1957, MOL, MSZMP iratai [Documents of the Hungarian Socialist Workers' Party], M-Ks, 288. f. 32. cs. 2. őe. 1957.
39. Aczél György előterjesztése az MSZMP KB titkárságához: A zenei ünnepségek rendezése 1960–61-ben [Proposal of György Aczél to the Central Committee: Organizations of the Musical Festivities in 1960–61], 6 January 1960; Az 1961-es Liszt-Bartók ünnepség terve [Planning of the Liszt-Bartók Festivities in 1961], 31 March 1960 and Losonczi Ágnes jelentése az 1960 évi Erkel-ünnepségekről [Report of Á. Losonczi on the Erkel Festivities in 1960], [?] October 1960, MOL MSZMP iratai [Documents of the Hungarian Socialist Workers' Party], M-Ks, 288. f. 33. cs. 15. őe. 1960.
40. Köpeczi Béla, a Kiadói Főigazgatóság vezetőjének jelentése Szarka Károly külügyminiszter-helyettesnek és a párizsi magyar könyvkiállítás forgatókönyve, 1959. november 27–december 11 [Köpeczi's Report to the Vice-Minister of Foreign Affairs on the Hungarian Book Exhibition in Paris, 27 November–11 December 1959], 18 November 1959, MOL, KÜM, XIX-J-1-k, Franciaország [France], 18/d, 004624/1-10, Box 30.
41. Péter János feljegyzései [Reports of János Péter], 22 January 1959, MOL, KÜM, XIX-J-1-j, Franciaország [France], 4/a, 001090/1959, Box 2.

42. Rácz Pál jelentése a Külügyminisztériumnak [Report of Pál Rácz to the Ministry of Foreign Affairs], 30 June 1959, XIX-J-1-j, Franciaország [France], 17/b, 003230/2/1959, Box 14.
43. The main incident was the protest movement of the so-called Déry Committee, headed by Louis de Villefosse, a writer who opposed Hungary's official diplomatic agenda. Their manifesto—distributed during the exhibition and published by *Le Monde, Le Figaro,* and other French newspapers—sought to mobilize French public opinion and raise awareness that Hungarian writers, such as Tibor Déry, remained in prison long after the violent repressions in the wake of the revolution. Western intellectuals who signed the manifesto included Albert Camus, Jean-Paul Sartre, T. S. Eliot, Bertrand Russell, Karl Jaspers, Ignazio Silone, Alberto Moravia, Carlo Levi, and others.
44. On the French book show in Budapest (24 October to 8 November 1959), see AMAE, série Europe 1944–1960, Hongrie, Dossier 106: Relations culturelles avec la Hongrie.
45. Összefoglaló a kulturális kapcsolatok helyzetéről [Summary on Cultural Relations], MOL, Művelődésügyi Minisztérium [Ministry of Culture], 7 March 1959, XIX-J-4-rrr, Aczél György miniszterhelyettes iratai [Papers György Aczél, Vice-Minister of Culture], 575/A/1959, Box 3; Áttekintés Magyarország külföldi kulturális tevékenységéről [Summary on Hungary's Cultural International Activities], 9 April 1959, MOL, MSZMP iratai [Documents of the Hungarian Socialist Workers' Party], M-Ks, 288. f. 33. cs. 28 őe. 1959.
46. Irányelvek kulturális kapcsolataink alakításához a kapitalista országokkal [Directives on Our Cultural Relations with Capitalist Countries], 22 July 1960, MOL, XIX-J-1-k, 005529/1960. Cited in Cseh, Kalmár, and Pór, *Zárt, bizalmas, számozott,* 466–471.
47. NATO Archives, Committee on Information and Cultural Relations, AC/52-WP/13 — AC/52-WP/63 and AC/52- D(58), D(271), D(265), D(190) and D(224).
48. Követi értekezlet jegyzőkönyve, A NATO országokban működő követeink regionális értekezlete [Documentation on the Special Meeting of Hungarian Plenipotentiary Diplomats Accredited to NATO Countries], 8 December 1959, MOL, MSZMP iratai [Documents of the Hungarian Socialist Workers' Party], M-Ks, 288. f. 32. cs. 6. őe. 1959.
49. A NATO országokba akkreditált követek értekezlete, Kulturális életünk, kulturális kapcsolataink a kapitalista országokkal, a Külügyminisztérium és a külképviseletek feladatai [Documentation on the Special Meeting of Hungarian Plenipotentiary Diplomats Accredited to NATO Countries: Our Cultural Life, Our Cultural Relations with Capitalist Countries, Tasks of the Ministry of Foreign Affairs and Tasks of the Legations], 26 July 1960, MOL, MSZMP iratai [Documents of the Hungarian Socialist Workers' Party], M-Ks, 288. f. 32. cs. 12. őe. 1960.
50. A magyar követség jelentései Hruscsov franciaországi utazásáról [Reports of the Hungarian Legation in Paris on Khrushchev's Visit to Paris], 6–7 May, 1960, MOL, KÜM, XIX-J-1-j, Franciaország [France], 5/b, 00395/6, 00395/7 and 00395/8, Box 5.
51. A londoni magyar követség jelentése [Report of the Hungarian Legation in London], 4 December 1960, MOL, Művelődésügyi Minisztérium [Ministry of Culture], XIX-J-4-rrr, Aczél György miniszterhelyettes iratai [Papers György Aczél, Vice-Minister of Culture], 2848/A, Box 2 and Béla Köpeczi tájékoztatója a Politikai Bizottság tagjai részére a magyar íródelegáció angliai és franciaországi tanulmányútjáról [Report of Béla Köpeczi to the Political Committee on the Trip of the Hungarian Delegation in France and in Great Britain], 30 December 1960,

MOL, MSZMP iratai [Documents of the Hungarian Socialist Workers' Party], M-Ks, 288. f. 33. cs. 17. őe. 1960. The British Council invited the following Hungarian intellectuals from 16 November to 2 December 1960: Béla Köpeczi, Tibor Kardos, Áron Tamási, Ferenc Juhász, Géza Ottlik. Passuth László beszámolója angliai tanulmányútjáról [Report of L. Passuth on his Trip in Great Britain], 5 March 1960, MOL, KÜM, XIX-J-1-u, Miniszterek és miniszterhelyettesek iratai [Documents of Ministers and Vice-Ministers], Péter János iratai [Papers János Péter], Box 47. The Hungarian writer L. Passuth was also invited by the British Council to travel to London, from 27 February to 18 March 1960.

52. Anikó Macher, "Les paradoxes de la politique culturelle internationale de la Hongrie de 1957 à 1963," in Marès, *Culture et politique étrangère des démocraties populaires,* 169–192.
53. Nemzetközi kulturális tevékenységünk megjavítása [Improvement of Our International Cultural Activities], [?] 1960, MOL, KÜM, XIX-J-1-r, Külügyminisztérium titkársága [Secretariat of the Ministry of Foreign Affairs], Sík Endre iratai [Papers Endre Sík], 92/1960, Box 5. The party's political committee decided to create the CIC on 29 March 1960.
54. The ICR was set up in 1949 under the supervision of the Ministry of Foreign Affairs to centralize foreign cultural exchanges in order to make them easier to control by the party. Naturally, Western diplomats were looking for direct contacts with Hungarian cultural life and cultural exchanges took place directly, without the authorization of the institute.
55. József Bognár, born in 1917, was a member of the Hungarian parliament in 1945 and president of the Hungarian Smallholders' Party in 1946. He was minister of information in 1946–47 and minister of home and trade affairs from 1949 to 1953. On 27 October 1956, he was nominated to become vice-president of the Council of Ministers and minister of foreign trade affairs in the Imre Nagy government. In 1960, he was guest lecturer in Economics at the University of Budapest before going on to preside over the Institute of Cultural Relations from 1961 to 1969.
56. Decrees of the Council of Ministers on 30 June 1962, number 1016/1962, and 27 June 1962, number 3184/1962. A Kulturális Kapcsolatok Intézete és az Ügyvezető Elnökség feladatai [The Institute of Cultural Relations and the Tasks of Their Presidency], 7 September 1962, MOL, KÜM, XIX-J-1-j, Vegyes [Miscellaneous], 4/fd, 006934/1962, Box 40.
57. Kulturális kapcsolataink irányelvei és feladatai [Directives and Tasks of Our Cultural Relations], 5 December 1961, MOL, KÜM, XIX-J-1-u, Miniszterek és miniszterhelyettesek iratai [Documents of Ministers and Vice-Ministers], Mód Péter iratai, [Papers Péter Mód], 1961, Box 37 and Nemzetközi kulturális és tudományos kapcsolataink irányelvei a nem szocialista országok viszonylatában [Directives of Our Cultural and Scientific Relations with Nonsocialist Countries], 26 November 1962, MOL, KÜM, XIX-J-1-j, Vegyes [Miscellaneous], 4/fh, 008791/1962, Box 73.
58. Cultural diplomacy had a positive outcome even before the normalization of the American-Hungarian relationships, for instance concerning the relations between Hungary and some American foundations. Shepard Stone, the president of the Ford Foundation, visited Hungary in 1963, whereupon Hungary began receiving Ford scholarships. On American-Hungarian cultural relations, see John Richardson, az Amerikai Külpolitikai Társaság igazgatójának magyarországi utazása: A washingtoni követség jelentése [Trip of the Director of the American Foreign Policy Society, John Richardson, to Hungary: Report of the Hungarian Legation in Washington], 21 March 1960, MOL, Művelődésügyi Minisztérium,

[Ministry of Culture], XIX-J-4-rrr, Aczél György miniszterhelyettes iratai [Papers of György Aczél, Vice-Minister of Culture], 720/A/1960, Box 2 and Feljegyzés a Ford Foundation-ról [Note on the Ford Foundation], 21 November 1963, MOL, KÜM, XIX-J-1-j, Vegyes [Miscellaneous], 17/d, 007536/1963, Box 87.

59. Értekezlet az európai integrációval kapcsolatos de Gaulli-i politikáról, Medvegy Pál francia referens feljegyzése [Meeting on de Gaulle's European policy, Note of Pál Medvegy], 7 June 1962, MOL, KÜM, XIX-J-1-j, Franciaország [France], 4/a, 006303/1962, Box 3; A párizsi magyar követség külpolitikai összefoglalója Budapest, [Summary of the Hungarian Legation in Paris on Foreign Affairs], 5 March 1962, MOL, KÜM, XIX-J-1-j, Franciaország [France], 5/b, 00311/2/1962, 194/szig. titkos, Box 5; Franciaország kapcsolatainak romlása a nyugati szövetségesekkel: A párizsi magyar követség jelentése [Deterioration of the Relations between France and Other Western Countries: Report of the Hungarian Legation in Paris], 3 February 1962, MOL, KÜM, XIX-J-1-j, Franciaország [France], 002011/1962, no. 117/szig.titkos, Box 5; Franciaország kulturális kapcsolatai a szocialista országokkal: A párizsi magyar követség jelentése [France's Cultural Relations with the Socialist Countries: Report of the Hungarian Legation in Paris], 19 July 1962, MOL, KÜM, XIX-J-1-j, Franciaország [France], 18/b, 005524/1962, no. 599, Box 25; Előterjesztés az MSZMP Politikai Bizottságához a magyar-francia államközi kapcsolatokról [Proposal to the Political Committee on Hungarian-French Relations], 22 December 1964, MOL, KÜM, XIX-J-1-r, Külügyminisztérium titkársága [Secretariat of the Ministry of Foreign Affairs], Péter János iratai [Papers János Péter], 390/1964, « B », Box 7; A párt külügyi osztálya előterjesztése az MSZMP Politikai Bizottságához a magyar-francia kapcsolatokról [Proposal of the Party's Section of Foreign Affairs to the Political Committee on the Hungarian-French Relations], 26 October 1964, MOL, Kulturális Kapcsolatok Intézetének iratai [Documents of the Institute of Cultural Relations], XIX-A-33-b, 003/30, Box 32; Note du directeur de l'Institut pour la DGACT, le 9 January 1962, CADN, Archives de l'ambassade de France à Budapest, DI/4/62, Box 172 and Rapport d'activité de l'Institut français de Budapest de l'année 1962, 30 March 1963, CADN, Archives de l'ambassade de France à Budapest, Box 172.

60. Cf. Anthony Haigh, *Cultural Diplomacy in Europe* (Strasbourg: Council of Europe, 1974).

61. On the trip of a delegation of Hungarian writers, see for example Magyar íródelegáció franciaországi utazása, 1962. december 7–28. [Travel of the Delegation of Hungarian Writers in France, from 7 to 28 December 1962], 5 January 1963, MOL, KÜM, XIX-J-1-k, Franciaország [France], 18/d, 0082/1-4, Box 30. On the Hungarian planning for the invitation of Western writers (Louis Aragon, Jean-Paul Sartre, Daniel Mayer, Raymond Queneau, and Jean Cocteau), see for example Francia írók meghívása a KKI 1963. évi belső terve alapján [Invitation of French writers Allowed by the Institute of Cultural Relations in 1963], 1 February 1963, MOL, KÜM, XIX-J-1-k, Franciaország [France], 18/d, 00902, Box 30. However, Western writers, notably Jean-Paul Sartre, refused to go to Hungary, mainly because their eminent Hungarian colleague István Bibó was still imprisoned.

62. A magyar-olasz kapcsolatok helyzete [Hungarian-Italian Relations], 16 January 1960, MOL, MSZMP iratai [Documents of the Hungarian Socialist Workers' Party], M-Ks, 288. f. 32. cs 2. őe. 1960.

63. Előterjesztés az 1962–63. évi magyar-olasz kulturális egyezmény tárgyában [Proposal Concerning the Hungarian-Italian Cultural Agreement], 10 August 1962, MOL, MSZMP iratai [Documents of the Hungarian Socialist Workers' Party], M-Ks, 288. f. 33. cs. 31. őe. 1962.

64. Note du directeur de l'Institut français de Budapest pour la Direction générale

des Affaires culturelles et techniques, 13 December 1961, CADN, Archives de l'ambassade de France à Budapest, no. 21/61, Box 165.

65. A kultúrdiplomáciai továbbképző tanfolyam tervezete [The Program of the Cursus of Cultural Diplomacy], 18 April 1962, MOL, KÜM, XIX-J-1-u, Miniszterek és miniszterhelyettesek iratai [Documents of Ministers and Vice-Ministers], Péter János iratai [Papers János Péter], 51/1962, Box 55.
66. A külföldi Magyar Intézetek helyzete, feladatai és működésük fejlesztéséhez szükséges feltételek [Situation, Tasks of the Hungarian Cultural Institutes and the Conditions of their Work], 21 July 1960, MOL, KÜM, XIX-J-1-j, Vegyes [Miscellaneous], 17/c, 005515, 1960, Box 87. At the same time, the Hungarian leadership wanted to renew the role of the Hungarian cultural attachés in Western countries. Greater importance was attached to more concrete, less rhetorical cultural work from the beginning of the 1960s, when a cultural attaché was also sent to Rome.
67. Házi Vencel feljegyzése a párizsi nagykövetség részére [Note of Vencel Házi to Hungarian Embassy in Paris], 10 December 1964, XIX-J-1-j, Franciaország [France], 17/b, 00175/4/1964, Box 14.
68. Conversation à cinq. Echanges culturels avec l'Est, Réunion du 1er au 2 mars 1960 à Paris, Note adressée au Cabinet du Ministre, 10 October 1960, AMAE, série Affaires culturelles, 1949–1960, Dossier 29. Anikó Macher, "Le Groupe de travail des échanges Est-Ouest: acteur ou simple observatoire occidental des relations culturelles entre les deux Europe (1960–1966)?" in *Les deux Europes/ The Two Europes,* ed. Guia Migani and Christian Wenkel (Bruxelles, Bern, Berlin, Frankfurt am Main, New York, Oxford, Wien: Peter Lang, 2009).
69. Relations culturelles entre pays occidentaux et pays de l'Est, Note adressée au Cabinet du Ministre, 22 May 1962, CDAN, Archives de l'ambassade de France à Budapest, no. 768, Box 169.
70. New research has shown how secret negotiations were planned between Hungarian and American political leaders from 1960 onward to resolve the "Hungarian question" and to secure an amnesty for political prisoners in Hungary. The Hungarian leadership agreed to the amnesty in 1963.

Bibliography

Baráth, Magdolna. "Magyarország a szovjet diplomáciai iratokban, 1957–1964." [Hungary in Soviet Diplomatic Documents, 1957–1964]. In Rainer, *Múlt századi hétköznapok: Tanulmányok a Kádár rendszer kialakulásának időszakáról.*

Bart, István. *Világirodalom és könyvkiadás a Kádár-korszakban* [Literature and Book Publishing during the Kádár Regime]. Budapest: Osiris Kiadó, 2002.

Békés, Csaba. *Európából Európába: Magyarország konfliktusok kereszttüzében, 1945–1990* [From Europe to Europe: Hungary in the Crossfire of Conflicts, 1945–1990]. Budapest: Gondolat, 2004.

———. "The Hungarian Question on the UN Agenda: Secret Negotiations by the Western Great Powers October 26th–November 4th 1956, British Foreign Office Documents." *Hungarian Quarterly,* no. 157 (2000): 103–122.

———. "Titkos válságkezeléstől a politikai koordinációig: Politikai egyeztetési mechanizmus a Varsói Szerződésben, 1954–1967" [From Secret Crisis Management to Political Coordination: Political Coordinating Mechanism in the Warsaw Pact, 1954–1967]. In Rainer, *Múlt századi hétköznapok: Tanulmányok a Kádár rendszer kialakulásának időszakáról.*

Du Bois, Pierre. "Cold War, Culture and Propaganda, 1953 to 1975." In Loth and Soutou, *The Making of Detente: Eastern and Western Europe in the Cold War, 1965–75.*

Borhi, László. *Hungary in the Cold War (1945–1956): Between the United States and the Soviet Union.* Budapest and New York: Central European University Press, 2004.

Cseh, Gergő Bendegúz, Melinda Kalmár, and Edit Pór, eds. *Zárt, bizalmas, számozott: Tájékoztatáspolitika és cenzúra 1957–1963* [Secret, Confidential, Numbered: Policy of Information and Censure, 1957–1963]. Budapest: Osiris Kiadó, 1999.

Deák, István. "'On the Leash' Review of *Az írók és a hatalom, 1956–1963* [Hungarian Writers and Government Power, 1956–1963] by Éva Standeisky." *The Hungarian Quarterly,* no. 156 (winter 1999). www.hungarianquarterly.com/no156/054.shtml (*The Hungarian Quarterly,* June 2010)

Duboscl ard, Alain, Laurent Grison, Laurent Jeanpierre, Pierre Journoud, Christine Okret, and Dominique Trimbur. *Entre rayonnement et réciprocité: Contribution à l'histoire de la diplomatie culturelle.* Paris: Publications de la Sorbonne, 2002.

Frank, Robert, ed. *Les identités européennes au XXe siècle.* Paris: Publications de la Sorbonne, 2004.

Fülöp, Mihály. "Mémoires de guerre froide et identité européenne." In Frank, *Les identités européennes au XXe siècle.*

Garadnai, Zoltán. "La Hongrie de János Kádár et le processus d'Helsinki." In du Réau and Manigand, *Vers la réunification de l'Europe Apports et limites du processus d'Helsinki de 1975 à nos jours.*

Glennon, John P., Edward C. Keefer, Ronald D. Landa, and Stanley Shaloff, eds. *Foreign Relations of the United States, 1955–1957: Eastern Europe.* Washington: U.S. Government Printing Office, 1990.

Gomart, Thomas. *Double détente: Les relations franco-soviétiques de 1958 à 1964.* Paris: Publications de la Sorbonne, 2003.

Gould-Davies, Nigel. "The Logic of Soviet Cultural Diplomacy." *Diplomatic History,* no. 27 (April 2003): 193–214.

Gönyei, Antal, ed. *Dokumentumok Magyarország nemzetközi kulturális kapcsolatainak történetéből, 1945–1948* [Documents on the History of Hungarian International Cultural Relations, 1945–1948]. Budapest: Téka, 1988.

Haigh, Anthony. *Cultural Diplomacy in Europe.* Strasbourg: Council for Cultural Cooperation, 1974.

Hixson, Walter L. *Parting the Curtain: Propaganda, Culture and the Cold War 1945–1961.* New York: St. Martin's Press, 1997.

Kalmár, Melinda. *Ennivaló és hozomány.* [Nourishment and Dowry] Budapest: Magvető, 1998.

Kecskés, Gusztáv. "Les caractéristiques de la politique étrangère de la Hongrie de 1945 à 1990." In Marès, *Culture et politique étrangère des démocraties populaires.*

———. "Franciaország politikája az ENSZ-ben a 'magyar ügy' kapcsán, 1956–1963" [France's Policy on the "Hungarian Question" within the UN, 1956–1963]. *Századok,* no. 5 (2000): 1171–1194.

Köpeczi, Béla. *Trente années de la culture hongroise: une révolution culturelle.* Budapest: Corvina, 1982.

Loth, Wilfried, and Georges-Henri Soutou, eds. *The Making of Detente: Eastern and Western Europe in the Cold War, 1965–75.* London and New York: Routledge, 2008.

Macher, Anikó. "La diplomatie culturelle franco-hongroise (1945–1950)." In Roche, *La culture dans les relations internationales.*

———. "Les paradoxes de la politique culturelle internationale de la Hongrie de 1957 à 1963." In Marès, *Culture et politique étrangère des démocraties populaires.*

———. "Le Groupe de travail des échanges Est-Ouest: acteur ou simple observatoire des relations culturelles entre les deux Europe (1960–1966)?" In Guia Migani and Christian Wenkel, eds., *Les deux Europes/ The Two Europes.* Bruxelles, Bern, Berlin, Frankfurt am Main, New York, Oxford, Wien: Peter Lang, 2009.

Marès, Antoine, ed. *Culture et politique étrangère des démocraties populaires.* Paris: Institut d'études slaves, 2007.

Murber, Ibolya. "A bécsi Collegium Hungaricum újjászervezése (1963)" [The Reorganization of the Collegium Hungaricum in Vienna (1963)]. *Levéltári Szemle,* no. 4 (2005): 26–40.

Rainer, M. János, ed. *"Hatvanas évek" Magyarországon.* [The "Sixties" in Hungary]. Budapest: 1956-os Intézet, 2004.

———. *Nagy Imre: Politikai életrajz 1896–1953* [Nagy Imre: Political Biography]. Vol. 1. Budapest: 1956-os Intézet, 1996.

———. *Nagy Imre: Politikai életrajz 1953–1958* [Nagy Imre: Political Biography]. Vol. 2. Budapest: 1956-os Intézet, 1999.

———, ed. *Múlt századi hétköznapok: Tanulmányok a Kádár rendszer kialakulásának időszakáról* [Everyday in the Last Century: Essays on the Period of the Formation of the Kádár Regime]. Budapest: 1956-os Intézet, 2003.

———. *Ötvenhat után* [After Fifty-Six]. Budapest: 1956-os Intézet, 2003.

Du Réau, Elisabeth, and Christine Manigand, eds. *Vers la réunification de l'Europe Apports et limites du processus d'Helsinki de 1975 à nos jours.* Paris: L'Harmattan, 2005.

Roche, François, ed. *La culture dans les relations internationales.* Rome: Editions de l'École française de Rome, 2003.
Romsics, Ignác. "Francia-magyar kulturális kapcsolatok és a párizsi 'Magyar Intézet' a két világháború között" [French-Hungarian Cultural Relations and the Hungarian Institute in Paris between the Two World Wars]. *Magyarságkutatás,* A Magyarságkutató Intézet évkönyve, 1989 (1989): 193–202.
Rosenberg, Victor. *Soviet-American relations, 1953–1960: Diplomacy and Cultural Exchange During the Eisenhower Presidency.* Jefferson, NC: McFarland Publishers, 2005.
Sőtér, István. *L'esprit français en Hongrie.* Budapest: Officina, 1944.
Standeisky, Éva. *Az írók és a hatalom, 1956–1963* [Hungarian Writers and Government Power, 1956–1963]. Budapest: 1956-os Intézet, 1996.
Szabó, József N. *Hungarian Culture—Universal Culture: Cultural Diplomatic Endeavours of Hungary, 1945–1948.* Budapest: Akadémiai Kiadó, 1999.
Turbet-Delof, Guy. *La révolution hongroise de 1956: journal d'un témoin.* Paris: Ibolya Virág, 1996.

Chapter 4

CATHOLICS IN OSTPOLITIK?

Networking and Nonstate Diplomacy in the Bensberger Memorandum, 1966–1970

Annika Frieberg

Introduction

In March 1968, a Catholic lay group called the Bensberger Circle published a document on West German–Polish relations. The Bensberger memorandum emphasized the importance of a West German Catholic initiative to improve contacts with Poland. Written from a Catholic perspective, the memorandum promoted the recognition of the Oder-Neisse line and criticized the Adenauer government's passive stance toward West Germany's eastern neighbors. The memorandum primarily attempted to influence public opinion in West Germany and encourage the overcoming of an antagonistic and difficult past, but it was directed specifically to the Polish Catholic Church. The Bensberger Circle came to assume a role as cultural diplomats in the field of tension between state, society, and nation in the Federal Republic and Poland.

An analysis of the individuals who created, and assigned meaning to, the Bensberger memorandum—the end result of a collective effort initiated in 1966—provides evidence that nonstate activism can play a decisive role in political change. Traditional discussions of Ostpolitik have focused on change from above, in which American allies exerted pressure to push West Germany toward détente within the changing international climate, or in which Willy Brandt's new vision of Ostpolitik came about because of superpower geopolitics

Notes for this section begin on page 129.

and the West German–East German situation.[1] However, a new body of international relations theory has introduced the work and role of nonstate actors in processes of political transformation. My research specifically draws from notions of "transnational advocacy networks" and the dynamics between state and nonstate actors in shaping foreign relations.[2] I argue for the importance of a group of nonstate actors, examining their influence through media on foreign relations.

One way in which nonstate actors like the creators of the memorandum could play a larger role was through media-generated discussions influencing public opinion. Across the spectrum during the cold war, all West German politicians had to take into consideration their own domestic constituencies in developing foreign policy. This was particularly true for the years of 1967 and 1968, preceding the elections in 1969. The relationship with Poland and the Eastern bloc was a central question in the election of 1969, which would end in a victory for Willy Brandt's concept of a foreign policy overhaul in Eastern Europe. At the same time, all major West German parties felt restricted by the need to take into consideration the feelings and agendas of the West German expellee groups. Though increasingly marginal compared to their status in the 1950s, the expellees still potentially could represent a decisive percentage of voters.[3] The Bensberger memorandum, an independent position loosely connected to church and media, shaped policy in the court of public opinion.

The memorandum was a diplomatic document created by nonstate actors who, in the name of a nation, people, or larger ethical questions, attempted to accomplish a shift in Polish-German relations. The fact that the circle came from Catholic intellectual elites was important because it facilitated contact with Polish groups. These elites appealed to shared Christian ideals to escape the traditional national antagonisms that underlay official political problems. The networks surrounding the Bensberger Circle were to a large extent founded on Catholic cross-border structures. In addition, since state-to-state relations were also complicated by the lack of legitimacy of the communist state, the Bensberger interactions with the Polish Catholic circles had the potential to stabilize relations further and create long-term continuities in the dialogue between the two societies.

At times of upheaval, weakness, or passivity in the state, other societal groups or institutions can assume roles as mediators in cross-border relations.[4] In Polish-German relations, Catholic groups found themselves in a position to become cultural diplomats, particularly because of the strong position of the Polish Catholic Church.

By considering the Bensberger Circle's role as public opinion formers and, more importantly, as mediators and builders of contacts across the borders, this study defines cultural diplomacy as diplomatic activity by nonstate actors in a vacuum of state strength and action. The West German government was not at the head of the shift in geopolitical thought taking place with regard to Poland in the 1960s but acted on it only when it became clear, through election results and media discussions, that public opinion had begun to turn. The Bensberger memorandum was a final push before the official political change, but more than that, it was an attempt at direct dialogue with Poland at a time when the West German state was largely focused on domestic political debates about foreign policy in which nonstate and noncommunist Polish voices had no place.

Background and Context

Official diplomatic relations did not exist between Warsaw and Bonn before 1970. Since its foundation in 1949, the Federal Republic had refused to recognize the Polish postwar borders, which had been moved eastward to the rivers Oder and Neisse at the 1945 Potsdam Conference, causing Germany to lose one third of its territory.[5] In addition, the creation of the German Democratic Republic complicated the relationship, geographically and politically. From 1955 on, the Federal Republic adhered to the Hallstein Doctrine. According to this doctrine, named after State Secretary Walter Hallstein, the Federal Republic was the sole representative of Germany and would not recognize, or maintain diplomatic relations, with any state that recognized the German Democratic Republic. This included Poland and all other Warsaw Pact states except for the Soviet Union. On both sides, memories of war, occupation, genocide, and expulsions plagued the relationship between Poles and Germans. Poland in particular feared and protested West Germany's rearmament and nuclear armament plans in combination with German calls for border revisions. Since1945 Poland had become a fairly weak state protectorate of the Soviet Union, an authoritarian regime plagued by conflicts with its powerful Catholic Church and occasional popular protests. The Polish People's Republic used the territorial conflict and supposed enmity with West Germany to unify its own population and distance it from Western Europe.

Official relations in these years were characterized by half-hearted initiatives and neglected opportunities for improvement, equally disappointing for both states' governments. In 1956, a relaxation in Poland's communist regime created hopes for an improvement of relations with West Germany. In 1963, a partial political opening initiated by Bonn led to the exchange of trade missions with Poland. For the Polish communists, however, the trade agreement could not replace official diplomacy, and the diplomat sent to head the Warsaw trade mission, Dr. Mumm von Schwarzenstein, remained politically isolated. In West Germany, leading Christian Democrats in the parliament continued to believe in a hard-line stance toward the Soviet Union and feared a weakening of the Hallstein Doctrine. On these grounds, they rejected renewed Polish proposals of a mutual Central European nuclear-free security zone in 1964 (the Rapacki Plan, first proposed by Polish foreign minister Adam Rapacki at the United Nations in 1957). The repeated rejections of this plan offended Gomułka and contributed to the diplomatic standstill.[6] Meanwhile, the Polish state embarked on a gradual reversal of the freedoms from 1956, culminating in the 1968 anti-Semitic campaigns and party purge—a development that strengthened the West German opponents to cooperation with Poland.

The Bensberger Circle and Memorandum

While the state policy between Poland and the Federal Republic was reduced to terse statements in the media or in diplomatic notes, a series of religious memorandums and statements attempted to open lines of communication in the relations. One of these documents was the Bensberger memorandum, which was prepared between 1966 and 1968 by a group around the well-known left-wing Catholic journalist and publisher of the *Frankfurter Hefte,* Walter Dirks. The Bensberger Circle was originally connected to the international Catholic peace movement Pax Christi. The founding fifty to sixty members of the Bensberger Circle met for the first time on 7–8 May 1966 in the Thomas-Morus Akademie in Bensberg, near Cologne. At this meeting, the circle elected its Poland Commission, which composed a text on the Polish-German relationship over the following two years. The outline was drafted by Eugen Kogon, and the original text written by Walter Dirks and the young theologian Gottfried Erb. A larger group within the circle became involved with revisions to the document.

In its final format, signed by 128 Catholics, the 25-page Bensberger memorandum included four sections: (1) the idea of Christian reconciliation and, as a consequence of this religious task, (2) the points of conflict between Poles and Germans; (3) issues surrounding the Oder-Neisse Line; and (4) proposed steps toward reconciliation and improved relations. The document was intended as a Catholic equivalent to a 1965 memorandum on Germany's relationship to its eastern neighbors published by the Protestant Church. More importantly, the memorandum was to be a more accommodating answer to the Polish Catholic bishops' 1965 letter to the German Catholic bishops. In short, there were at least three target audiences: Polish Catholics, the West German domestic audience, and the West German Catholic establishment.

Intellectual Origins of the Memorandum

In a 1947 article in the Catholic journal *Frankfurter Hefte,* Eugen Kogon and Walter Dirks discussed the relationship between Poland and Germany and introduced their vision of a united Germany within postwar Europe. The authors argued that Polish-German relations must be seen through the lens of the war and Nazi Germany's crimes in the East. Dirks commented, on the stories of ruthless expulsions of Germans from the eastern territories, that the methods struck him as similar to those used by the Nazis in the concentration camps, and that they indicated a desire for revenge among the Poles. "They have not forgotten that they were injured 'in the name of the German people' and they also have not forgotten the eyes of the travelers, whom they encountered during their transports."[7] In the formerly German territories, "the word 'German' had come to represent extermination politics and concentration camps such as Stutthof, Treblinka, Majdanek and Auschwitz."[8] German war crimes and German foreign policy during the Hitler era were also the root cause of the loss of the eastern territories. In Dirks's words, "Churchill did not go to Yalta because of Stalin's pretty eyes but because *we* forced him there."[9]

In these early years, the *Frankfurter Hefte* was very concerned with questions of German war guilt. It was one of the few journals belonging to the religious press that discussed Poland from a perspective critical of Germany's role in World War II.[10] In terms of the Germans' relationship with the Nazi past, Kogon and Dirks believed that it was a Christian duty to acknowledge, and come to terms with, guilt for the crimes committed by Germans during the war. This repentance should involve not only prayer and internal work but also concrete attempts at restitution to those injured. On the other hand, they rejected ideas of collective guilt and denazification imposed by the Allies from above in the postwar era. Coming to terms with the Nazi past should occur voluntarily, through individual acts of conscience.[11]

The two authors ultimately blamed nationalism for the brutalities between Poles and Germans. Kogon commented that "nationalism as an ordering principle in Europe overall has failed, and it has failed particularly in the European east."[12] Against antagonistic nationalism in both Poland and Germany, they posed the Christian duty to forgive and the need to break the "circle of evil" by understanding the other perspective.[13] Finally, they asked for "a realistic policy ... [since] the mutual pursuit of demands and reasons in centuries of a shared history of conflict, does not lead to any sensible solutions."[14] In this way, they utilized Christian ideals and a sense of the two countries' common European heritage to offset the traditional confrontational and competitive view.

Walter Dirks and Eugen Kogon had firm backgrounds as public intellectuals involved in the foundation of a postwar German state. Dirks, who had studied theology, was a well-known journalist for the left-wing Catholic press during the Weimar era. During the Allied occupation and license press era, he was listed as politically clean and had no difficulty receiving a publishing license from the American occupation authorities. The same was true for Kogon, who spent six years in the Buchenwald concentration camp until he was liberated in 1945. Kogon wrote one of the first standard works on Nazi Germany, *Der SS-Staat: Das System der deutschen Konzentrationslager,* in 1946, and he participated in early debates on the Nazi war crimes and their connection with German society at large. Kogon and Dirks founded the *Frankfurter Hefte* in 1946. Thus the Bensberger memorandum was drafted by men who were not focused exclusively on Polish-German issues but took a larger responsibility for the moral and political rebuilding of a German state. Strengthening Germany's relationships with its neighboring states in the aftermath of the war was central to this project. Dirks was involved in French-German reconciliation efforts as well, and he envisioned the project of Polish-German reconciliation within a larger context of restored foreign relations for Germany on the European continent.

Christian activism and media influence were the foundation of their political involvement from the very beginning. Dirks argued for political activism based on Christian responsibility as early as the 1920s. After the war, *Frankfurter Hefte* ran a feature on the Catholic philosopher Jacques Maritain, who argued for a necessary Christian cultural impact on politics.[15] Maritain's works became inspirational texts for the Christian Democratic movement in postwar Europe, in which Dirks played an early prominent role. Also active in founding the Christian Democratic Party in Frankfurt, Dirks ultimately became disillusioned with its political direction and left it to focus exclusively on journalistic activism.[16]

Maritain's writings also inspired Polish Catholic intellectuals in the interwar movement called *Odrodzenie* (Rebirth). His ideas became a point of intersection as some of these young Polish interwar intellectuals became leading members of postwar intelligentsia and the Bensberger Circle's primary contacts in Poland. While Dirks's attempts to combine socialist ideals with Catholicism did not take root in the CDU, his influence was strong in that his particular vision of Christian politics was expressed in radio and in the *Frankfurter Hefte.* Associating his name with the memorandum and networking on its behalf, Dirks gave it a high public profile that it would otherwise have lacked.

The Church Memorandums and Media: Religious Activism In Public Opinion

In the mid 1960s, the West German churches and media began to take an increased interest in Bonn's policies toward Eastern Europe. In addition, churches and religious groups published a series of statements and memorandums on Polish-German relations. The religious and media efforts were more entwined than they appeared publicly, since several elite figures were active in both realms. By the early 1960s, a greater interest in Poland had begun surfacing in the West German media. Television documentaries such as Jürgen Neven du Mont's *Breslau* (1963) and Hansjakob Stehle's *Polens Osten-Deutschlands Westen* (1964) created debate about postwar Poland and the formerly German territories. Leading press such as *Die Zeit, Stern,* and television and radio stations featured Polish culture and history. Walter Dirks himself had been a commentator on the radio station Südwestfunk since 1948, and from 1965 to 1967 he led the cultural desk at the radio station Westdeutscher Rundfunk. Eugen Kogon was a controversial television reporter for the Norddeutscher Rundfunk's popular political magazine *Panorama.* Klaus von Bismarck, the director-general of the Westdeutscher Rundfunk and a close friend of Walter Dirks, was one of the initiators of the 1962 Tübingen memorandum.

Through the Tübingen memorandum, the German Protestant Church first became publicly engaged in Ostpolitik. This document, published by eight leading lay Protestants, criticized the existing Eastern policy as based on unrealistic expectations for postwar Europe, and though it was not an officially church-sponsored document, it triggered an internal discussion. In October 1965, the Chamber of Public Responsibility (*Kammer für öffentliche Verantwortung*) of the Protestant Church published a memorandum named "The Situation of the Expellees and the Relationship of the German People to Its Eastern Neighbors: An Evangelical Memorandum." Recommending acceptance of the territorial losses, this document provoked a violent debate about the Oder-Neisse Line in the Federal Republic and great frustration in the expellee organizations.[17] Some of these memorandums were apolitical, whereas others, like the Bensberger and Tübingen memorandum, criticized the government's foreign policy stance.

German and Polish Catholic clergy and prominent laity had additional opportunities to interact with each other during the Second Vatican Council in Rome between 1962 and 1965. Their meetings inspired the bishop of Wrocław, Bolesław Kominek, to write a reconciliatory letter to the German hierarchy. The letter, which was signed by the Polish Primate, Cardinal Stefan Wyszyński and all the Polish bishops, invited the German bishops to the Polish Church's millennial celebration in May 1966. It also addressed the difficulties of Polish-German reconciliation. The letter included the famous phrase "We forgive and ask for forgiveness," which was reproduced in all articles describing the letter. Promptly responding to the letter, the German Catholic bishops stated "we take the outstretched hands," but they carefully avoided any reference to the territorial question dividing Poles and Germans.[18] The cautiously phrased answer disappointed the Polish episcopate.

In 1965 Dirks visited the Second Vatican Council in Rome. His *Frankfurter Hefte* report "In Rome, Late Fall 1965," described the last session of the Second Vatican Council and was published in January 1966. It ended with a comment about the Polish initiative. He wrote, "Finally, the message of the Polish episcopate was quietly being prepared. Will the Council, since this message is its fruit, in its last moments contribute also to the relaxation of certain domestic German tensions? With this hope, absolutely no certainty, I have returned to the chilly German late fall." The article added in a footnote that "the Polish bishops' high-minded offer was accepted by the Germans without reservations."[19] However, in the following months Dirks began to feel that the German bishops' answer was inadequate and too reticent. In Rome, he met for example with the editor of *Tygodnik*

Powszechny, Jerzy Turowicz, as well as Bishop Bolesław Kominek.[20] Through his Polish contacts, he became aware that the Polish Catholics were frustrated with the response from the German Catholic Church, due to its lack of political substance.

The memorandums and ongoing debates encouraged the original initiators of the Bensberger memorandum. They believed that it was high time for German Catholic groups to play a role in the larger geopolitical debates about the future of Europe. The official invitation letter to the founding meeting in Bensberg on 8 May 1966 spoke of the need to follow up on the efforts made at the Second Vatican Council and to contribute to the 1965 Protestant document. "We owe it not only an answer but also a supplement; the community of faith with the Polish Catholics gives us specific sources of recognition, relations and responsibilities. We also owe the Polish bishops an answer to their appellation, which on a foundational level goes beyond the German bishops and addresses us all."[21] In this way, the letter referred to earlier efforts and drew on the mutual Catholic faith to explain its particular duty to open a dialogue with the Polish Catholics.

West German Politics and the Memorandum

While functioning as a focal point at its early stages, Dirks was not formally the leader of the Bensberger Circle. The group invited to compose and sign the memorandum was at first politically varied, but over time its sympathies shifted more clearly to the left. From the outset, the Bensberger activists believed that a position independent of politics was desirable for their purposes of influencing public opinion. In letters from the planning stages in 1966, the originators discussed the necessity of gathering "some intelligent Catholics" and creating their own document on the relationship with Poland.[22] A letter exchange between Gottfried Erb and Walter Dirks considered the form this gathering should take, deciding also that the gathering should be a group of Catholic laity independent of church structures and Pax Christi in order to make it "politically freer and more flexible."[23] Other prominent members, such as Karlheinz Koppe, who joined in 1967 and became one of the speakers for the circle, were closely associated with the Social Democrats. Koppe wrote in his memoirs:

> As I was already an SPD party member, I had the opportunity to speak with Herbert Wehner about the memorandum and the debate about

> recognizing the Oder-Neisse Line connected with it. He agreed with our ideas without reservations but was of the opinion that the time – especially considering the [upcoming] Bundestag elections in 1969 – was not ripe for SPD to openly support the proposition.[24]

The statement made clear that the document was not politically anchored in either parties or the church. Their document faced firm opposition from the CDU and had only unofficial support from Social Democratic politicians. The Bensberger Circle also became involved in domestic politics and published memorandums on, for example, the Vietnam War and conscientious objection to military service.

A New Concept of Polish-German Relations?

The Bensberger Circle approached Polish-German relations based on their understanding and application of Christian peace, reconciliation, and forgiveness between peoples. The argument for improved relations with Poland involved the notion of an internal process of confessing one's own guilt, overcoming hostility, and giving and receiving forgiveness that Dirks and Kogon had expressed already in their 1949 article. In the memorandum, they wrote, "The Christian message of salvation refers in its central promises – reconciliation, justice, peace – also to the world changing forces of contemporary society. In the service of this message, Christians are charged to assume public responsibility in a critical and liberating manner."[25] The memorandum pointed out that this responsibility for reconciliation was also the message of the two most recent popes, John XXIII and Paul VI, and of the Second Vatican Council. The reconciliation with Poland was described as a concrete challenge for West German Christians to enact the Vatican II message of peace.

This responsibility to reconcile with Poland had not been fulfilled by the German Catholics up to this point. "In the light of the terrible injustice committed against the Poles," the German Catholics had not protested in a way "which would do justice to the fate of the victims beyond all diplomacy and political calculations." To protest the perceived injustice of the state had a precedent in the New Testament. The early section of the memorandum indicated this by stating that Jesus, by proclaiming this message of peace, had also often come into conflict with the "official powers of his time."[26] Christian responsibility was reinterpreted to mean the right to follow one's conscience against the decisions of the ruling authorities or the state, as well as the church authorities.

The Bensberger memorandum was largely inspired by the 1965 Evangelical memorandum. The two documents together created a trend in West German Christian thought regarding Polish-German relations. The Evangelical memorandum had proclaimed a similar but more moderate line on the Christian responsibility for politics. It gave assurance in its introduction that the Protestant Church was not attempting to replace elected political representatives.[27] The church was not responsible for formulating detailed political goals and solutions. "However, it belongs to the political service of Christianity to represent the structural and human preconditions for politics that serve humanity and peace." Because of this responsibility, stated the Protestant document, the church should confront political mistakes. It made clear that it considered the "German Eastern Policy" one of these problems and proposed that it should be reformulated.[28]

Like the Bensberger memorandum, the Evangelical memorandum justified its political commentary with the argument that Christians must contribute to a moral foundation of politics in contemporary society. The Evangelical memorandum was more careful in outlining the limitations of this responsibility, partially because it was a document created by the church itself and not by an independent group. The greatest difference between these documents, however, was that the Evangelical memorandum was directed at a German audience with the Polish side as approving observers, whereas the Bensberger memorandum was a communiqué to the Poles themselves. Being Catholic, the Bensberger Circle had an advantage over the Protestant Church in the dialogue with Poland, given the prevalence of Catholicism there.

Two concepts were at the foundation of the memorandum's concept of peace. First, it built on the idea of national self-determination. This idea had been the foundation for the Potsdam Conference decisions of "humane and orderly population transfers" of German ethnic minorities out of Eastern European countries and was now becoming accepted as premises for long-term peace. However, a large segment of the West German population belonged to the very ethnic minority that had been forced to leave the formerly multiethnic border areas, and both the Bensberger memorandum and the other German church memorandums were forced to address the problem of peace with this group in mind. On the one hand, the German nation had lost part of its territorial body—as the memorandum put it, "We Germans experienced the loss of East Germany as an amputation."[29] On the other hand, Poland's loss of eastern territories to the Soviet Union meant that the nation depended on its new western territories for its very survival. The memorandum stated: "We thank the Polish bishops for ... placing the emphasis of their argumentation for the Polish territorial claims on the contemporary facts; the territorial loss in the east of Poland, the hardship in its middle part where the war passed through twice, and life and work for the new settlers."[30] In the interest of peace and the survival of an independent Poland, the ethnically cleansed postwar nation-states and their borders had to be accepted, however painful the territorial loss and uprooting of the German ethnic minorities.

Secondly, the creators of the Bensberger memorandum based its political argument on the idea that Polish-German reconciliation must largely be carried out through normalization between the states. On the second page, the memorandum assured the reader that German Catholics would "support with all their powers, that the German people respect the Polish people's national right to existence."[31] The phrase came out of the intertwined Polish-German past: the Prussian participation in the partitions of Poland, followed closely by the Nazi occupation and the Molotov-Ribbentrop Pact. The memorandum hinted that the Polish nation had been stateless and occupied by foreign powers (including Prussia) for over one hundred years. The Federal Republic, adhering to the Hallstein Doctrine, had refused from the moment of its creation in 1949 to recognize either the Polish state borders or the communist state itself. From both a geopolitical and historical perspective, Bonn ought to recognize the existing Polish state and ensure the security of the nation before any form of reconciliation could take place. This was the background and context to the opening comment that German Catholics must respect the Polish people's right to its national existence. By this line of reasoning, the Bensberger Circle arrived at the necessity of coexistence with Poland's communist state.

The notion of applying the national right to self-determination to communist Poland was problematic in several ways. In light of Stalinism in the 1950s, and the fear that a new war would break out again, anti-communism had been a major obstacle to accepting any of the communist states.[32] Many conservative Catholics and media in West Germany believed that it was both naïve and immoral to attempt to compromise with the communist dictatorships, and that negotiating with any communist meant negotiating with the Soviet Union.[33] *Die Welt* had reacted to the Polish bishops' message with the comment, "Even the message of the Polish bishops cannot switch off the hard facts of politics ... for this dialogue would have to take place under the hard and suspicious eyes of a third power (the Soviet Union), which has pushed the two of us into a diabolical conflict."[34] The Bensberger memorandum acknowledged this difficulty when it stated: "Certainly, the differences in political and societal systems are obstacles to cultural cooperation. We are assuming however that after the first and highest barriers are cleared out, much more is possible than that which is sketched out today."[35]

As a pretext for the development of an active policy of coexistence with the Eastern European states, the memorandum referred to global political developments. Pointing out that the Great Powers had agreed on a non-aggression pact after the Cuban crisis, they argued that West Germany risked being left behind if it did not actively develop its relations to the East as well. The Federal Republic could not afford to be excluded from the broader world political arena. On the contrary, the state should play a key role in overcoming East-West tensions in the cold war. The memorandum also played with the idea that a united Europe would both offset nationalism and strengthen Germany's and Poland's roles in the word. It stated: "Reconciliation between the two peoples is also necessary for the success of either a comprehensive European state order or a functional world organization within a foreseeable future. A European solution would simplify the task of reconciliation. Especially the territorial issues would lose their edge if the borders lost their present nation-state–oriented and divisive connotations."[36] While the idea of a Europe without national boundaries seemed far-fetched, it appeared to solve several of Germany's problems by negating nationalism, disconnecting the country from the recent past in the interest of reconciliation, reducing the tensions of the border conflicts, and strengthening Europe in the cold war arena.

Preparing the Memorandum: Media Reactions and the Bensberger Circle

The memorandum played a distinct role in the 1960s media debates on the relations with Poland. Indeed, it drew media attention as early as 1966, before it was published or even completed. Because of this, its composition was significantly influenced by the media's responses and considerations. Between 1966 and 1968, the Bensberger Circle collected over 1,500 press clippings concerning issues related to the memorandum.[37] This collection—kept in the archives of the

Friedrich Ebert Foundation—indicated that the circle was highly interested in media reactions, strategizing to offset criticism and use the attention to maximum effect. Because of the importance of publicity and media contacts, the circle elected speakers who were responsible for public relations and formal statements to a larger public. The media debates also actively influenced the document's shape and content, changing and expanding its mission.

An incident within the circle showed how closely intertwined the circle's work was with the media response. Between the summers of 1966 and 1967, work on the memorandum was almost completely put aside. Eugen Kogon had developed an outline for a draft but had not found time to write the full text, and Walter Dirks was in poor health and also otherwise engaged.[38] A third member of the commission, Hans Werhahn, felt that the memorandum would not be interesting to a greater public if its publication was delayed too long. He kept urging the commission to use the momentum of the earlier church documents and finally wrote a first draft himself. This draft was rejected by a majority of the circle but did serve the purpose of spurring the Poland commission into renewed action. In June 1967 Dirks and Erb retreated to the Schwarzwald for a week and developed an alternative draft that became the foundation of the memorandum in its final form.[39] Timing and content became crucial in light of their public relations effect.

In 1967 and 1968, three leaks about the memorandum's content appeared in the West German press, which ultimately determined its date of publication. In the fall of 1967, the conservative Catholic weekly *Echo der Zeit* reported that the memorandum indicated the "radical leftist orientation of German Catholics" and would demand the recognition of the German Democratic Republic.[40] The leaks also worried the German episcopate. Cardinal Döpfner, the president of Pax Christi, wrote to the Bensberger leadership after the *Echo der Zeit* article to request more information on the group's work, since people were "writing to [him] from all sides."[41] The media attention had forced the West German episcopate to become involved, if hesitantly, with the memorandum.

It was also at the episcopate's urging that on 4 February 1968, representatives of the Bensberger Circle met with representatives of Catholic expellee organizations to investigate whether the groups could reach a consensus or at least open an internal Catholic dialogue between different groups. Nine expellee representatives who had read the draft participated in the meeting. Among their many criticisms, the most frequent and important for this discussion was the memorandum's ignorance of the role of Russia and the Soviet Union in the Polish past and present. They emphasized that accepting the borders from 1945 also meant accepting Stalin's theft of Poland's eastern territories in 1939 and ignoring the Russian crimes against the Polish people in those territories. An acceptance of the 1945 borders and states would implicitly condone Stalin's role in Eastern Europe. They also stated their belief that the Soviet Union, not Poland and the Federal Republic, was the first key to creating change in Eastern Europe.[42] All in all, the expellee representatives realized that a reunited Germany within the borders of 1937 in a completely non-communist Europe was an unrealistic expectation. At the same time, they were as unwilling to accept the Bensberger Circle's conception of the West German state as they were the Polish communist state. They did not think that smaller states, such as Poland and the Federal Republic, let alone smaller independent groups, could have an impact on cold war political relations.

Later during the same month, *Die Welt* reported that the authors had tried, but failed, to win the German episcopate's support for their project. Shortly thereafter, the German Press Agency (DPA) gained access to drafts of the text through an unknown contact and published them.[43] The Bensberger Circle decided to go ahead and publish the text in its entirety to prevent further rumors from spreading. The Bensberger memorandum was released to the public in March 1968.

The newspapers responsible for the leaks hoped to sabotage the internal negotiations of the circle and alienate the general public from its aims and intents, and in fact, the circle found the leaks problematic at the time. The media attention alienated moderate to conservative Catholics and disturbed the difficult negotiations with the Catholic organizations of German expellees from the Polish borderlands. In hindsight, however, the leaks also had positive effects. According to Gottfried Erb, the quality of the memorandum improved after the Poland commission came under external pressure from the press. He wrote later: "All the intrigues led to a greater effort to improve the style and content of the statements since it had become clear that we could no longer formulate analyses and requirements in peace and quiet, noticed by only a few."[44] They brought the memorandum into the public eye, prevented its marginalization, and improved its overall quality. The publicity around the document took on a life of its own in the media debates and drove the project forward.

After Publication

While the memorandum had already been thoroughly discussed, its publication made it available to a larger audience. A few of the letters of protest sent to the circle illustrated the problem of creating acceptance for the redrawn border and resettlement of populations. These problems involved both personal feelings of hurt and anger and a wide-spanning paradigm shift. A furious Silesian expellee wrote, "I tell you that it is a disgrace when people who call themselves 'Germans' move toward treason. *Pfui Teufel!*" The same person went on to claim that it was against both divine and natural laws to give away the homeland of a "highly civilized people" to a population that could barely read and write, and was guilty of terrible brutalities. He then described the treatment he and his family had received at the hand of the Poles.[45] Such statements were evidence of the bitterness created by the war as well as of a lingering antagonistic nationalism in which the Germans considered themselves culturally superior to the Poles. Some anonymous protesters went even further. They sent Karlheinz Koppe a letter with a picture of a coffin intended for him, a package containing with a rope to hang himself, and finally a package of feces.[46] While these statements and actions were not endorsed by the expellee organizations and were limited to only a few individual cases, they illustrate vividly how new emerging concepts clashed with older images of Polish-German relations in domestic debates. The expellee organizations protested vehemently against the religious memorandums and saw them as attempts by the mass media to sabotage the expellees.[47] The extreme cases of attacks on the Bensberger Circle might have been very few in number, but as Koppe commented in his memoirs, several of the circle members felt seriously threatened at the time.

The disputes between the Bensberger Circle and their critics showed how closely the understanding of the German nation, state, and national territorial boundaries related to the question of Polish-German relations. Not only did the border question and value judgment of whether one's own people was more civilized than or equal to the other contribute to the conflicting views on the Eastern policy, but there was also the question of which role nonstate participants should and could play in formulating foreign policy. The attention the memorandum received elevated the effort into something larger than the statement of an unattached group—an airing of historical conflicts and clashing national concepts that preceded the foreign relations change. However, it was the Polish Catholic response to the memorandum that might ultimately have been a more important result of the document.

The Polish Response

In Poland, journalists in the Catholic intellectual press such as Tadeusz Mazowiecki and Jerzy Turowicz welcomed the initiative. They had appreciated the efforts of the German Protestants, but as a country with a Catholic population of over 90 percent they were especially concerned with German *Catholic* opinion. The Polish Catholic press familiarized a broader readership with the memorandum.[48] These journalists primarily belonged to the Znak circle in Poland.[49]

The position of the Znak circle within communist Poland warrants a separate explanation. Beginning in 1956, the Znak circle had attempted to work within the communist system for change. At that time, the Polish Thaw and the rise of the national communist Władysław Gomułka created hope that certain freedoms, such as freedom of the press or even some forms of democratic parliamentary organization, might be instituted. The Znak circle quickly realized that democratic reform would not occur. However, it concluded that cooperation with the national communists, led by Gomułka, would be a more efficient strategy of reform-oriented opposition than violent resistance. This position, which they called neopositivism, had roots in the particularities of Polish history, when the country was partitioned between the neighboring empires for over a hundred years. The Polish positivist movement emerged in 1863 after a failed uprising against Russia. Those held responsible for the uprisings, the romantics, had argued that revolution was the one suitable reaction to oppression and had prided themselves on being willing to die for their nation. To bolster their position, the positivists argued that violent resistance changed nothing. Cooperation with the system, the philosophy of "organic work" or moderate change and self-improvement from within, would better serve the nation and contribute to Poland's future independence.

The neopositivists in the Znak circle stated clearly that while they were not supporters of communism, they considered the postwar state, whether communist or not, a precondition for the continued existence of the Polish nation. Stanisław Stomma, one of the Znak circle's leading figures, explained that he wished for the new government to "count with the will of the nation, to take into consideration the nation such as it really is and not some abstract hypothetical representation of it."[50] He defined neopositivism as the acceptance of the existing Marxist *raison d'état* and the alliance with the Soviet Union, the opposition to ideology, political method in contrast to political romanticism, compromise, and the rejection of risks, violence, and prestige politics.

Privileged in Gomułka's Poland, the members of the Znak circle had traveled several times to the Federal Republic after 1956 and were already familiar faces to the West German Catholics with an interest in Poland. In 1969, after the memorandum's publication and upon the election of Social Democrat Willy Brandt as chancellor, Stomma visited the Federal Republic again. During the visit, he participated in a general meeting of the Bensberger Circle. Then in 1970, a small Bensberger group visited Poland as the special guests of the Znak circle, which, as a lay group loyal to Wyszyński with a professed interest in Polish-German relations, was an appropriate host for the Germans. The two groups also suited each other well as cooperation partners since they shared not only a Catholic foundation but also a belief that present-day politics, including international relations, must be based on a compromise with the existing Polish communist state, even though neither of them supported communism as an ideology.

The Znak circle functioned as a bridge between the Polish episcopate and the state. The episcopate supported the group but was not always pleased with its position on either foreign policy or Polish domestic politics. Thus, in understanding the position of the Bensberger memorandum, the stance of the Polish Catholic Church must also be taken into consideration. While the church cooperated with the state within certain limits, it remained anti-communist and considered itself the rightful representative of the nation. The main accusation of the Polish communist rulers after the episcopate's letter in 1965 had been that the Catholic episcopate was intruding on the state's areas of responsibility for foreign policy. The episcopate responded that it was concerned only with the spiritual development of the Polish people and the relations with the German Catholic episcopate. As the biographer of Wyszyński, Andrzej Micewski, later observed: "The Party was upset because Stefan Wyszyński was speaking in the name of the nation. Wyszyński never thought of it that way, *even though as Primate he had the moral right to do so* [my emphasis]."[51] The Polish episcopate was less than interested in a peaceful coexistence because the cardinal believed that a sense of tension and external oppression strengthened the Catholic faith among the population.[52] Overall, the state-church relationship in Poland was characterized by complexity and constant negotiation; navigating was thus difficult for mediating insiders such as the Znak circle and especially so for outsiders.

In 1963, Wyszyński disagreed with the Znak circle about the nature of the compromise between state and church and relations with the Vatican. The Cardinal wanted a stricter line against the state than did the Znak circle. After the episcopate's letter in 1965, which the Znak circle criticized publicly, relations between the episcopate and the group were chilly, but in the ensuing escalation of tensions between the state and church, they improved again.[53] Wyszyński agreed with the Znak circle's positive evaluation of the Bensberger memorandum. In September of 1968, he sent a letter of acknowledgement to the Bensberger Circle. The letter first thanked the Bensberger Circle cordially for their "courageous phrasing" of the document, then added, "As shepherds of the Polish people, we evaluated the letter less from a political than from a social-religious point of view." It commended the Bensberger Circle's "Christian courage, honest good will and international outlook on the world."[54] Again, the bishops elected to speak as the representatives (shepherds) of the Polish nation while distancing themselves from state politics.

However, an incident in 1970 proved the complexity and fragility of a peace strategy founded on a normalization with the Polish communists. When a group from the Bensberger Circle visited Poland in April 1970, Wyszyński canceled his audience with them because the group had met with Catholic groups loyal to the regime. Karlheinz Koppe remembered in a 2005 interview that when he went to the Polish military mission in West Berlin to apply for entrance visas, he had to agree as a precondition to meet also with these groups. He had to make this decision alone, on a moment's notice, and in accordance with the circle's concept of normalization he accepted the precondition without fully realizing the extent of the Polish cardinal's disassociation from the state-sponsored groups. Afterward the Znak circle, in particular Stomma, tried to mediate between the cardinal and the visitors. In the end, as an alternative solution, the group was received by the Archbishop Kominek in Wrocław in the name of the Polish episcopate.[55] The incident showed that the Polish state took an interest in the visit of the Bensberger Circle as symbolizing a new relationship with West Germany, and tried to manipulate the visit to its own advantage. It also showed that the Catholic Church was not willing to accept a peace in which both itself and the communist state were involved.

By 1970 the Znak circle's compromise with the state had become discredited domestically.[56] The circle still had the cardinal's full support, but in the aftermath of the 1968 party purge it had largely lost its political independence in relation to the party. Yet its profile in the West German media was still high, as Polish-German relations played a central role in the West German political debates and the Bensberger Circle and the Znak circle were respected pioneers whose meetings and word carried weight when it came to Polish-German questions. The Bensberger Circle's close connection with the Znak circle brought it to the heart of the Polish Catholicism, and in later years Wyszyński often gave special consideration to the members of the Bensberger Circle despite his hesitations during their first visit.[57] These groups had the advantage of good media access and positive symbolic status in the Catholic-driven reconciliation. Gomułka was removed in 1970 soon after signing the agreement with the Federal Republic. Meanwhile, the bishops and intellectuals involved with developing and signing the 1960s religious documents and exchanges remained politically and socially active and influential even after the end of communism in 1989. Among these individuals were two future popes, Bishop Karol Wojtyła and Cardinal Josef Ratzinger, parliamentary members Stanisław Stomma and Jerzy Turowicz, and the prime minister of Poland's first noncommunist government, Tadeusz Mazowiecki.

Conclusion

In this case study, groups in both states took responsibility for international relations with the other state and consciously interacted to improve these relations. The Bensberger memorandum was a statement representing "all who are prepared to agree with [our] considerations and suggestions."[58] It was addressed to the Polish Catholic bishops, who received it as representatives for the Polish nation. In taking responsibility for the relations, the Bensberger Circle was also motivated by its perception of a universal Christian responsibility for peace. Initiated outside of states or state leadership, the group's activities thus differed from the American or Soviet cases, as well as from state initiatives that emerged elsewhere in two states, such as in Polish–East German relations and West German–French relations. The initiatives taken in cooperation with Polish Catholics were also unique cases, since the Poles traditionally thought of nation and state as separate from the nineteenth century forward. The Znak circle believed in cooperation with the communists, even though they were of the conviction that the state in Poland did not fully represent its population. Meanwhile, the Polish Catholic hierarchy took an even stronger stance on this issue, feeling that the church was a truer representative of historical Poland than the state.

The Bensberger circle's efforts benefited from the group's greater political flexibility and power to attract media attention. The memorandum showed not only that nonstate actors can play a crucial role in foreign relations, but also that cultural diplomacy as it is understood here can serve as a stabilizing factor in cases of state weakness or state discontinuity. Nonstate actors and well-organized, cross-border institutions such as church and media gained a powerful yet complicated mediating position between and parallel to the Polish and West German states. In view of the Polish–West German case, in which the state and nation acted as separate though entwined entities, the study of cultural diplomacy is incomplete without consideration of international contacts in which a strong state is not present as a driving force.

Endnotes

1. See for example Werner Link, "Ostpolitik: Détente German-Style and Adapting to America," in *The United States and Germany in the Era of the Cold War, 1968–1990,* ed. Detlef Junker (New York: Cambridge University Press, 2004), 33–39; or Timothy Garton Ash, *In Europe's Name: Germany and the Divided Continent* (New York: Random House, 1993).
2. Jeremi Suri, "Non-Governmental Organizations and Non-State Actors," in *Palgrave Advances in International History,* ed. Patrick Finney (New York: Palgrave Macmillan, 2005), 223–247; Thomas Risse-Kappen, "Bringing Transnational Relations Back," in *Bringing Transnational Relations Back In: Non-State Actors, Domestic Structures and International Institutions,* ed. Thomas Risse-Kappen (Cambridge and New York: Cambridge University Press, 1995); Margaret E. Keck and Kathryn Sikkink, *Activists Beyond Borders: Advocacy Networks in International Politics* (Ithaca, NY: Cornell University Press, 1998); Akira Iriye, *Global Community: The Role of International Organizations in the Making of the Contemporary World* (Berkeley: University of California Press, 2002).
3. Garton Ash, *In Europe's Name,* 227. For a discussion of the relationship between expellees and West German foreign policy, see Pertti Ahonen, *After the Expulsion: West Germany and Eastern Europe 1945–1990* (Oxford and New York: Oxford University Press, 2003).
4. In *Global Television and the Shaping of World Politic,* Royce Ammon lists among the functions of traditional diplomacy (1) the activities associated with supporting a country's citizens as they travel abroad and conduct business in foreign countries, a function known as performing routine consular affairs; (2) the gathering and interpretation of information; (3) the signaling and receiving of governments' positions on various issues; (4) the official representation of a diplomat's home (sending) government before his or her host (receiving) government; (5) the conduct of international public relations; (6) negotiation, and

(7) crisis management. Few if any of these functions could be successfully carried out by state actors before 1970 in the Polish–West German case. Royce J. Ammon, *Global Television and the Shaping of World Politics: CNN, Telediplomacy and Foreign Policy* (Jefferson, NC: McFarland, 2001), 9.
5. This statement is in comparison to the German borders of 1937.
6. Dieter Bingen, *Die Polenpolitik der Bonner Republik von Adenauer bis Kohl, 1949–1991* (Baden-Baden: Nomos, 1998), 83–86.
7. Walter Dirks and Eugen Kogon, "Verhängnis und Hoffnung im Osten: Das Deutsch-Polnische Problem," *Frankfurter Hefte,* no. 2 (May 1947): 470–483, here 470.
8. Ibid., 479.
9. Ibid., 476.
10. Robert Żurek, *Zwischen Nationalismus und Versöhnung: Die Kirchen und die deutsch-polnischen Beziehungen, 1945–1956* (Cologne: Böhlau, 2005), 102.
11. Claire Flanagan, *A Study of German Political-Cultural Periodicals from the Years of Allied Occupation, 1945–1949* (Lewiston, NY: E. Mellen, 2000), 186–192.
12. Dirks and Kogon, "Verhängnis und Hoffnung," 475, 483.
13. Ibid., 473.
14. Ibid., 479, 482.
15. Flanagan, *A Study of German Politico-Cultural Journals,* 211.
16. Ibid., 184.
17. Also in the German Democratic Republic, efforts at reconciliation with Poland occurred within the Protestant Church in the 1960s. An example was the "Aktion Sühnezeichen," in which young East German Protestants traveled to Poland and worked to restore Jewish memorials and memorial sites from World War II.
18. Hans-Adolf Jacobsen and Mieczysław Tomala, eds., *Bonn-Warschau 1945–1991: Die deutsch-polnische Beziehungen. Analyse und Dokumentation* (Cologne: Verlag Wissenschaft und Politik, 1992), 142, 145.
19. Walter Dirks, "In Rom, Spätherbst 1965," in *Frankfurter Hefte,* no. 20 (January 1966): 30–34, here 34.
20. Letter from Walter Dirks to Bolesław Kominek, 12 February 1966, Nachlass Walter Dirks, Box 128, Friedrich Ebert Stiftung (FES); Letter from Bolesław Kominek to Walter Dirks, undated (May 1966?), Nachlass Walter Dirks, Box 128, FES.
21. Letter from Bensberger Circle to Heinz Missala, 13 April 1966, Bensberger Kreis, BK Protokoll, Erklärungen, Bensberger Kreis 54, FES.
22. Letter from Gottfried Erb to Walter Dirks, 25 February 1966, Nachlass Walter Dirks, Box 128, FES.
23. Letter from Walter Dirks to Gottfried Erb, 4 January 1966, Nachlass Walter Dirks, Box 128, FES.
24. Karlheinz Koppe, *Dreimal getauft und Mensch geblieben* (Berlin: Rohnstock, 2004), 170.
25. Bensberger Kreis, ed., *Ein Memorandum deutscher Katholiken zu den polnisch-deutschen Fragen* (Mainz: Matthias-Grünewald-Verlag, 1968), 7.
26. Ibid., 7.
27. Kirchenkanzlei der Evangelischen Kirche in Deutschland, ed., *Die Lage der Vertriebenen und das Verhältnis des deutschen Volkes zu seinen östlichen Nachbarn: Eine evangelische Denkschrift,* 5th ed. (Hannover: Verlag des Amtsblattes der Evangelischen Kirche in Deutschland, 1965), 5.
28. Ibid., 41.
29. Bensberger Kreis, *Memorandum,* 8.
30. Ibid., 20.
31. Ibid., 4.

32. See Tony Judt, *Postwar: A History of Europe since 1945* (New York: Penguin, 2006), 242.
33. See Ahonen, *After the Expulsion,* 130.
34. *German-Polish Dialogue,* 118, translated from *Die Welt,* 4 December 1965.
35. Bensberger Kreis, *Memorandum,* 21.
36. Ibid., 24.
37. Gottfried Erb, "Das Memorandum des Bensberger Kreises zur Polenpolitik," in *Ungewöhnliche Normalisierung: Beziehungen der Bundesrepublik Deutschland zu Polen,* ed. Werner Plum (Bonn: Verlag Neue Gesellschaft, 1984), 182. Folders with press clippings also in Friedrich Ebert Stiftung.
38. Letter from Manfried Seidler to the members of the "smaller circle" of the Poland commission, 31 May 1967, Bensberger Kreis, Polen, Mi 60, FES.
39. Letter from Norbert Greinacher to Manfred Seidler, 1 September 1967, Bensberger Kreis, Polen, Mi 60, FES.
40. "Ostdruck bei den Katholiken: Kardinal Döpfner's Bistumsblatt für Anerkennung der Oder-Neisse-Grenze," *Die Zeit,* 24 November 1967.
41. Letter from Julius Döpfner to Alfons Erb, 6 December 1967, Bensberger Kreis Polen, Polen, Mi 60, FES.
42. Author unknown, "Aktennotiz. Betr.: Gespräch mit den Vertriebenenvertretern vom 4.2.1968 im Kolping-Haus von Frankfurt," 4 February 1968, Bensberger Kreis, Polen, Mi 60, FES.
43. Gottfried Erb, "Das 'Bensberger Memorandum' / Geschichte und erste Stellungnahmen," *Frankfurter Hefte, no. 23* (April 1968): 219.
44. "Bei allen Umtrieben wurde die Anstrengung grösser, die Qualität der Aussagen in Stil und Inhalt zu steigern, denn es war klar geworden, dass wir nun nicht mehr in betulicher Ruhe analysen und Forderungen formulieren konnten, die nur wenige registrierten." Erb, "Das Memorandum des Bensberger Kreises zur Polenpolitik," 182.
45. Letter from Gerhard Denkmann to Alfons Erb, 4 March 1968, Bensberger Kreis, Gottfried Erb Dokumentation zum Polen-Memorandum des BK (Anerkennung der Oder-Neisse-Linie), FES.
46. Koppe, *Dreimal getauft,* 170.
47. Ahonen, *After the Expulsions,* 205.
48. Tadeusz Mazowiecki, "Polska-Niemcy i memorandum 'Bensberger Kreis,'" *Więż* (1968), 4–5; Jerzy Turowicz, "Memorandum 'Bensberger Kreis,'" *Tygodnik Powszechny,* 17 March 1968, 1,5.
49. In Polish, the Koła Posłów Znak, meaning the circle of parliament members Znak (the Sign), to distinguish it from the journal with the same name.
50. Stanisław Stomma, "Dlatego kandyduję do Sejmu," *Tygodnik Powszechny,* 20 January 1957, 4.
51. Andrzej Micewski, *Cardinal Wyszynski: A Biography,* trans. W. R. Brand and K. Mroczkowska-Brand (San Diego: Harcourt Brace Jovanovich, 1984), 256. Still, Hansjakob Stehle argued in his book *Eastern Policy of the Vatican 1945–1979* that whereas Wyszyński was involved in heated rhetoric with the communist state, he would always back up and advise calm in a time of crisis for the country. See Hansjakob Stehle, *Eastern Politics of the Vatican 1945–1979,* trans. Sandra Smith (Athens, OH: Athens University Press, 1981), 342.
52. Stehle, *Eastern Policy of the Vatican 1945–1979,* 346.
53. Robert Jarocki, *Czterdzieści pięć lat w opozycji (o ludziach "Tygodnika Powszechnego"),* (Krakow: Wydawn. Literacki, 1990), 221; Wolfgang Pailer, *Stanisław Stomma: Nestor der polnisch-deutschen Aussöhnung* (Bonn: Bouvier, 1995), 103.

54. Letter from Stefan Wyszyński to the Bensberger Circle, 12 September 1968, Bensberger Kreis, Polen 60, FES.
55. Karlheinz Koppe, interview with Annika Frieberg, Bonn, 23 February 2005.
56. Andrzej Friszke, *Koło posłów „Znak" w Sejmie PRL 1957–1976* (Warsaw: Wydawnictwo Sejmowe, 2002), 108.
57. Winfried Lipscher, a theology student and Bensberger member who later became an official translator at the West German Consulate in Warsaw, has given examples of Wyszyński's preferential treatment. Winfried Lipscher, interview with Annika Frieberg, Berlin, 18 May 2005.
58. The opening statement of the Bensberger memorandum claimed to represent neither all Germans nor all Catholics but all who were prepared to agree with the suggestions in the text, an imprecise group that could either be considerably smaller than all Germans and Catholics, or substantially larger.

Bibliography

Ahonen, Pertti. *After the Expulsion: West Germany and Eastern Europe 1945–1990.* Oxford and New York: Oxford University Press, 2003.

Ammon, Royce J. *Global Television and the Shaping of World Politics: CNN, Telediplomacy and Foreign Policy.* Jefferson, N.C.: McFarland, 2001.

Bensberger Kreis, ed. *Ein Memorandum deutscher Katholiken zu den polnisch-deutschen Fragen.* Mainz: Matthias-Grünewald-Verlag, 1968.

Bingen, Dieter. *Die Polenpolitik der Bonner Republik von Adenauer bis Kohl, 1949–1991.* Baden-Baden: Nomos, 1998.

Dirks, Walter. "In Rom, Spätherbst 1965." *Frankfurter Hefte,* no. 20 (January 1966): 30–34.

Dirks, Walter, and Eugen Kogon. "Verhängnis und Hoffnung im Osten: Das Deutsch-Polnische Problem." *Frankfurter Hefte,* no. 2 (May 1947): 470–483.

Erb, Gottfried. "Das Memorandum des Bensberger Kreises zur Polenpolitik." In *Ungewöhnliche Normalisierung: Beziehungen der Bundesrepublik Deutschland zu Polen,* ed. Werner Plum. Bonn: Verlag Neue Gesellschaft, 1984.

———. "Das 'Bensberger Memorandum' / Geschichte und erste Stellungnahmen," *Frankfurter Hefte, no. 23* (April 1968).

Flanagan, Claire. A Study of German Political-Cultural Periodicals from the Years of Allied Occupation, 1945–1949. Lewiston, NY: E. Mellen, 2000.

Friszke, Andrzej. *Koło posłów „Znak" w Sejmie PRL 1957–1976.* Warsaw: Wydawnictwo Sejmowe, 2002.

Garton Ash, Timothy. *In Europe's Name: Germany and the Divided Continent.* New York: Random House, 1993.

Iriye, Akira. *Global Community: The Role of International Organizations in the Making of the Contemporary World.* Berkeley: University of California Press, 2002.

Jacobsen, Hans-Adolf, and Mieczysław Tomala, eds. *Bonn-Warschau 1945–1991: Die deutsch-polnischen Beziehungen. Analyse und Dokumentation.* Cologne: Verlag Wissenschaft und Politik, 1992.

Jarocki, Robert. *Czterdzieści pięć lat w opozycji (o ludziach „Tygodnika Powszechnego").* Krakow: Wydawn. Literackie, 1990.

Judt, Tony. *Postwar: A History of Europe since 1945.* New York: Penguin, 2006.

Keck, Margaret E., and Kathryn Sikkink. *Activists Beyond Borders: Advocacy Networks in International Politics.* Ithaca, NY: Cornell University Press, 1998.

Kirchenkanzlei der Evangelische Kirche in Deutschland, ed. *Die Lage der Vertriebenen und das Verhältnis des deutschen Volkes zu seinen östlichen Nachbarn: Eine evangelische Denkschrift.* 5th ed. Hanover: Verlag des Amtsblattes der Evangelischen Kirche in Deutschland, 1965.

Koppe, Karlheinz. *Dreimal getauft und Mensch geblieben.* Berlin: Rohnstock, 2004.

Link, Werner. "Ostpolitik: Détente German-Style and Adapting to America." In *The United States and Germany in the Era of the Cold War, 1968–1990,* ed. Detlef Junker. New York: Cambridge University Press, 2004.

Mazowiecki, Tadeusz. "Polska-Niemcy i memorandum 'Bensberger Kreis.'" In *Więż* (1968): 4–5.

Micewski, Andrzej. *Cardinal Wyszynski: A Biography.* Trans. W. R. Brand and K. Mroczkowska-Brand. San Diego: Harcourt Brace Jovanovich, 1984.

"Ostdruck bei den Katholiken: Kardinal Döpfner's Bistumsblatt für Anerkennung der Oder-Neisse-Grenze." *Die Zeit,* 24 November 1967.

Pailer, Wolfgang. *Stanisław Stomma: Nestor der polnisch-deutschen Aussöhnung.* Bonn: Bouvier, 1995.

Risse-Kappen, Thomas. "Bringing Transnational Relations Back." In *Bringing Transnational Relations Back In: Non-State Actors, Domestic Structures and International Institutions,* ed. Thomas Risse-Kappen. Cambridge and New York: Cambridge University Press, 1995.

Stehle, Hansjakob. *Eastern Policy of the Vatican 1945–1979.* Trans. Sandra Smith. Athens: Ohio University Press, 1981.

Stomma, Stanisław. "Dlatego kandyduję do Sejmu." *Tygodnik Powszechny,* 20 January 1957.

Suri, Jeremi. "Non-Governmental Organizations and Non-State Actors." In *Palgrave Advances in International History,* ed. Patrick Finney. New York: Palgrave Macmillan, 2005.

Turowicz, Jerzy. "Memorandum 'Bensberger Kreis.'" *Tygodnik Powszechny,* 17 March 1968.

Żurek, Robert. *Zwischen Nationalismus und Versöhnung: Die Kirchen und die deutsch-polnischen Beziehungen 1945–1956.* Cologne: Böhlau, 2005.

Part III

CULTURAL DIPLOMACY IN THE MIDDLE EAST

Chapter 5

INTERNATIONAL RIVALRY AND CULTURE IN SYRIA AND LEBANON UNDER THE FRENCH MANDATE

Jennifer Dueck

In April 1940, the celebrated French orientalist Henri Laoust drafted an influential note that was to appear on the desks of many officials at the Ministry of Foreign Affairs for years to come. This note stated that the Arabic language was emerging to take its rightful place among the "great languages of civilization." This fact, Laoust wrote, would necessitate a profound alteration in the foundations of France's cultural policy toward Arab countries. Two points in particular stand out in his missive. First, the Arabic and French languages should not be seen as competitors, but rather as close associates in a process of rich cultural and intellectual exchange. Second, and no less significant, was his contention that there should be a complete dissociation between France's political and cultural activities in the region.[1]

Laoust's note reflected two interrelated elements of France's position in the region that are both relevant to discussions of cultural diplomacy. The first pertains to French bilateral relations with Syria and Lebanon. The French Mandate over Syria and Lebanon between 1920 and 1945 represented a time of transition, most notably with regard to the political independence of Middle Eastern states. The independence that these two Levantine states earned during World War II followed hundreds of years of imperial rule by the Ottoman Empire and then, during the interwar years, by France. The progress

Notes for this section begin on page 155.

toward independence had a profound impact on France's cultural relationship with the Levant. The second, less explicit element in Laoust's note concerns other Western powers with interests in the Middle East: in particular it acknowledged the cultural competition that these foreign states posed for France. This international rivalry for cultural influence in Syria and Lebanon allows us to explore and analyze the French conception of cultural diplomacy. Furthermore, the case study of Syria and Lebanon illustrates the dynamics of cultural diplomacy in a region full of internal political instability and the development of local nationalisms, as well as European competition for influence in an imperial context.

In defining their own approach to cultural diplomacy, French government actors' rhetoric contained deep-rooted contradictions. Notably, we find insecurity about the status of French cultural influence, coexisting alongside an enduring confidence in French cultural superiority. Laoust's insistence, echoed by others at the Ministry of Foreign Affairs, that the Arab language and heritage be treated with respect is just one example of this insecurity:[2] it meant a tacit recognition that the French were facing powerful competition for cultural influence among educated Arabs. However, in spite of this insecurity, French officials also asserted a remarkable degree of confidence in French language and learning as an undisputed "international instrument."[3] The long-standing confidence in French culture among elites around the world was tenacious, as can be seen in Louis XIV's promotion of French culture in the Russian courts, or in the Third Republican colonial civilizing mission. French policymakers remained convinced that their culture was superior and would continue to mold Arab and international elites. This belief paradoxically persisted alongside French insecurity.

Another apparent contradiction in French discourse about cultural diplomacy was the French desire to separate the nation's cultural policies from its political agenda while at the same time using culture as a political tool. Many officials at the Ministry of Foreign Affairs remained convinced that culture was an effective means to gain political influence, and Laoust himself was in some ways the incarnation of this idea. While holding a research position, he also served as an adviser to various departments of the French High Commission for the Levant.[4] The clear tie that administrators in both political and cultural bureaus saw between culture and politics appears fundamentally inconsistent with their will to keep their nation's cultural and political agendas separate. However, the Ministry of Foreign Affairs was concerned about this separation only to ensure that the

Syrian and Lebanese populations did not perceive culture as part of a political project and hence associate it with negative images of imperialism. The promotion of French culture abroad was undeniably motivated by powerful underlying political objectives. Indeed, historians increasingly regard culture as an integral component of international political relations. According to Dominique Trimburs on culture and diplomacy, negotiations over cultural dissemination during the 1930s became a significant palliative to an otherwise aggressive international political scene. As part of that process, culture itself emerged as an object to be exported by the state in a more deliberate and systematic way than ever before.[5] Consequently, French cultural diplomacy, at its most basic level, consisted of nurturing the institutional structures that allowed France to disseminate its culture overseas.

In order to understand the French conception of cultural diplomacy in the Middle East, we must situate the notion within both imperial and noncolonial contexts. The relationship between culture and imperial power has been a subject of great debate in the last two decades. One need only evoke the vigorous discussions provoked by the work of Edward Said or Samuel Huntington to appreciate the significance of culture in international power struggles. A close relation to "culture" in this wave of thought is "knowledge." Edward Said, in his influential work *Orientalism,* borrowed from Michel Foucault's notions about the relationship between knowledge and power, arguing that the epistemological framework that dominates collective thought also controls social and political structures of power. Applying this model to the colonial situation, Said argued that the West used the management of knowledge as a tool to rule the East. Although Foucault and Said have both long been discounted as historians, namely because their conclusions outweigh the evidence they presented and their work contains many empirical flaws, their ideas remain relevant to an understanding of how cultural diplomacy works in the colonial context.[6]

The importance of culture and knowledge to the colonial context is especially significant in France's case, given the centrality of culture to France's philosophy of imperialism, dubbed the "civilizing mission." In the late nineteenth century this specifically French concept evolved into a coherent colonial ideology as a justification and a motivation for imperial conquest. French colonialists framed a political, economic, and military presence overseas as a cultural gift to the imperial subjects, bringing them better institutions of justice and government along with more effective economic organization, technology, and medicine, as well as the French language and French reasoning.[7] Although for a long time historians considered the civilizing mission to be little more than superficial rhetoric, Alice Conklin has shown that it was a more potent force in shaping French imperial politics than had previously been assumed.[8]

Curiously, however, documents relating to cultural missions in Syria and Lebanon refer to the civilizing mission far less frequently than one might anticipate, in spite of the fact that the Levant was part of the French Empire. More often, cultural missions in the Levant were associated with a general notion of cultural dissemination, a process carried out by diplomatic bureaus that was not restricted to imperial lands. What, then, differentiated cultural policies within the civilizing mission from cultural diplomacy in non-imperial lands?

The civilizing mission, as it was understood by Third Republic citizens, was a specifically colonial doctrine meant to justify imperial expansion. Cultural diplomacy, by contrast, extended well beyond the empire and lacked the explicit colonial baggage of the civilizing mission, which was intended to facilitate direct rule and military conquest. Secondly, there is a central distinction to be made between cultural diplomacy and the civilizing mission insofar as each entails a different balance in the relationship between culture and political power. Conklin suggests that the central principle of the civilizing mission is the concept of mastery over nature and society, which the French were confident they had achieved. They were also confident that "primitive" colonial citizens had not attained such mastery, and that it was their duty to assist colonial subjects in developing it. Moreover, this duty, according to the principles of the civilizing mission, was to be carried out in all domains—political, economic, and cultural. The civilizing mission targeted individuals and societies in their entirety.[9] An engagement in cultural diplomacy, on the other hand, contained no inherent convictions about mastery, and certainly did not prescribe action on such a vast scale.

Interestingly, for a variety of reasons the Syrian and Lebanese Mandates fell somewhere in between the respective paradigms of cultural diplomacy and the colonial civilizing mission. French authority in the Levant was weak, facing opposition from internal and external quarters, and French officials did not feel the sense of mastery inherent in the doctrine of the civilizing mission. The Mandates were, at the outset, on a path toward independence, and an application of the holistic ideology of general civilizing was inconceivable. In addition, the Mandates were under the purview of the Ministry of Foreign Affairs, rather than the Ministry of Colonies.

Given that these features of French rule in Syria and Lebanon made the paradigm of the civilizing mission difficult to apply comprehensively there, we need to elucidate how the French government used culture abroad in noncolonial situations. One of the main issues requiring clarification is the relationship between cultural diplomacy and propaganda. Indeed, the French phrase that often appears in Foreign Ministry documentation referring to overseas cultural policy is "oeuvres de propagande." For this reason, it is useful to discuss how conceptions of propaganda should fit into our understanding of cultural diplomacy.

In reference to the term "propaganda," historians inevitably face the same problem of defining what it is. Many have resolved the issue by studying propaganda in times of exceptional trouble, such as war, when messages become more dogmatic and the means used to convey them more brutal, thereby making them easier to delimit.[10] Some studies examine propaganda by unraveling the rapport between various press agencies and the government, or by focusing on the development of a specific technique of transmission, such as magazines, radio, television, posters, or illustrations. Although valuable in many contexts, none of these approaches is appropriate for French cultural dissemination abroad as envisaged by the French Ministry of Foreign Affairs.

There is, however, an even larger problem in using the term "propaganda" with reference to cultural diplomacy: there is usually a moral judgment attached to the term. A fundamental conviction reigns among many academics and the wider public that propaganda is something bad, employed only by nasty politicians who make selective use of the truth and actively manipulate information in order to suppress intellectual freedom. This is true of Leonard Doob's influential study in 1948, which defined propaganda as "the attempt to affect the personalities and to control the behavior of individuals towards ends considered unscientific or of doubtful value at a particular time."[11] Jacques Ellul's similarly influential work attempted to move beyond Doob by rejecting the assumption that propaganda is "evil" and that it always consists of lies. Nevertheless, Ellul begins with the Foucauldian premise that "the force of propaganda is a direct attack against man" and that propaganda makes the exercise of true democracy impossible.[12] Philippe Amaury's study of French propaganda and Michael Balfour's examination of British and German propaganda both distinguish between pure information, which invites inquiry, and propaganda, which causes "people to leap to conclusions without adequate examination of the evidence."[13] More recent definitions of propaganda have deliberately moved away from such value-laden conceptions to envisage propaganda as any technique used to persuade a target audience to think or behave in a way that would benefit the propagandist. Philip Taylor argues that propaganda is not inherently good or bad but is rather a unilateral exercise, in which one party presents ideas to an audience in order to persuade without allowing a critical examination of the evidence.[14]

Such definitions are important and appropriate in many environments, as is the examination of the moral implications of propaganda. Nevertheless, this conceptual framework differentiating knowledge or education from propaganda poses problems for the French case. French cultural dissemination abroad was based precisely on knowledge and education, channeled through art, music, and the cinema, literature and scholarship, and schools and language instruction. The terms "*propagande*" and "*rayonnement*" often seem almost synonymous in government documents. Very often this "propaganda" involved the study and appraisal of literature and history. The French language, considered a propaganda tool in and of itself, was meant to constitute the basis of rational thought and understanding. R. A. Leeper of the British Foreign Office was one of few in British government circles to understand this vision of propaganda. Lamenting his nation's disdain for overseas self-promotion and suspiciousness of propaganda in 1935, he called on his countrymen to embrace cultural propaganda "*à la française,*" which he described as follows: "the French example shows that there is a legitimate form of propaganda which benefits directly those who receive it and indirectly those who conduct it, and that this kind of propaganda is a most valuable contribution to international relations."[15]

While one should not accept wholesale this altruistic image of French cultural propaganda, it should nevertheless color our interpretation. Leeper's notion of legitimate overseas propaganda corresponds very well to French ideas about cultural diplomacy. Philippe Amaury's study of how French governments managed information between 1939 and 1944 demonstrates the hostility of French citizens toward official attempts to control information. Overseas propaganda was, however, an exception to this rule. Even for skeptical French Republic citizens, overseas propaganda consisted of "*rayonnement de la culture française*" and could be defended on the understanding that it had to be honest, sanctioned by the foreign government, and reliant on locally established cultural institutions. As Robert Young has noted, this was "*propagande de la vérité,*" which was distinct from "black" propaganda.[16]

Can this conception of propaganda be reconciled with those that define it as a tool to benefit the propagandist and, in its more sinister guises, to control public behavior despotically? Even philanthropic ventures, which appear to improve people's lives and enrich their minds, would be interpreted by scholars such as Ellul as subtle endeavors to manipulate an unsuspecting target audience.[17] Such contentions make it difficult to dispel the pervasive Foucauldian suspicion that any method for transmitting knowledge through cultural or social ventures is really just another attempt by the powerful to control the weak.

It is mainly because of these negative connotations that many historians have eschewed the term "propaganda" entirely and opted instead for "cultural diplomacy." Albert Salon, who produced the first serious study of French cultural diplomacy, assembled a lexicon to describe the use of culture in international relations. He differentiates very clearly between propaganda, as the attempt to spread an opinion or ideology for a political purpose, often as an auxiliary to armed conflict, and other, less offensive-sounding concepts, such as "*action culturelle*," "*politique culturelle*," and "*diffusion culturelle*."[18]

The difference, it should be said, is not that cultural action, policy, or diffusion abroad was disinterested or apolitical. As suggested earlier, French cultural dissemination in Syria and Lebanon was designed to make politics and culture appear separate only in order to make culture a more effective political tool. If its goals are fundamentally political, how does this cultural diplomacy differ from the definitions of "propaganda" cited above as, at worst, an evil and dishonest attempt to brainwash, or at best an honest but single-minded attempt to convince without leaving room for contested opinions? Trimbur asks at which point cultural diplomacy becomes "*une propagande pure et simple*" and suggests that there is a difference between a "*bonne foi française*" and a "*propagande agressive, allemande et italienne, faisant pièce aux prétentions des autres pays.*"[19] Marc Blancpain, secretary general of the Alliance Française, notes in his preface to Salon's lexicon: "*je crains toujours qu'elle* [cultural action abroad] *soit le déguisement du mot propagande.*"[20] According to Salon, there are two very significant distinctions between propaganda and cultural diplomacy. First, cultural action abroad allows conflicting viewpoints, while propaganda does not. Because of this openness, cultural diplomacy is not subversive or anti-democratic. Salon's second distinction is that cultural policy overseas requires mutual exchange and reciprocal relationships with the foreign government and institutions. It cannot simply be a unilateral exercise.[21]

French officials considered that the purpose of cultural diplomacy was not to organize structures that would engage in direct propagandistic persuasion, but rather to foster institutions that would create certain predispositions. To predispose an audience meant engendering loyalties in a less pointed and less direct manner than is suggested by the terms "propaganda" or "persuasion." Its objectives are also far less precise, and its methods can be much more discreet.[22] The French desire for discretion in self-promotion was especially conspicuous in countries where French influence was less secure, and in regions where France's political role was less entrenched. French language instruction, for example, was seen by officials as a tool that would foster predispositions with the prospect that, at some unidentified future moment, the audience would feel an affinity for France. These sorts of projects, which were clearly long-term ventures with uncertain and far-off results, were the main focus of French cultural diplomacy.

Although the French had quite a clear conception of their cultural objectives overseas, the implementation of these objectives in Syria and Lebanon met with a number of obstacles, namely the internal conflicts between the French government and the private organizations involved in cultural diplomacy, the local situation in the Levant, and international competition. The French government was, of course, a composite body whose parts did not always communicate effectively or work together. Its players were positioned in a vast bureaucratic maze of ministries, departments, and commissions. The first steps toward centralized management of overseas information were taken in 1910 with the inauguration of the Bureau des écoles et œuvres françaises à l'étranger, which in 1920 was turned into a full-blown Service des œuvres françaises à l'étranger under the jurisdiction of the Ministry of Foreign Affairs. It was composed of four sections, which were respectively responsible for schools and universities, literature and the arts, tourism, and miscellaneous "*œuvres.*" The Service des œuvres was aided by a multiplicity of other government branches, including the Service d'information et de presse, also under the Ministry of Foreign Affairs as well as the Ministries of National Education, Fine Arts, and Commerce. Its broad range of activities included broadcasting, cinema, athletic events, tourism, medical assistance, and education. In 1924 this service granted special funds to the Levantine portfolio, and the Middle East became second only to Europe as an area of French cultural investment.

Alongside these cultural offices, there was also growing concern for information management. The interministerial Commission à l'information was created in 1936 and expanded in 1939 into the Commissariat général à l'information, which was responsible for informational management at home and abroad. A central focus of the commissariat was cultural dissemination, as can be seen in the composition of its personnel. The employees included "*littérateurs*," artists and academics, with the celebrated playwright Jean Giraudoux as their director. It was fitting, then, that the commissariat took the Service des œuvres under its umbrella.[23] A formal Ministry of Information was set up by the Reynaud government only after the start of World War II. Under the Vichy regime, information was completely controlled by the state. After the war, it devolved to a peacetime Ministry of Information, directed by the left-wing writer André Malraux.

The changing bodies responsible for administering the empire were similarly disorganized and disparate. The French Empire was constructed rather haphazardly over the course of the nineteenth century, and its administration mirrored its acquisition. Although the French conquered Algiers in 1830 and soon afterward boasted colonial territories from the West African coast to Indochina, a proper Ministry of Colonies was established only in 1894. Even this did not result in a uniform and centralized colonial administration. Formal colonies, such as Indochina, French West Africa, and Madagascar fell under its jurisdiction, but the departments of Algeria were administratively assimilated to France and governed by the Ministry of the Interior. The Protectorates in Tunisia and Morocco fell to the Ministry of Foreign Affairs, as did the Syrian and Lebanese Mandates. Thus, three completely independent Ministries administered the empire.[24] Within Syria and Lebanon, French administrative authority was further subdivided between the Quai d'Orsay in Paris, the High Commission in Beirut, and various "*detachés*" scattered throughout the region, in addition to the military officers responsible for keeping the peace.[25]

The government's administrative structure meant that French cultural policy in Syria and Lebanon often lacked coherence. This was not the only problem, however. In its desire to separate the cultural from the political, and to be discreet in its cultural self-promotion, the French government in the Levant relied almost exclusively on nongovernmental intermediaries for cultural interaction with the local population. These intermediaries included both religious and secular associations, which had diverse objectives and served different target populations. This diversity speaks to an important feature of French cultural diplomacy, which tended toward multilateral projects and exhibited an inability or unwillingness to impose uniformity. Cultural programs did not consist of unilateral initiatives projecting highly controlled messages from French ruling authorities onto indigenous masses. Rather, they depended on the cooperation of a plethora of nongovernmental participants who had their own independent agendas.

The most prominent of the private French intermediaries were the Catholic missionaries, such as the Jesuits, the Lazarists, and the Marist Brothers. These congregations had long-established missions in the Levant dating in some cases back to the seventeenth century.[26] They enjoyed the greatest personal contact with the local population and constituted the primary cultural intermediaries used by the French government. However, although they often acted as intermediaries, they were not under the direct administrative jurisdiction of any government and cannot be seen simply as government agents.[27]

While the French government did often equate its own interest with that of these religious intermediaries, the bonds between the government and private missions were variable in strength and format. Particularly problematic in this regard was the long-standing debate over the role of the clergy in French society, a debate that culminated dramatically in France at the turn of the twentieth century, when the secular Third Republican government banned clerical participation in public education and seized a hefty chunk of church assets. Nevertheless, this early-1900s legislation separating church and state left French missions in the Ottoman Empire relatively untouched. The Levant, indeed, became the "*terre d'exil*" for the missions, and the defence of their stronghold in the Levant became a key strategy in the French Catholic struggle against secularism. With the creation of the Mandate after World War I, a fundamental tension emerged between France's anti-clericalism at home and its clerical representatives in Syria and Lebanon.[28] Such tension often impeded effective cooperation between the French government and missionaries in cultural projects in the colonial context.

The second element that hindered effective implementation of cultural diplomacy between France, Syria, and Lebanon was the changing local politics of these countries during the Mandate period, and the mutual distrust between French and local actors that emerged as part of that process. The 1930s had already seen great challenges to French power and stability with the much-contested election of a left-wing "popular front" government in 1936, along with increasing local agitation for political rights in the empire. Nowhere was the growing colonial unrest stronger than in the Levantine Mandates, where local leaders garnered sufficient clout to negotiate and sign the Franco-Syrian and Franco-Lebanese treaties for independence in 1936. Although the French parliament refused to ratify them in 1938, the texts are much bolder than reform efforts elsewhere in the imperial domains.

The two states, it is crucial to remember, were not proper colonies or even protectorates. They were placed under French trusteeship by the League of Nations only after World War I and the fall of the Ottoman Empire. France was charged with the task of guiding them toward independence in the foreseeable future. Such a formulation of imperial governance was exceptional in the context of the French Empire, and it meant that French political control was not as firm there as it was elsewhere. The Syrian and Lebanese leaders were unique in extracting a treaty for independence from the French government in 1936, and this in itself attests to France's weakness there, relative to its other colonies and protectorates.[29] By 1945, both Levantine states had gained formal independence, and soon after, they successfully forced the removal of the French military from the region. In addition, the Mandate states were very new creations, relative to most other imperial territories. The legitimacy of the actual Mandate administration was conferred by the League of Nations, itself a new organization.[30] As a result of the political formula for French control and its recent establishment, French authority was subject to great internal and external opposition. In order to carry out a successful cultural policy in such a turbulent political climate, the French had to cajole hostile or indifferent local forces into choosing France as a partner in culture, while at the same time sustaining the loyalty of those already predisposed to support French cultural "*œuvres.*"

The Institut français de Damas, which hosted French academics doing research in Syria and fostered ties with the local intelligensia, is a good example of successful collaboration. Laoust, cited above, proved one of the most adept French cultural representatives in adapting to the new political realities. After becoming director of the Institut in 1941, he steered it through the minefield of political agitation, shielding it from much criticism and from closure by anti-French political forces by charting an apolitical course.[31] The missionary schools, by contrast, weathered the anti-French nationalist unrest with less skill. Politically influential under French rule, owing to their close ties with the Mandate authorities, missionary orders such as the Jesuits and Lazarists fought to maintain special rights and privileges without due consideration for nationalist sentiment. Moreover, as outspoken promoters of French culture and language, they were poorly placed to dissociate themselves from the unpopular Mandate regime and found themselves the targets of anti-French public aggression and government legislation. Once the Syrian government took over from the French administration, many French missionaries needed the protection of local Christian communities in order to continue their work.[32]

Cultural cooperation thus existed through a haphazard collection of coalitions, some ephemeral, some enduring, and all of them subject to the vagaries of Syrian and Lebanese politics. Nationalist demands forced the French to reconsider their policies not only in the economic and political spheres but also in the domain of culture. Given this, one of the main quandaries facing the French government was the variety of agendas of the local collaborators participating in France's cultural program, which will be considered next. In wealthy and powerful target countries, financial and material support from the local government and private organizations might make them the primary conduits of French influence.[33] In the context of the Mandates, the balance of material resources available for cultural projects was generally on the side of the French. What the French could not unilaterally command, however, were indigenous government policies granting special privileges to French establishments, especially as power over domestic administration was progressively transferred to new Syrian and Lebanese assemblies and then parliaments during the 1920s and 1930s. The French were even less able to coerce the manifold Christian and Muslim religious authorities. Not only did the Christian Patriarchs and Islamic Muftis hold considerable spiritual and financial resources, they also had enormous political influence and exercised a great deal of power to stir or quell public agitation against France. In this sense cultural diplomacy in the Levant both demonstrates how colonizers wielded power and belies the notion that the colonized people were powerless.

This latter point is particularly significant in light of Edward Said's influential conception of power and knowledge in the colonial environment as the function of a binary opposition between homogenous groups of powerful colonizers and powerless subjects. In reality, there were far too many factors in most colonized regimes to allow this type of homogeneity or passivity on the part of the local population. The Syrian and Lebanese political factions operating in the incipient governments, the urban notables, and the religious leaders must be seen as cultural agents in their own right. Their behavior illustrates how colonialism involved a "constant negotiation of power relationships and identities."[34]

The multilateral nature of French cultural policy was all the more complex owing to the religious diversity in the Levant, which made Syria and Lebanon unique in the Middle East and North Africa. In Syria just after World War I, 69 percent of the population was Sunni Muslim, 16 percent was Alawite, Druze, or Isma'ili, and 14 percent was Catholic or Orthodox Christian. Lebanon in 1932, according to government census records, had a Christian population of 51.3 percent, which just outnumbered the Muslims at 48.8 percent. Broken down, Lebanon was 19.9 percent Shiite, 6.8 percent Druze, and 22.4 percent Sunni.[35] France's imperial policies in the Middle East and Africa generally sought to empower non-Muslim or non-Arab Muslim minorities at the expense of the Sunni majority. In Lebanon, the Christians were the principal beneficiaries of French rule, having enjoyed privileged relations with France since the sixteenth century.[36] In Syria, the French worked to diminish Sunni prominence by granting semi-autonomy to the Alawite and Druze regions, and by ceding Syrian territory, such as the Biqa Valley, to Lebanon and Alexandretta to Turkey. The French decision to capitalize on the Christians' support clearly alienated the region's Muslims.[37] Given the tensions caused by the mesh of intra- and interconfessional rivalries, it should come as little surprise that the French could not simply establish cultural partnerships with local groups in a vacuum. Rather, they had to cope with a range of different religious and political identities, which inevitably affected cultural affiliation.

The international environment was another factor hampering French cultural diplomacy in the Middle East, not least because other powers were similarly seeking to use culture to gain political clout in the region. During the 1930s, the French government faced increasing cultural competition from Germany and Italy, as well as Britain and the United States. The Italians set up language courses and sports teams, and the American Protestants founded schools and encouraged Levantine leaders to favor Anglo-Saxon culture over that of France.[38] Of these four, only Britain equaled, and indeed surpassed, the French in imperial prowess. After World War I, the British government grew increasingly attached to the idea of an independent federation of Arab states as a British sphere of influence. Such a vision flew in the face of French policies, which encouraged distinct minority identities to counter regional Sunni Arab solidarity.

The German, Italian, and American imperial efforts were materially and historically far less substantial than those of the British. Nevertheless, cultural competition from them grew quite dramatically during the 1930s and 1940s.[39] Interference in the Levant by Hitler and Mussolini, most prominent until 1941, was marked by a discretion that seems at odds with their domestic conduct. Unwilling to provoke open diplomatic conflict with Britain in the Middle East before the war, they attempted to promote themselves through cultural endeavors that were sufficiently quiet not to cause formal dispute. American opposition to colonial empires drew considerable impetus from Woodrow Wilson's Fourteen Points in 1919, the fifth of which called for increased indigenous voice in colonial government and suggested that the administration of colonies be handed over to international committees. The Americans had little political interest in the Middle East before World War II. They were inspired, rather, by the ideology of "open door" economics, anti-imperialism, support for self-determination, and, most significant, a desire to spread the benefits of their society overseas.[40] After World War II began, British and American attempts to gain influence were likewise tempered by an unwillingness to create an atmosphere of open conflict, especially after 1941, when Free French and British forces were jointly responsible for the security of the Levant. Given the urgent daily exigencies of war, one might expect cultural propaganda to fall somewhat by the wayside. However, a large portion of Allied attention between 1941 and 1945 was devoted to artistic, literary, and educational initiatives, and these projects increased rather than decreased in importance during this period.

In order to illustrate the role that cultural diplomacy played in a colonial territory on the cusp of independence at a time when the international balance of power was being realigned, it is useful to consider the following example from Syria at the end of World War II. Amid the domestic and international turmoil between 1944 and 1946, a series of negotiations and incidents took place involving foreign schools. Education was a cornerstone of French cultural policies overseas, and the controversy over foreign schools in Syria demonstrates how different players used cultural institutions to gain leverage in international diplomacy.

As noted above, education was likely the most significant element in French cultural diplomacy. It is thus necessary to understand the administration of education under the French Mandate before looking at the changes that came about as Syria moved toward independence. The greatest governmental advocate for French education in the Levant throughout the interwar period was Gabriel Bounoure, a graduate of the prestigious *École Normale Supérieure* in Paris. Having arrived in the Middle East in 1923, he directed the Service des œuvres, overseen by the Ministry of Foreign Affairs, and the Service de l'instruction publique, attached to the High Commission, from 1929 until well after World War II. A key component of the government's cultural policy was to provide financial support for French education carried out by either French organizations or local institutions. After 1923, financial subsidies to private schools and other French cultural endeavors fell under the jurisdiction of the Service des œuvres at the Ministry of Foreign Affairs in Paris, while the High Commission's Service de l'instruction publique was responsible for coordinating the Syrian and Lebanese Ministries of Public Instruction.

When Bounoure was assigned as director of both the Service des œuvres and the Service de l'instruction publique, he made a concerted effort to separate the two offices, though in practice he directed both. The significance of this division lay in the role he envisaged for each service after independence. Bounoure expected the Service de l'instruction publique to be abolished along with the High Commission when Syria and Lebanon gained their independence. The Service des œuvres, by contrast, was a diplomatic department that operated all over the world and, in his view, did not need to diminish its work after the Mandate ended. Its continued work to promote French culture in the Levant would not be a remnant of the colonial Mandate, but rather a regular component of diplomatic relations.[41] Thus, Bounoure was taking administrative measures early on to separate French cultural institutions from the imperial Mandate administration.

Bounoure, however, was unusual in his efforts to organize the structures that would allow for a smooth transition from an imperial relationship to a diplomatic one. In 1944, French officials who perceived that the Mandate would soon end attempted to negotiate a Franco-Syrian treaty that would secure special economic, political, and cultural privileges for France in an independent Syria. One component of the treaty the French presented to the Syrian negotiators was a convention to define the parameters for Franco-Syrian cultural relations and to protect existing French cultural interests, most notably schools.[42] The Syrians saw the proposals as an attempt to undermine their independence and rejected the entire process.

Nationalist politics in Syria were dominated by a large and amorphous coalition called the National Bloc, which was formally established in 1931 but had already gathered some momentum by 1927. Composed mainly of Sunni Muslim notables of the ruling elite from the pre-Mandate era, it was supplemented by a new generation of nationalists who were more pan-Arab in orientation.[43] Although divided in many respects, Syrian nationalists were united insofar as they would negotiate with the French only after they had achieved full independence and could establish regular diplomatic relations without according any special rights to France. The Syrian refusal to negotiate in 1944 was matched by the thoroughly intransigent attitude of the French leaders in their dealings with the Syrians throughout 1944 and 1945, particularly over military issues. This intransigence culminated in the French bombardment of Damascus in May 1945 in order to reestablish political control. At this point the British, who had a significant troop presence in the region, stepped up pressure for a full military withdrawal, which was implemented by 1946.

The very pronounced Syrian public and governmental animosity toward the French, resulting from the latter's intractability, clearly affected cultural diplomacy. To illustrate this, it is useful to compare the draft text of the 1945 University Convention with an earlier version mooted in the late 1930s, and also to examine the involvement of another foreign power, namely the United States, in Franco-Syrian relations.

In the pre-independence period, a successful agreement about educational establishments would have secured a privileged place for the French language in the national curriculum as well as special consideration for French representatives on pedagogical and examination councils. By 1945, success for the French no longer meant maintaining the status of a privileged nation but rather ensuring parity with the rights of other foreign powers, especially the United States.[44] The strongest Syrian objections to the 1945 draft convention were reserved for section six, the first clause of which promised to grant France all educational privileges that Syria had accorded to any other nation. Syrian President Hashim al-Atasi was unwilling to confer any special privileges on France, and in contrast to Syria's stance in the prewar period, insisted that France establish bilateral diplomatic ties like any other nation.[45] As the French tried to maintain a colonial legacy, the Syrians sought to force France into a standard mode of diplomatic agreement.

The international diplomatic discussions arising from draft university convention primarily involved the United States, whose government was keen to use American Protestant missionaries to undermine French power in the Middle East. Although not a colonial power, the United States was, by the end of the war, becoming increasingly active in establishing spheres of influence, and American representatives in the Levant had worked consistently throughout the war to promote Syrian independence. The main conduits of American activity in Syria consisted of educational institutions, which, like their French equivalents, were protected by certain agreements. The most important of these, signed by the French government in 1924, stipulated that Americans be allowed to operate schools and philanthropic associations without hindrance.[46] With the Allied occupation of the Levant in 1941 and the progress toward Syrian independence, the short- and long-term validity of this accord was called into question. As early as October 1941, the US State Department made overtures designed to ensure the protection of the Protestant missions in an independent Syria and Lebanon. This in itself was an indirect means of affirming the future independence of the Mandate states. De Gaulle's Free French administration refused throughout the war to countenance any change in the 1924 accord, in the hope that France would gain its own cultural concessions from the Syrian government before anyone else had a hearing.[47]

For much of the war, American demands were restricted to protecting American institutions. In 1945, however, American officials sought not only to protect the status quo but also to challenge it. They were particularly unhappy that the French language remained obligatory in all schools, and that the French authorities wanted to safeguard their position as the most significant cultural influence in Syria and Lebanon. By 1945 Washington refused to accept any special treatment for France in the cultural domain. The Syrians proved very responsive to American pressure, which was all the more irritating to the French.[48]

American diplomatic pressure on the French was exercised not only by official government representatives but also by nongovernmental bodies, such as the American Protestants. The latter coordinated their work in the Levant through the American Board of Commissioners for Foreign Missions, which had been founded in 1810 and oversaw the missionary initiatives.[49] The US government, which clearly supported the agenda of the Protestant missions, progressed from defensive to offensive just as the Franco-Syrian negotiations over the still unresolved University Convention resumed in 1945. Much of the French weakness at this time derived from the American support offered to the Syrian government. The American officers saw French educational institutions as a direct obstacle to both their own establishments and their political vision for the region, particularly insofar as the French schools emphasized sectarian divisions. The US government's wider conception of the Middle East was geared toward establishing a regional Arab federation. The Syrians, for their part, were keen to accept American support, and the French found them far too eager to adopt American suggestions in exchange for political recognition.[50] Even more frustrating for French officials in the Franco-Syrian talks was the Syrians' use of American arguments against them in order to undermine the French educational missions.

In October 1945 this growing diplomatic pressure on France to renounce its privileges in the cultural arena coincided with measures taken by the Syrian government to curb the freedom of French schools. The legislation, passed in 1944 but effective only in autumn 1945, stipulated that all private schools needed written authorization from the Syrian Ministry of National Education to operate. All schools were ordered to close until this was granted. The Syrian government required that schools wishing to obtain permission have a national name, a Syrian head teacher, and an exclusively Arab staff. Schools were also required to adopt the official curriculum and submit their finances and teaching to national inspection.[51] These regulations conflicted with the terms of the University Convention proposed by the French, which would have granted considerable weight to their language and educational advisers. The rejection of formal French influence in the education system was both de jure and de facto. Moreover, the French soon noted that non-French foreign schools had been granted permission to reopen much more quickly, and claimed that Syrian officials systematically singled out French schools for harassment.[52] Attendance statistics confirm this: declines in enrollment occurred almost entirely in French schools, while attendance at other foreign institutions remained steady.[53]

Faced with hostile Syrian and American intervention in the running of French schools, the French government's transition from colonial cultural policy to cultural diplomacy bore little fruit. In spite of the very clear French conception of how to engage in cultural diplomacy overseas, the application in this imperial context was fraught with difficulty owing to conflicts within the French camp as well as opposition from local leaders and foreign powers. The conception of French cultural diplomacy rested on the twin pillars of an apolitical institutional infrastructure and the principle of reciprocity in cultural dissemination. The Mandate regime certainly allowed the French greater latitude to foster nongovernmental bodies, such as the Francophile missionaries, that could be used as intermediaries to the local population. At the same time, the French exercised that very access through the channels of an unpopular imperial regime. This connection helped paint the institutions of cultural diplomacy with the political brush of French imperialism, thereby hindering their effectiveness. Reciprocity was another conceptual feature of French ideas about cultural diplomacy. Ultimately, the success or failure of foreign initiatives was entirely dependent on their reception on the ground, where they might be welcomed, dismissed, or absorbed and reinvented as a local enterprise. France's evident political agenda in Syria and Lebanon impeded the development of genuine relationships of trust with local partners that could have enabled a genuinely reciprocal flow of ideas.

Endnotes

This chapter draws on material from the author's book *The Claims of Culture at Empire's End: Syria and Lebanon under French Rule* (Oxford: Oxford University Press, 2009).

1. Ministère des Affaires Étrangères (henceforth MAE), Levant, 1944–65, 364, note by Henri Laoust, 24 April 1940. Copies of the note or a discussion of it appear in the following: MAE, Levant, 1944–65, cartons 39, 40, 364; MAE, Relations culturelles (henceforth RC), Enseignement, 1945–1961, 109. On Laoust and his work at the French Institute in Damascus see Renaud Avez, *L'Institut Français de Damas au Palais Azem (1922–1946): À travers les archives* (Damascus: L'Institut Français de Damas, 1993), 148.
2. MAE, RC, Enseignement, 1945–1961, 97, MAE (Afr-Lev) to RC, note "Coopération intellectuelle entre la France et les pays Arabes," 25 May 1945. See also MAE, Levant, 1944–65, 364, Ostrorog to Bidault, 30 April 1945; MAE, RC, Enseignement, 1945–1961, 109, du Chayla to Bidault, 30 July 1946.
3. MAE, RC, Enseignement, 1945–1961, 109, MAE (Afr-Lev) to RC, 16 August 1946.
4. Avez, *L'Institut Français,* 208–209, 213–214.
5. Dominique Trimbur, "Introduction," in *Entre rayonnement et réciprocité: Contributions à l'histoire de la diplomatie culturelle,* ed. Alain Dubosclard et. al. (Paris: Publications de la Sorbonne, 2002), 18. Young uses a similar conception of cultural diplomacy. Robert J. Young, *Marketing Marianne: French Propaganda in America, 1900–1940* (New Brunswick, NJ: Rutgers University Press, 2004), 102.
6. On Foucault and historians see Jan Goldstein, ed., *Foucault and the Writing of History* (Oxford: Blackwell, 1994); Allen Megill, "The Reception of Foucault by Historians," *Journal of the History of Ideas* 48, no. 1 (1987): 117–141; John M. MacKenzie, *Orientalism: History, Theory and the Arts* (Manchester and New York: Manchester University Press, 1995). On Samuel Huntington and the Middle East see James L. Gelvin, *The Modern Middle East: A History* (New York: Oxford University Press, 2005), 1–7.
7. Robert Aldrich, *Greater France: A History of French Overseas Expansion* (New York: St. Martin's Press, 1996), 92, 98–99; Alice L. Conklin, *A Mission to Civilize: The Republican Idea of Empire in France and West Africa, 1895–1930* (Stanford: Stanford University Press, 1997), 2–3.

8. Conklin, *Mission to Civilize,* 1–27, 254–56. Classic political and military interpretations are C. M. Andrew and A. S. Kanya-Forstner, *The Climax of French Imperial Expansion, 1914–1924* (Stanford: Stanford University Press, 1981); Henri Brunschwig, *Mythes et réalités de l'impérialisme colonial français, 1871–1914* (Paris: A. Colin, 1960).
9. Conklin, *Mission to Civilize,* 5–6.
10. A. Peter Foulkes, *Literature and Propaganda* (London and New York: Methuen, 1983), 6–8. See for example Denis Peschanski and Laurent Gervereau, eds., *La propagande sous Vichy, 1940–1944* (Nanterre: Bibliothèke de documentation internationale contemporaine and Paris: Diffusion, Editions La Découverte, 1990); Dominique Rossignol, *Histoire de la propagande en France de 1940 à 1944: L'utopie Pétain* (Paris: Presses universitaires de France, 1991).
11. Leonard W. Doob, *Public Opinion and Propaganda* (London: Cresset, 1949), 240.
12. Jacques Ellul, *Propaganda: The Formation of Men's Attitudes,* trans. Konrad Kellen and Jean Lerner (New York: Vintage Books, 1973), xv–xvi.
13. Philippe Amaury, *Les deux premières expériences d'un 'Ministère de l'Information' en France: l'apparition d'institutions politiques et administratives, d'information et de propagande sous la IIIe République en temps de crise (juillet 1939–juin 1940), leur renouvellement par le régime de Vichy (juillet 1940–août 1944)* (Paris: Librairie générale de droit et de jurisprudence, 1969), 4; Michael Balfour, *Propaganda in War, 1939–1945: Organisations, Policies, and Publics, in Britain and Germany* (London: Routledge & Kegan Paul, 1979), 421.
14. Philip M. Taylor, *Munitions of the Mind: A History of Propaganda from the Ancient World to the Present Era* (Manchester and New York: Manchester University Press, 1995), 1–15, quote on 14; Garth S. Jowett and Victoria O'Donnell, *Propaganda and Persuasion* (Thousand Oaks: Sage, 1999), 6.
15. R. A. Leeper, "British Culture Abroad," *Contemporary Review,* no. 148 (August 1935): 203.
16. Amaury, *Les deux premières expériences d'un 'Ministère de l'Information' en France,* 16; Young, *Marketing Marianne,* xv–xvi, 81, 126.
17. Ellul, *Propaganda,* 70–79.
18. Albert Salon, *Vocabulaire critique des relations internationales dans les domaines culturel, scientifique et de la coopération technique* (Paris: La Maison du dictionnaire, 1978), 12–13, 47, 112, 115–116. For studies of French cultural diplomacy, see Alain Dubosclard et al., eds., *Entre rayonnement et réciprocité: Contributions à l'histoire de la diplomatie culturelle* (Paris: Publications de la Sorbonne, 2002); Antoine Marès, "Puissance et présence culturelle de la France: L'exemple du Service des œuvres françaises à l'étranger dans les années 30," *Relations internationales,* no. 33 (spring 1983): 65–80; Gilles Matthieu, *Une ambition sud-américaine: Politique culturelle de la France, 1914–1940* (Paris: L'Harmattan, 1991); Mathew Burrows, "'Mission civilisatrice': French Cultural Policy in the Middle East, 1860–1914," *The Historical Journal* 1, no. 29 (1986): 109–136.
19. Trimbur, "Introduction," 18–19.
20. Preface to Salon, *Vocabulaire,* 1.
21. Salon, *Vocabulaire,* 12–3, 47, 112, 115–116.
22. Matthieu, *Une Ambition sud–américaine,* 67–68.
23. Amaury, *Les deux premières expériences d'un 'Ministère de l'Information' en France,* 27–58; Avez, *L'Institut Français,* 193; Marès, "Puissance et présence culturelle de la France," 65–80; Matthieu, *Une Ambition sud–américaine,* 65–71; Young, *Marketing Marianne,* 80–81, 102–103, 126–127, 141–143.
24. There are many general histories of the French Empire, one of the most comprehensive being the two-volume set by Jean Meyer et al., *Histoire de la France*

coloniale, vol. 1.: *Des origines à 1914* (Paris: A. Colin, 1991) and Jacques Thobie et. al., *Histoire de la France coloniale,* vol. 2.: *1914–1990* (Paris: A. Colin, 1990).

25. Nadine Méouchy, "Introduction thématique," in *France, Syrie et Liban, 1918–1946: Les ambiguïtés et les dynamiques de la relation mandataire,* ed. Nadine Méouchy (Damascus: Institut français d'études arabes de Damas, 2002), 24–26.
26. Jean-Pierre Valognes, *Vie et mort des Chrétiens d'Orient: Des origines à nos jours* (Paris: Fayard, 1994), 502–519.
27. Jérôme Bocquet, "Le Collège Saint-Vincent, un agent de la présence française?" in Méouchy, *France, Syrie et Liban, 1918–1946,* 105–124; Elizabeth Thompson, "Neither Conspiracy nor Hypocrisy: The Jesuits and the French Mandate in Syria and Lebanon," in *Altruism and Imperialism: Western Cultural and Religious Missions in the Middle East,* ed. Eleanor H. Tejirian and Reeva Spector Simon (New York: Middle East Institute, Columbia University, 2002), 66–87.
28. Pierre Fournié, "Le Mandat à l'épreuve des passions françaises: L'affaire Sarrail (1925)," in Méouchy, *France, Syrie et Liban, 1918–1946,* 125–168.
29. Tony Chafer and Amanda Sackur, "Introduction," in *French Colonial Empire and the Popular Front: Hope and Disillusion,* ed. Tony Chafer and Amanda Sackur (New York: St. Martin's Press, 1999), 1–2.
30. Political accounts of the Mandates can be found in Philip S. Khoury, *Syria and the French Mandate: The Politics of Arab Nationalism, 1920–1945* (Princeton: Princeton University Press, 1987), 33–43; Meir Zamir, *The Formation of Modern Lebanon* (London and Dover, NH: Croom Helm, 1985); Meir Zamir, *Lebanon's Quest: The Road to Statehood, 1926–39* (London and New York: I. B. Tauris, 1997); Raghid El-Solh, *Lebanon and Arabism: National Identity and State Formation* (London and New York: I. B. Tauris, 2004); Elizabeth Thompson, *Colonial Citizens: Republican Rights, Paternal Privilege, and Gender in French Syria and Lebanon* (New York: Columbia University Press, 2000).
31. Avez, *L'Institut Français,* 148–150.
32. Jennifer Dueck, "Educational Conquest: Schools as a Sphere of Politics in French Mandate Syria, 1936–1946," in *French History: Special Issue on Spaces and Places* 20, no. 4 (2006): 442–459.
33. Young has shown, for example, that French cultural propaganda in the United States targeted the educated elite and subsidized publications with such considerations in mind. Young, *Marketing Marianne,* 29–30, 35, 171–172.
34. Thompson, *Colonial Citizens,* 1–3.
35. Khoury, *Syria and the French Mandate,* 14–15; R. Maktabi, "The Lebanese Census of 1932 Revisited: Who Are the Lebanese?" *British Journal of Middle Eastern Studies 26,* no. 2 (1999): 219–241.
36. Valognes, *Vie et mort,* 77–79, 268–269.
37. See El-Solh, *Lebanon and Arabism;* Zamir, *The Formation of Modern Lebanon;* Zamir, *Lebanon's Quest.*
38. MAE (Nantes), Beyrouth, Sûreté Générale, 2, SGA (Aleppo), Info., 7 November 1936, 11 December 1936; MAE, RC, Enseignement, 1945–1961, 109, report by Documentation extérieure et contre-espionnage, 8 August 1946.
39. On Germany and the French Empire see Chantal Metzger, *L'empire colonial français dans la stratégie du Troisième Reich (1936–1945),* vol. 1 (Brussels and New York: Peter Lang, 2002). On Italy see Renzo de Felice, *Il fascismo e l'oriente: arabi, ebrei e indiani nella politica di Mussolini* (Bologna: Il Mulino, 1988); Manfredi Martelli, *Il fascio e la mezza luna: i nazionalisti arabi e la politica di Mussolini* (Rome: Settimo sigillo, 2003).
40. Phillip J. Baram, *The Department of State in the Middle East, 1919–1945* (Philadelphia: University of Pennsylvania Press, 1978); John A. DeNovo, *American Inter-*

ests and Policies in the Middle East (Minneapolis: University of Minnesota Press, 1963); James A. Melki, "Syria and the State Department, 1937–47," *Middle Eastern Studies* 1, no. 33 (January 1997): 92–106.
41. Pierre Fournié, "La carrière de Gabriel Bounoure à Beyrouth, 1923–1952," in *Vergers d'exil*, ed. Gérard D. Khoury (Paris: Geuthner, 2004), 60–64.
42. See Salma Mardam Bey, *La Syrie et la France: Bilan d'une équivoque, 1939–1945* (Paris: L'Harmattan, 1994), 162–175.
43. Khoury, *Syria and the French Mandate*, chap. 1, 400–427.
44. MAE, RC, Enseignement, 1945–1961, 108, Ostrorog to Bidault, 7 May 1945; "Projet de Convention Universitaire Franco-Syrienne," 28 February 1945; MAE (RC) to the Ministry of National Education, 30 March 1945; Ostrorog to MAE, 29 April 1945; Ostrorog to MAE, 29 April 1945; Beynet (signed Ostrorog) to MAE, 9 March 1945.
45. MAE, RC, Enseignement, 1945–1961, 108, Ostrorog to MAE, 29 April 1945; Ostrorog to Bidault, 7 May 1945; "Projet de Convention Universitaire Franco-Syrienne," 28 February 1945, Titre VI.
46. See MAE, Guerre, 1939–45, Londres (CNF), 45 for a copy of this text.
47. MAE, Guerre, 1939–45, Londres (CNF), 45, Commissariat aux affaires étrangères to State Department, 2 October 1941.
48. MAE, Office du Levant, 7, report of meeting between Massigli, Chauvel and Shone, 13 September 1945.
49. MAE, Guerre, 1939–45, Londres (CNF), 45, International Missionary Council to René Pléven, 16 October 1941. J. A. DeNovo, "On the Sidelines: The United States and the Middle East between the Wars, 1919–1939," in *The Great Powers in the Middle East, 1919–1939*, ed. Uriel Dann (New York: Holmes & Meier, 1988), 225–226.
50. MAE, RC, Enseignement, 1945–1961, 108, Ostrorog to MAE, 29 April 1945; High Commission to MAE, 8 March 1945. MAE, Office du Levant, 7, Beynet to Bidault, 16 February 1945.
51. This was Law 121, passed 21 December 1944. MAE, RC, Enseignement, 1945–1961, 108, Beynet to Bidault, 22 October 1945; Service de l'Instruction Publique (Aleppo) to the head of the Ecole de Saint-Joseph des Filles Azizié.
52. MAE, Office du Levant, 7, MAE (Afr-Lev) to British embassy in Paris, November 1945.
53. R. D. Matthews and M. Akrawi, *Education in Arab Countries of the Near East: Egypt, Iraq, Palestine, Transjordan, Syria, Lebanon* (Washington, D.C.: American Council on Education, 1949), 326–327, 388–392, 391.

Bibliography

Aldrich, Robert. *Greater France: A History of Overseas Expansion*. New York: St. Martin's Press, 1996.

Amaury, Philippe. *Les deux premières expériences d'un 'Ministère de l'Information' en France: l'apparition d'institutions politiques et administratives, d'information et de propagand e sous la IIIe République en temps de crise (juillet 1939–juin 1940), leur renouvellement par le régime de Vichy (juillet 1940–août 1944)*. Paris: Librairie générale de droit et de jurisprudence, 1969.

Andrew, C. M., and A. S. Kanya-Forstner. *The Climax of French Imperial Expansion, 1914–1924*. Stanford: Stanford University Press, 1981.
Avez, Renaud. *L'Institut français de Damas au palais Azem (1922–1946): À travers les archives*. Damascus: L'Institut Français de Damas, 1993.
Balfour, Michael. *Propaganda in War, 1939–1945: Organisations, Policies, and Publics, in Britain and Germany*. London: Routledge & Kegan Paul, 1979.
Baram, Phillip J. *The Department of State in the Middle East, 1919–1945*. Philadelphia: University of Pennsylvania Press, 1978.
Bocquet, Jérôme. "Le Collège Saint-Vincent, un agent de la présence française?" In *France, Syrie et Liban, 1918–1946: Les ambiguïtés et les dynamiques de la relation mandataire,* 105–124, ed. Nadine Méouchy. Damascus: Institut français d'études arabes de Damas, 2002.
Brunschwig, Henri. *Mythes et réalités de l'impérialisme colonial français, 1871–1914*. Paris: A. Colin, 1960.
Burrows, Mathew. "'Mission civilisatrice': French Cultural Policy in the Middle East, 1860–1914." *Historical Journal* 29, no. 1 (1986): 109–136.
Chafer, Tony, and Sackur, Amanda . "Introduction." In *French Colonial Empire and the Popular Front: Hope and Disillusion,* ed. Tony Chafer and Amanda Sackur. New York: St. Martin's Press, 1999.
Conklin, Alice L. *A Mission to Civilize: The Republican Idea of Empire in France and West Africa, 1895–1930*. Stanford: Stanford University Press, 1997.
DeNovo, John A. "On the Sidelines: The United States and the Middle East between the Wars, 1919–1939." In *The Great Powers in the Middle East, 1919–1939,* ed. Uriel Dann. New York: Holmes & Meier, 1988.
———. *American Interests and Policies in the Middle East*. Minneapolis: University of Minnesota Press, 1963.
Doob, Leonard W. *Public Opinion and Propaganda*. London: Cresset, 1949.
Dubosclard, Alain et al., eds. *Entre rayonnement et réciprocité: Contributions à l'histoire de la diplomatie culturelle*. Paris: Publications de la Sorbonne, 2002.
Dueck, Jennifer. *The Claims of Culture at Empire's End: Syria and Lebanon under French Rule*. Oxford: Oxford University Press, 2009.
———. "Educational Conquest: Schools as a Sphere of Politics in French Mandate Syria, 1936–1946," in *French History: Special Issue on Spaces and Places* 20, no. 4 (2006): 442–459.
Ellul, Jacques. *Propaganda: The Formation of Men's Attitudes*. Trans. Konrad Kellen and Jean Lerner. New York: Vintage Books, 1973.
El-Solh, Raghid. *Lebanon and Arabism: National Identity and State Formation*. London and New York: I. B. Tauris, 2004.
Felice, Renzo de. *Il fascismo e l'oriente: arabi, ebrei e indiani nella politica di Mussolini*. Bologna: Il Mulino, 1988.
Foulkes, A. Peter. *Literature and Propaganda*. London and New York: Methuen, 1983.

Fournié, Pierre. "La carrière de Gabriel Bounoure à Beyrouth, 1923–1952." In *Vergers d'exil,* ed. Gérard D. Khoury. Paris: Geuthner, 2004.

———. "Le Mandat à l'épreuve des passions françaises: L'affaire Sarrail (1925)." In *France, Syrie et Liban, 1918–1946: Les ambiguïtés et les dynamiques de la relation mandataire,* ed. Nadine Méouchy. Damascus: Institut français d'études arabes de Damas, 2000.

Gelvin, James L. *The Modern Middle East: A History.* New York: Oxford University Press, 2005.

Goldstein, Jan, ed. *Foucault and the Writing of History.* Oxford: Blackwell, 1994.

Jowett, Garth S., and Victoria O'Donnell. *Propaganda and Persuasion.* Thousand Oaks: Sage Publications, 1999.

Khoury, Philip S. *Syria and the French Mandate: The Politics of Arab Nationalism, 1920–1945.* Princeton: Princeton University Press, 1987.

Leeper, R. A. "British Culture Abroad." *Contemporary Review,* no. 148 (August 1935): 203.

MacKenzie, John M. *Orientalism: History, Theory and the Arts.* Manchester and New York: Manchester University Press, 1995.

Maktabi, Rania. "The Lebanese Census of 1932 Revisited: Who Are the Lebanese?" *British Journal of Middle Eastern Studies 26,* no. 2 (1999): 219–241.

Mardam Bey, Salma. *La Syrie et la France: Bilan d'une équivoque, 1939–1945.* Paris: L'Harmattan, 1994.

Marès, Antoine. "Puissance et présence culturelle de la France: L'exemple du Service des œuvres françaises à l'étranger dans les années 30." *Relations internationales* 33 (spring 1983): 65–80.

Martelli, Manfredi. *Il fascio e la mezza luna: i nazionalisti arabi e la politica di Mussolini.* Rome: Settimo sigillo, 2003.

Matthews, R. D., and M. Akrawi. *Education in Arab Countries of the Near East.* Washington, D.C.: American Council on Education, 1949.

Matthieu, Gilles, *Une ambition sud-américaine: Politique culturelle de la France, 1914–1940.* Paris: L'Harmattan, 1991.

Megill, Allen. "The Reception of Foucault by Historians." *Journal of the History of Ideas 48, no. 1* (1987): 117–141.

Melki, James A. "Syria and the State Department, 1937–47." *Middle Eastern Studies* 33, no. 1 (January 1997): 92–106.

Méouchy, Nadine. "Introduction thématique." In *France, Syrie et Liban, 1918–1946: Les ambiguïtés et les dynamiques de la relation mandataire,* ed. Nadine Méouchy. Damascus: Institut français d'études arabes de Damas, 2002.

Metzger, Chantal. *L'empire colonial français dans la stratégie du Troisième Reich (1936–1945).* Vol. 1. Brussels and New York: Peter Lang, 2002.

Meyer, Jean et al. *Histoire de la France coloniale,* vol. 1: *Des origines à 1914.* Paris: A. Colin, 1991.

Peschanski, Denis, and Laurent Gervereau, eds. *La propagande sous Vichy, 1940–1944.* Nanterre: Bibliothèke de documentation internationale contemporaine and Paris: Diffusion, Editions La Découverte, 1990.
Rossignol, Dominique. *Histoire de la propagande en France de 1940 à 1944: L'utopie Pétain.* Paris: Presses universitaires de France, 1991.
Salon, Albert. *Vocabulaire critique des relations internationales dans les domaines culturel, scientifique et de la coopération technique.* Paris: La Maison du dictionnaire, 1978.
Taylor, Philip M. *Munitions of the Mind: A History of Propaganda from the Ancient World to the Present Era.* Manchester and New York: Manchester University Press, 1995.
Thobie, Jacques et al. *Histoire de la France coloniale*, vol. 2: *1914–1990.* Paris: A. Colin, 1990.
Thompson, Elizabeth. "Neither Conspiracy nor Hypocrisy: The Jesuits and the French Mandate in Syria and Lebanon." In *Altruism and Imperialism: Western Cultural and Religious Missions in the Middle East,* ed. Eleanor H. Tejirian and Reeva Spector Simon. New York: Middle East Institute, Columbia University, 2002.
———. *Colonial Citizens: Republican Rights, Paternal Privilege, and Gender in French Syria and Lebanon.* New York: Columbia University Press, 2000.
Trimbur, Dominique. "Introduction." In *Entre rayonnement et réciprocité: Contributions à l'histoire de la diplomatie culturelle,* ed. Alain Dubosclard et al. Paris: Publications de la Sorbonne, 2002.
Valognes, Jean-Pierre. *Vie et mort des Chrétiens d'Orient: Des origines à nos jours.* Paris: Fayard, 1994.
Young, Robert J. *Marketing Marianne: French Propaganda in America, 1900–1940.* New Brunswick, NJ: Rutgers University Press, 2004.
Zamir, Meir, *The Formation of Modern Lebanon.* London and Dover, NH: Croom Helm, 1985.
———. *Lebanon's Quest: The Road to Statehood, 1926–39.* London and New York: I. B. Tauris, 1997.

Chapter 6

The United States and the Limits of Cultural Diplomacy in the Arab Middle East, 1945–1957

James R. Vaughan

In the dozen years between the end of World War II and the proclamation of the Eisenhower Doctrine, cultural diplomacy came to play an increasingly prominent role in the conduct of foreign relations in the Middle East. A growing number of governments created or expanded cultural diplomacy programs, and academics, artists, sportsmen, publishers, broadcasters, and film stars found themselves cast in new ambassadorial roles. Here, the cultural diplomacy program of the United States between 1945 and 1957 was in many respects a period of lost opportunity. In 1945 much of the Arab world was fertile ground for cultural diplomacy, yet by January 1957, large swaths of the Arab world, particularly in the urban and intellectual centers, had come to regard the United States with deep suspicion, if not outright hostility.

One might ask why, despite increased levels of investment and activity, cultural diplomacy proved unable to prevent this precipitous decline in American prestige. This draws upon the observation, set out by the editors of this volume, that much of the existing scholarship on cultural diplomacy has a one-dimensional quality, the result of its treatment of cultural diplomacy as an arm of American cold war strategy. The problematic relationship that developed between an idealized concept of cultural diplomacy as an act of mutual exchange and trust-building on the one hand, and the demands

---

Notes for this section begin on page 179.

of a national security agenda dominated by cold war concerns on the other, was at the heart of an awkward dilemma that US officials proved unable to resolve satisfactorily in the postwar Middle East. A strong awareness of the unpopularity of particular US policies persuaded many of the value of "cultural" alternatives to traditional diplomatic channels. At the same time, however, the failure of American statesmen to address the political causes of American unpopularity made the successful conduct of cultural diplomacy immeasurably more difficult. Apparently, the inability of the State Department and the United States Information Agency (USIA) to resolve this dilemma stemmed from the subordination of the cultural diplomacy program, for which they were responsible, to cold war priorities that often were of negligible concern to the Arab citizens of the Middle East.

The essay developed as part of a broader analysis of American and British propaganda in the Middle East during the early cold war.[1] It draws on historiographical developments since the mid-1990s which have collectively constituted, if not a complete turn, then at least a cultural twist in Cold War history. As Scott Lucas noted in 2003, "culture" became important for historians of the cold war because of "the development for the first time during 'peace' of a comprehensive state strategy, which incorporated culture into the campaign to defeat its adversary." A broad range of social sectors and groups, including "business, labor, journalists, youth, women, African Americans, athletes," all played important roles.[2] Several scholars subsequently responded to Lucas's demand for historians to move "beyond the stale and unrewarding evaluation of propaganda as an adjunct to policy" and began to engage fully with the relationship between propaganda, ideology, and diplomacy.[3] Susan L. Carruthers is among those who have expressed dissatisfaction with classing "propaganda" as a self-contained category of historical analysis, urging historians to integrate the study of propaganda within more nuanced investigations of ideology, culture, and power.[4]

"Cultural diplomacy," following Jessica Gienow-Hecht's definition, is treated here as the use of culture as "an instrument of state policy"[5] (albeit a form of state policy with a complex set of links to the private sector). In this respect, it can be readily distinguished from the concept of "cultural relations," which, as the editors point out in their introduction to this volume, tend to grow "naturally and organically," independently of direct government sponsorship. As such, cultural diplomacy has provided historians with a valuable arena in which to seek insights into the ideological clash at the heart of the cold war system. Exploring the nature of that ideological clash serves as an important reminder that the cold war, though rooted in competing ideas derived from an essentially European vision of modernity, was rapidly transformed into a genuinely global confrontation. "Washington and Moscow," as Odd Arne Westad has pointed out, "needed to change the world in order to prove the universal applicability of their ideologies."[6]

The study of cultural diplomacy is important, one might therefore argue, because it can cast fascinating light on the links between ideology and diplomacy, whilst helping to blur and break down the traditional chronological distinctions between the cold war and post–cold war eras.[7] The contest for cultural supremacy, played out within the international and domestic structures of the cold war, allows us to challenge the idea that the collection of integrative processes known as "globalization" belongs specifically to the post–cold war era. The emphasis that historians of culture and the cold war have placed on the relationship between the state and the private sector has, as Gienow-Hecht states, "moved the object under investigation from politics to capitalism in ways very different from the 1960s and 1970s."[8]

The Middle East offers the student of cultural diplomacy a fascinating field of study, albeit one not without its fair share of problems. The most immediate is the limited quantity of existing research in the area. Whilst there is developed literature on the cultural cold war in Europe,[9] the Middle East (despite J. M. Lee's claim that it was the challenge of Arab nationalism that forced British policymakers to appreciate the importance of cultural diplomacy[10]), has not generally been afforded extended treatment. Nevertheless, there is plenty of evidence to suggest that the Arab world was far from a marginal backwater in the cultural cold war, and the sheer scale of cultural activities in the region after 1945 ought to attract researchers.

American diplomats, even when spending on information and cultural activities was severely reduced during the eighteen-month period immediately following the end of World War II, remained fiercely protective of the cultural diplomacy program. One report from Baghdad in 1946 argued that it would be "folly to slash American cultural efforts," on the grounds that "the Arab world's leading statesmen and spokesmen have been, and for the present, will continue to be products of American cultural influences."[11] In truth, this was an exaggerated claim. Though there was a long tradition of American cultural influence in the Middle East, it was by no means the only tradition; nor, arguably, was it the dominant one. In 1933, Britain's High Commissioner in Egypt complained that

> The failure of England to make use of the forty years from 1882 to 1922 to create for herself a strong cultural position in Egypt is one of the most extraordinary phenomena of our illogical Imperial story ... The net result is that the declaration of Egyptian Independence in 1922 found France still predominant in the cultural field.[12]

Postwar American officials in Cairo also acknowledged the dominant cultural influence of France, citing an editorial in the *Egyptian Gazette* that argued that as far as the news media in Egypt were concerned, operating in English was a disadvantage. "Nothing can alter the fact," it was argued, "that Napoleon and his savants preceded the British connection with this country and that the French, being much more alive to the value of cultural work, established a hold two great wars and a national renaissance could not destroy."[13] In the interwar period, the French had consolidated their cultural influence in the Levant through their position as the League of Nations mandatory power in Syrian and Lebanon. The British, meanwhile, established as the dominant power in Iraq, Transjordan, Palestine, and Egypt, expanded their cultural diplomacy apparatus in response to French cultural preeminence and Mussolini's aggressive ambitions in the Mediterranean.[14]

Not all the cultural programs in the Middle East were imposed upon the region from the outside. In the interwar years, one of the leading theorists of Arab nationalism, Sati al-Husri, used his position as Iraq's minister of education to push a pan-Arab educational agenda across the Arab world.[15] Sati al-Husri was especially keen to spread pan-Arab ideas in Egypt—and with good reason, for Egypt was widely regarded as the political, intellectual, and cultural center of the Arab world. US officials certainly thought so: by 1947, Egypt was said to offer great opportunities for US cultural diplomacy programs because "information, technical knowledge and ideas which are exposed in Egypt spread through publications, newspapers and Egyptian technical experts to other Arab countries."[16] In the 1950s, when Nasser despatched Egyptian teachers to Arab countries across the region and launched the "Voice of the Arabs" radio program, he was simply building upon a long tradition of Egyptian cultural influence.

The cultural diplomacy program of the United States was both a part of and a reaction to the international expansion of cultural activities in the Middle East. American cultural influence can be traced back to the mid-nineteenth century, particularly through the efforts of the missionaries and philanthropists who founded the Robert College in Istanbul in 1863, the Syrian Protestant College, later known as the American University at Beirut, in 1866, and the American University at Cairo in 1919. Cultural diplomacy and information policy emerged as a recognized arm of US foreign policy in the 1930s, but it was only after World War II, initially under the administrative control of the State Department's Office of Information and Cultural Affairs (OIC), that such activities began to be organized systematically in the Arab world.

Why did the United States embark upon a systematic program of cultural diplomacy in the Arab Middle East after 1945? There are a number of plausible explanations. One stems from the frequently asserted belief that the dissemination of knowledge about America, its people and its values—the "projection of America"—was a positive and beneficial activity in itself. As one State Department officer argued in 1949, the assumption of usefulness of the cultural and informational arms of US diplomacy "rests upon the twin concepts that real knowledge will persuade, and mutual understanding will promote peace and friendship among all the peoples of the world."[17] Few US politicians, particularly those with a hand on Congressional purse strings and a businesslike eye on the value for money provided by investment in cultural diplomacy, were prepared to accept this idealistic line of argument at face value. The expansion of US cultural activities in the Middle East was inspired by rather less charitable impulses. Competition with European rivals was one such factor, fed by a gnawing inferiority complex and accompanying resentment at the often patronizing tone in which Europeans spoke of America. In this sense, the "projection of America" was a necessary corrective to the stereotypes and misrepresentations perpetuated by other countries active in the field. A fine example of this justification came from Cairo in 1947 when the head of the US diplomatic mission, S. Pinckney Tuck, complained that

> The major European countries are making far greater efforts to explain their position and to win friends in Egypt than we are ... Much of this effort is directed in a pointedly derogatory sense to the United States, its people, its aims and intentions, and its accomplishments ... It would be suicidal to our foreign policy to permit such impressions to be spread unhindered.[18]

The French were seen as particularly culpable, and United States Information Service (USIS) officials likened some French publicity material as the "projection of America through a needle." Material from official French sources published in the Egyptian press in January 1948 was said to be superficially friendly, but a closer reading revealed that it "damned America by snickers and the light touch ... leading the reader to conclude that Americans are feather-minded ...

love their meals above their fellowmen [and] are far more interested in political advantage than world affairs."[19] It was thus with some relish that US diplomats viewed the opportunities for cultural activities opening up in the Levant after the war—a consequence, as the Americans saw it, of Syria and Lebanon's "rejection of all [French] cultural development and language."[20] Similar tensions existed between American and British information and cultural officers in the Middle East. Indeed, "Western" cultural diplomacy in the region was on occasion characterized as much by disagreements and infighting as it was by the presentation of a united anti-Soviet or anti-Communist front.

The conflict between Arab nationalism and European imperialism was another important influence upon those responsible for "projecting America," as some officials argued that, historically, American prestige in the Arab world was at its greatest when the US was popularly associated with ideas and policies such as Woodrow Wilson's Fourteen Points or Roosevelt's Atlantic Charter statement.[21] Predictably, however, the single biggest spur to American investment in cultural diplomacy was the sense that the Soviet Union and its communist proxies had developed a subversive interest in the region and embarked upon their own campaign to denigrate America and to prove the superiority of Soviet values and culture.[22]

By the end of 1946, the Soviet legation in Cairo had embarked on a public campaign denouncing American archaeologists, professors, missionaries, doctors, agricultural missions, the American University at Beirut, and the Chicago Institute of Oriental Studies. These individuals and agencies, it was argued, in league with USIS officials, were responsible for '"a program of colonial expansion" that sought, through innocent-looking cultural activities, to achieve the "political slavery of all countries where there is American capital."[23] All this appeared to justify the analysis of one Cairo-based diplomat, Philip Ireland, who some months earlier had argued that "the economic and political discontents of this part of the world ... will continue to be exploited to their fullest by the Russians, to undermine and destroy British and American prestige and standing in the Middle East which, in the case of America, attained an unprecedented high place during the past war."[24] Ireland made no specific mention of Soviet cultural activities, but in the months that followed American officials became increasingly concerned about Soviet cultural initiatives, particularly in Beirut and Damascus. Here, "front organizations," such as the Lebanese chapter of the Friends of the Soviet Union, were said to be a particularly useful instrument for exerting Soviet control over "intellectuals sympathetic to Communist aims but who hesitated to join the party because they held official or important positions."[25]

In 1946, when the State Department created the Office of Information and Cultural Affairs to conduct overseas propaganda, it did so in the face of a widespread belief in American political circles that '"the responsibility for telling foreigners about the U.S. should be left to private agencies of information."[26] At the inaugural meeting of the US Advisory Commission on Information, Assistant Secretary of State for Public Affairs George V. Allen acknowledged that "the Government's role in the information job should remain supplemental to that done by private industry and that it should be limited to those fields where private industry can not or does not wish to enter."[27] By the end of the 1940s, however, private-sector cooperation had actually been institutionalized within the State Department's information and cultural diplomacy bureaucracy. Key institutions, such as the International Information and Educational Exchange program (USIE), the International Information Administration (IIA), and after 1953, the United States Information Agency (USIA), all included a Private Enterprise Cooperation office dedicated to the task of mobilizing private business and nongovernmental organizations behind American cultural diplomacy.[28]

In January 1953 the Advisory Commission on Information produced a report that summarized US thinking about the developing state-private networks of cultural diplomacy and propaganda. The IIA, it stated, should make as much use as possible of private organizations such as the international press services, motion picture studios, and publishing companies, all of which were identified as having key roles to play in exporting news, ideas, and features of American culture to overseas audiences.[29] There had been talk in the late 1940s about the possibility of mobilizing citizen volunteers behind an "American Committee for Democracy" in Egypt,[30] and the Truman administration's Psychological Strategy Board (PSB) later developed "a central and coordinated plan ... to indoctrinate and utilize Americans serving in the area in ... private capacities."[31]

This kind of approach to the practice of cultural diplomacy increased the significance of a number of private foundations dedicated to fostering closer relations with the citizens of the Middle East. Perhaps the most prominent was the American Friends of the Middle East (AFME), founded in June 1951. AFME existed, in its own words, "to further and intensify relations—especially cultural relations—between Americans and Middle Easterners."[32] To that end, its activities ranged from some fairly innocuous exchange programs and tours to some explicitly anti-Israeli and anti-British propaganda. Despite British protests, the organization was allowed to go about its business largely unhindered, and several historians have claimed that it received financial support from the CIA.[33]

By 1952, the State Department had joined forces with the private sector in numerous cultural diplomacy activities in the Middle East. These included so-called "symphony salutes" or concerts given by American orchestras in honor of particular overseas cities and broadcast by the Voice of America or the local radio station in the city being honored. Examples in the 1950s included a "salute" from Houston to Ankara and from Rochester to Tehran. Taking a "sister city" or "twinning," such as between Baton Rouge and Cairo, was also encouraged by the Private Enterprise Cooperation office. Such affiliations produced tangible examples of cultural exchange. The Baton Rouge–Cairo affiliation, for example, led to "an exhibit of Egyptian art in Baton Rouge," a "collection of sports equipment sent to Cairo for use by university students learning to play baseball and basketball," and the visit of Selim Bey, the Egyptian Minister of Information, to Baton Rouge.

US officials were quick to take advantage of the often highly developed public relations machinery of American corporations active in the region. USIA's Country Plan for Egypt in 1953 listed a number of companies capable of making important contributions, including the Trans World and Pan-American airlines, Coca-Cola, Pepsi-Cola, the Ford motor company, General Motors, major Hollywood studios, and private news agencies.[34] However, the relationship between the US government and the commercial news agencies did not always run smoothly. Roy Howard (director of Scripps-Howard Newspapers and a former president of the United Press) was perhaps USIA's most vehement critic, informing Eisenhower with some pomposity that the agency's news service was "a menace to the great asset inherent in the world-wide reputation for independence and freedom from propaganda taint that is the priceless and exclusive possession of the American agencies."[35] C. D. Jackson, a Time-Life executive and the White House's special advisor on psychological warfare, responded by tearing into Howard's "appalling display of selfishness, ignorance, and arrogance" and denouncing the United Press's international file as "250 words a day of the most unutterable below-the-belt tripe, which even a third-rate tabloid would not publish."[36] In fact, USIA had gone out of its way to assist the private news agencies and had even delayed improvements to its own news service in order to facilitate deals between the commercial agencies and Middle Eastern governments.[37] Indeed, the standard practice for American diplomats was to "take any steps necessary to adjust local activities, so as to eliminate causes for charges of competition, wherever private American news agencies operate."[38]

The central element of the American cultural diplomacy program in the Middle East was educational exchange. In 1945 the United States could look back on a distinguished history of involvement in Middle Eastern education dating back to the nineteenth-century missionary colleges. At the 1945 San Francisco conference to establish the United Nations Organization, it was noted with satisfaction that "29 of 40 Arab delegates ... had attended American schools in the Near East."[39] When the State Department came to consider US educational efforts in the region in 1946, it concluded that such schools would "continue to be the best American cultural influences in the Near East,"[40] and by 1952 there were said to be about 7,000 Middle Eastern students attending American educational institutions in the region.[41]

Private foundations played a major role. The AFME provided funds and facilities for exchanges and visits to the United States for Middle Eastern students and scholars. British observers were impressed by the work of both the Near East Foundation, which supported "a substantial program of public health, sanitation, education, home and family welfare and agricultural training in Syria, the Lebanon and Persia," and the Rockefeller Foundation, which engaged in "educational and health projects in Turkey, Egypt, Persia and the Lebanon."[42] When the US government looked to expand state-sponsored educational programs in the region, predominantly through the Fulbright exchange program, these were firm foundations upon which to build. In August of 1950, USIE staff noted that

> The inauguration of the [Fulbright] program in Syria has been so successful as to prompt a request from the Syrian Government for two additional American experts in the field of education for the coming year ... The careful selection of *potential* leaders for ... grants will contribute substantially toward winning friends for America. High priority should be given to this aspect of USIE activities.[43]

In 1946 the State Department had argued that "exchange of persons, and of students even more than those of mature age, is the most effective means of establishing understanding and sympathetic contacts with future moulders of opinion in other countries."[44] A decade later, in the face of Congressional threats to cut funding, Eisenhower declared himself willing to "fight, bleed, and die" for the exchange program.[45] Such determination resulted in the maintenance of an extensive Middle Eastern program throughout the 1950s, and USIA reports indicated that students from Iran and every Arab state except Libya were present at colleges and universities in the US during the mid 1950s. Numbers ranged from just two Sudanese students between 1950 and 1955, to 1,958 Jordanian and 4,478 Iranian students in the same period.[46]

Private academic institutions also provided opportunities for the educational arm of US cultural diplomacy. In September of 1953, the Library of Congress joined forces with Princeton University to stage a major conference on "Islamic Culture in the modern world." USIA took the opportunity to conduct a major publicity campaign about the conference, describing it as "primarily an occasion for increasing American knowledge of Islam, strictly on the non-political level."[47] This was rather disingenuous, as government agencies had been closely involved in organizing the conference from the beginning. In April of 1953 the IIA described how

> [o]n the surface, the conference looks like an exercise in pure learning. This in effect is the impression desired. The ostensible purpose is to promote good will and to further mutual understanding between Islamic peoples and the United States. The International Information Administration promoted the colloquium along these lines and has given it financial and other assistance because we consider that this psychological approach can make an important contribution to United States political objectives in the Moslem area at this time.[48]

The colloquium provides a fine example of the state-private network in action. At various points, the organizers contacted ARAMCO, Pan-American Airways, Trans World Airlines, and American Export in order to provide grants and travel facilities for delegates. The State Department's "private" publishing company, Franklin Publications, was also brought in to pay for and undertake the printing and publication in Arabic of the conference papers.[49]

Franklin Publications was the most important US asset in Arabic book publishing, translation, and distribution. The idea stemmed from the State Department's anxiety about the extent of Soviet publishing and book distribution activities across the region.[50] By June 1952, Franklin Publications had opened for business, describing itself as "a private and independent organization working in association with universities, foundations, government agencies, research institutes and various cultural groups." State Department officers were more candid, describing it as an example of "effective work in the field of cultural propaganda by a private organization under State Department cognizance."[51] Under official supervision, the company set out to study the book needs of the Arabic-speaking Middle East and to provide translations of American texts as required. By 1956 the National Security Council was noting that Nasser himself had praised the company for the educational titles it had made available,[52] and USIA added approvingly that "the operations of the corporation and USIA are closely allied and it is important ... that the Agency be kept ... fully informed of the corporation's activities, requests, problems, and achievements."[53]

Franklin Publications was by no means the only American intrusion into Arabic literary and publishing circles. The USIS Book Club in Syria, set up in 1954, was deemed successful in that it "acquainted an important group of Syrians with American books" and acquired a peak membership of nearly 2,500. It was, however, overly susceptible to charges that it was merely an American propaganda vehicle, so a reformed club was created in 1955, this time in partnership with the Syrian Librairie Universelle. The arrangement with the Librairie Universelle meant that USIS no longer had to distribute books carrying the imprint of a fictitious publisher but could rely on authentic Damascus companies, or the Librairie itself, to appear as the publisher.[54]

Given the power and appeal of America's entertainment media corporations, it is unsurprising to learn that efforts were made to exploit the popularity of American cinema for the benefit of US interests in the Middle East. Contacts with Darryl Zanuck, the power behind 20th Century Fox, proved especially useful. Zanuck, recalling his anti-Nazi propaganda work with Anthony Eden and Brendan Bracken in the 1930s and his role in the wartime production of "War Department films ... designed for the Home Front," appeared before the Jackson Committee[55] in 1953. "I have the definite feeling," he promised, "that ... someone from the motion picture industry should be able to make a worthwhile contribution."[56] Before long, USIA was working with Fox Movietone on the *News of the Day* newsreel and distributing it across the Middle East in English, French, and Arabic.[57]

When the Jackson Report was delivered at the end of June in 1953, it acknowledged that "75 percent of the free world's screen time is held by American commercial films," adding that "the American film industry, working with CIA and FBI, has cooperated in removing communists from production units." The report went on to claim that "[t]here is evidence that the film industry is prepared to cooperate with the Government, and every effort should be made by the latter to increase the positive contribution of commercial film to the United States propaganda and information program."[58] In the years that followed, the State Department and USIA would work closely with representatives of major Hollywood studios. In 1954, C. D. Jackson wrote to Eisenhower's Chief of Staff Sherman Adams, recalling Daryll Zanuck's testimony to the Jackson Committee, which had argued in favor of impressing upon key Hollywood figures the need to take American overseas propaganda objectives into account, and to "insert in their scripts and in their action the right ideas with the proper subtlety."[59]

USIA, therefore, developed its own plan to bring its influence to bear upon the Hollywood moguls, and Jackson requested that Eisenhower host a dinner for the key figures in the major Hollywood studios, including Zanuck, Cecil B. DeMille, the Warner brothers, and Walt and Roy Disney.[60] This meeting led to the appointment of DeMille as a chief consultant to USIA, and there is also evidence that US officials worked closely with representatives of MGM, 20th Century Fox, and RKO Pictures in the Middle East.[61] During this period, American representatives in the Middle East reported that "Disney cartoons,"[62] "westerns and slapstick humor of the Abbot and Costello variety"[63] were all popular with Arab audiences. British diplomats in Iraq agreed, reporting that "Baghdad at night resounds to swing and wild west shootings from the various open air cinemas."[64] The popularity of American popular culture inspired a State Department scheme to use US celebrities as informal "ambassadors." It was argued, for example, that if Bing Crosby were to make a tour of the Middle East, "the reception he would receive would be enormous." Crosby, it was thought, "would not be suspected of political chicanery. A few words about the world situation dropped strategically by him would have immeasurable effect."[65] Other stars identified as possible cultural ambassadors included Bob Hope, Jack Benny, Clark Gable, Lana Turner, Judy Garland, James Stewart, and Gary Cooper.

By the mid 1950s, USIA had come to see international sport as an important aspect of cultural diplomacy. The agency's deputy director, Abbott Washburn, declared in a 1954 memorandum entitled "International Athletics—Cold War Battleground," that "Communism has thrown down a challenge on the sports fields of the world," adding that "The recapturing of American prestige as a sports leader or at least the arresting of the depreciating of … American prestige in the minds of world youth necessarily depends on greater participation in important international competitions by United States athletes and sports teams."[66] US representatives in the Arab world had already attempted to use sport to forge bonds of friendship with those among whom they lived and worked. In 1952 the American legation in Jordan organized its own baseball game in Amman, using the opportunity to score some public relations points with the Jordanians. An American-produced Arabic publication picked up the story under the heading, "Jordanians Beat Americans at Own Game," reporting the 21–19 victory of the Amman team and noting how the American diplomats had presented the Jordanians with bats, balls, caps, and other equipment purchased by members of the legation.[67]

Sport provided another fertile area for cooperation between the government and the private sector. The Private Enterprise Cooperation office was always keen to use American sporting representatives as part of the cultural diplomacy program. In early 1952, a report for the Congressional Appropriations Committee announced that among the "unconventional devices and techniques" recently employed, "the [American] Amateur Athletic Union is giving full cooperation in the development of U.S. participation in the Olympics as a psychological factor in international affairs.'"[68] In the mid 1950s, USIA despatched Olympic athletes Mal Whitfield and Robert Mathias on goodwill tours of the Middle East in order to hold coaching sessions, give exhibitions, and provide advice to sports club organizers and youth groups.[69] The basketball exhibition team, the Harlem Globetrotters, made a successful visit to Beirut in 1953, and the State Department subsequently announced plans for another tour in 1955, this time taking in not only Beirut but also Tel Aviv, Alexandria, Cairo, Baghdad, and Istanbul. In an era of turbulent American race relations, the State Department's Herbert Hoover, Jr., was clear about the political benefits that such tours could bring, stressing the "unlimited possibilities for racial understanding and good will" that they produced.[70]

The projects and examples cited above would seem to suggest a far-reaching, well-organized, successful cultural diplomacy program. In April 1947 William Benton urged US diplomats in Cairo to recognize the importance of the international information and cultural affairs program, as well as the need for American leadership "at a time when the world is in the midst of what Secretary Marshall calls a 'riot of propaganda.'"[71] As the head of the Office of Information and Cultural Affairs, Benton clearly had a vested interest in stressing the value of the services provided by his department, but his words also reflected a broader enthusiasm about the possibilities for American influence in the Middle East. Yet by mid 1957, such enthusiasm had been replaced by a disappointed awareness that large swaths of Arab opinion viewed the United States with bitter suspicion. This is perhaps best illustrated by the sense of powerlessness that prevailed among those responsible for administering American cultural diplomacy in Syria. The educational exchange program was hampered by an edict of the Syrian Ministry of Education that expressively forbade teachers and government education officials to cooperate with American officials or visit the USIS library.[72] Contacts with army and air force officers, recognized as "the single most influential group in Syria," were similarly choked off after the Syrian government issued specific orders forbidding them to have any contacts with USIS staff.[73] Even the day-to-day administration of cultural activities was effectively shut down, and the US Public Affairs Officer in Damascus contended that "for some time to come, presentation of special exhibits, artists, lecturers, etc. will be imprudent ... The film section is also closed ... The library is also closed, since it has served in the past as the principal target for attacks on USIS—and now is no time to provide targets."[74]

Growing American unpopularity, along with its malign impact on US information and cultural activities, was certainly recognized as a problem, but few solutions appeared to be at hand. By 1956, USIA and the White House were stressing the need to "humanize" the projection of America and once again hoping that private citizens and institutions would play a key role.[75] This was by no means a novel suggestion, however, and when it had been considered by the State Department in previous years, it had generally been disregarded. In 1950 the idea had been attacked by the head of the American mission in Iraq, who, anticipating the later judgments of scholars seeking to differentiate between cultural diplomacy and cultural relations, argued against bringing private American citizens into the State Department's cultural diplomacy program in any official capacity, on the grounds that

> Those friends I mentioned and hundreds of others are friends of the Arabs because of themselves, not because they are officials. They went out there as missionaries, as teachers, as doctors, and lived among them and gave their lives to them. If you bring them in at this time you smear them a bit and I think they are more useful in reaching toward our ultimate objectives, as old friends rather than as new government officials.[76]

Two years later, State Department experts, still well aware of the good work done by private agencies, noted that "in order to keep operating in the Near East and keep the good-will of the people, they have been obliged to disown the policies of the U.S. Government in the area." The natural conclusion was that private American cultural representatives in the area "would have more to lose than gain, if we gave them any great amount of attention."[77] At such moments were the inbuilt contradictions within the US cultural "state-private network" clearly exposed.

Another consistent theme in American thinking on the challenges and obstacles facing the cultural diplomacy program was the question of mutuality. The bids to "humanize" the projection of America abroad and to promote Eisenhower's "person-to-person" exchange scheme were symptomatic of a real desire to elevate the principle of mutuality within the cultural diplomacy program. That this was still an objective in 1956 should have been a matter of no little concern, given the aims formulated a decade earlier by the State Department's Office of Information and Cultural Affairs. One memorandum, considering the implementation of the Middle Eastern program after World War II, was at pains to stress that any cultural diplomacy program that simply lectured its target audiences would be met with contempt. "There must," it was argued, "be some sense of mutual respect, some consultation on our part, as to their desires in the way of information and cultural services, and some demand on, our part for the exchange of their cultural goods against ours."[78]

In 1948 Assistant Secretary of State for Public Affairs George V. Allen told the first meeting of the US Advisory Commission on Information that "[c]ultural relations must be a two way street if we are to avoid a justified accusation of imperialism."[79] By the early 1950s, one disgruntled official was complaining to Theodore Streibert (later called upon by Eisenhower to serve as the first director of the United States Information Agency) that

> Our international information and education program is supposed to be a two way street ... I believe we can achieve very solid results by being interested in the other fellow's story, by ... promoting *mutual* understanding from which can grow mutual cooperation ... The great contribution ... would be to demonstrate to other countries, concretely and in a positive fashion, that we are *interested in them* as well as wanting them to be interested in us.[80]

It seems odd, therefore, that despite repeated official statements stressing the importance of treating foreigners as partners for cultural exchange rather than passive recipients of American exports, US cultural diplomats failed to convince foreigners that they were genuinely interested in what the rest of the world had to say.

In short, the US cultural diplomacy program in the Middle East failed to live up to the principles of mutual reciprocity and genuine cultural exchange. As early as 1946 the State Department had received warnings from officers in the field that "the principal of mutuality has often been disregarded in the hasty setting up of a program or the taking over of a war pressure program."[81] Huntington Damon, a State Department official who later became head of USIA's Middle Eastern operations, argued that among the Arab citizens, the task of showing that "the U.S. respects and admires their cultures [was] one of the most difficult and important long-term requirements for bringing the East and West together."[82] The dismissive attitude of some US officials toward the cultural achievements of the Arab world was a significant obstacle in itself, as in the case of the American diplomat responsible for cultural relations in Iraq in 1946, who stated bluntly that "Iraq has little to offer the United States of a cultural nature, the only exception being archaeological research facilities. Cultural cooperation between Iraq and the United States will be, therefore, virtually a one-way street."[83] Some officials, it seems, saw cultural diplomacy in the Middle East as a civilizing mission in which the principle of mutuality was either irrelevant or deployed merely as a cynical device to flatter the Arab objects of American enlightenment.

As far as US cultural diplomacy in the Middle East was concerned, what was characterized as a "two-way street" too often appeared to be a thoroughfare dominated by one-way traffic. Throughout the 1940s and 1950s, US cultural diplomacy was compromised by serious administrative and conceptual flaws. At the heart of the problem was the connection that had developed between the cultural and political aims of American foreign policy. That connection, perhaps inevitable to some degree, was fostered by key officials' insistence that cultural activities be understood as firmly in the service of political objectives. Throughout the formative decade of the cold war, the key agencies responsible for cultural diplomacy were located within the national security bureaucracy. The Jackson Report institutionalized a vision of defense, diplomatic, economic, information, and cultural policies as interconnected components of a "total cold war" strategy. This was probably advantageous, at least in theory, for the political warfare specialists and propagandists. It was far more questionable as a guiding philosophy for cultural diplomacy.

From an early stage in the developing cold war, American cultural diplomacy was justified and evaluated according to its ability to play a role in the pursuit of short-term political objectives. As one State Department official argued in October of 1947, "the acid test is not whether political information activities 'contaminate' the purity of cultural projects, but rather whether the latter impede the success of the former."[84] The primacy of short-term political objectives, driven by the contingencies of the cold war, was thus quickly established. In 1950, a US Information and Educational Exchange program officer explained that

> We would all prefer that the establishment of a healthy international community and the spreading of the democratic way of life were our main objectives. They still are our ultimate goals, but I think it would be healthier and make for a more effective political warfare operation if we recognized that for the time being they are secondary objectives.[85]

American cultural diplomacy was thus hampered by a school of opinion in the State Department that regarded it as "a minor appendage to Information, with little value or significance in itself."[86] To their own detriment, US officials created a cultural diplomacy program subservient to the political goals of the cold war national security establishment and consistently underestimated the extent to which an unpopular policy could render even the best-organized series of cultural activities meaningless.

The most obvious evidence of this is the impact of Arab perceptions of US policy toward Palestine. In 1946, when the State Department promoted a tour of the Middle East by the Lebanese-born, Princeton-based academic Philip K. Hitti, his tour was overshadowed by the crisis in Palestine. US diplomats in Cairo reported that

> Whatever [Hitti's] intentions were, and however sincerely he meant his statement that his mission was cultural and not political, Princeton's professor of Arabic was inextricably trapped in the Palestine question, and in this respect his arrival could not have been more unfortunately timed. He was the first to admit it. "In Cairo," he said sadly, "every time I tried to talk about books and learning I was interrupted and asked to explain America's stand on Zionism. It has been just the same in Lebanon."[87]

The Truman administration's role in securing the United Nations vote in favor of partition in Palestine in November of 1947 provoked a storm of anti-American feeling across the Arab world. It was hardly the fault of the cultural diplomacy program that by 1948 Iraqi press editorials were proclaiming: "We no longer require ... science, culture or education [from] a nation, which knows neither right nor justice."[88] By April 1948, just weeks before the outbreak of the first Arab-Israeli war, the State Department's cultural officer in Baghdad pointed out that his efforts were "dependent upon basic American policy" and that "[w]e are judged by our actions in the political field."[89] By 1951, State Department officers responsible for cultural activities found themselves in the farcical position of "trying to persuade [the Arabs] that we love them ... while in the meantime slugging them over the head on the Palestine issue."[90]

Whatever the merits of individual US cultural diplomacy projects, their incorporation into a cold war propaganda platform massively diminished their potential, leading to the alienation of Arab audiences in spite of the often attractive nature of the cultural products themselves. The more perceptive American cultural diplomats and information policy specialists understood this well, but because of the lowly status they held within the national security establishment, their voices were too often marginalized or ignored. They were left to issue unheeded warnings about the consequences of the failure they saw unfolding around them. "What do they [the Arabs] think of the Soviet Union?" one official enquired rhetorically at a meeting of the State Department's Information Policy Committee in 1951. "I don't know. But I do know that they don't think of us as they once did and some of them are beginning to think about looking in the other direction as a possibility. That, a year ago, two years ago, three years ago, just didn't exist."[91] When private US citizens in the Middle East were feeling "obliged to disown the policies of the U.S. Government" and the American University of Beirut was seriously considering dropping the word "American" from its name,[92] there was little for US cultural diplomats to do but bemoan the prevailing circumstances and wait for better times to come.

Endnotes

1. James R. Vaughan, *Unconquerable Minds: The Failure of American and British Propaganda in the Arab Middle East, 1945–1957* (Basingstoke and New York: Palgrave Macmillan, 2005).
2. Wm. Scott Lucas, "'Total Culture' and the State-Private Network," in *Culture and International History,* ed. Jessica C. E. Gienow-Hecht and Frank Schumacher (New York: Berghahn Books, 2003), 207–12.
3. Wm. Scott Lucas, "Beyond Diplomacy: Propaganda and the History of the Cold War," in *Cold War Propaganda in the 1950s,* ed. Gary Rawnsley (New York: St. Martin's Press 1999), 21.
4. Susan L. Carruthers, "Propaganda, Communications and Public Opinion," in *Palgrave Advances in International History,* ed. Patrick Finney (Houndmills, Basingstoke and New York: Palgrave Macmillan, 2005), 214.
5. Jessica Gienow-Hecht, "On the Diversity of Knowledge and the Community of Thought: Culture and International History," in Gienow-Hecht and Schumacher, *Culture and International History,* 3–41, here 4.
6. Odd Arne Westad, *The Global Cold War: Third World Interventions and the Making of Our Times* (Cambridge and New York: Cambridge University Press, 2005), 4.

7. For one of the most interesting recent efforts to move beyond the rigid chronological confines of the cold war, see Matthew Connelly, *A Diplomatic Revolution: Algeria's Fight for Independence and the Origins of the Post–Cold War Era* (Oxford and New York: Oxford University Press, 2002).
8. Jessica Gienow-Hecht, "Shame on U.S.? Academics, Cultural Transfer and the Cold War: A Critical Review," *Diplomatic History* 24, no. 3 (summer 2000): 465–494, here 493.
9. See, for example, David Caute, *The Dancer Defects: The Struggle for Cultural Supremacy during the Cold War* (Oxford and New York: Oxford University Press, 2003); Jessica Gienow-Hecht, *Transmission Impossible: American Journalism as Cultural Diplomacy in Postwar Germany, 1945–1955* (Baton Rouge: Louisiana State University Press, 1999); Robert Haddow, *Pavilions of Plenty: Exhibiting American Culture Abroad in the 1950s* (Washington, D.C.: Smithsonian Institution Press, 1997); Robert Hewison, *In Anger: British Culture in the Cold War, 1945–60* (New York: Oxford University Press, 1981); Walter Hixson, *Parting the Curtain: Propaganda, Culture, and the Cold War, 1945–1961* (Houndmills: Macmillan, 1997); Richard Kuisel, *Seducing the French: The Dilemma of Americanization* (Berkeley: University of California Press, 1993); Uta Poiger, *Jazz Rock and Rebels: Cold War Politics and American Culture in a Divided Germany* (Berkeley: University of California Press, 2000); Yale Richmond, *Cultural Exchange and the Cold War: Raising the Iron Curtain* (University Park: Pennsylvania State University Press, 2003); Giles Scott-Smith and Hans Krabbendam, eds., *The Cultural Cold War in Western Europe 1945–1960* (London: Frank Cass, 2003); Tony Shaw, *British Cinema and the Cold War: The State, Propaganda and Consensus* (London and New York: I. B. Tauris, 2001); Roland Wagnleitner, *Coca-Colonization and the Cold War: The Cultural Mission of the United States in Austria after the Second World War* (Chapel Hill: University of North Carolina Press, 1994).
10. J. M. Lee, "British Cultural Diplomacy and the Cold War, 1946–61," *Diplomacy and Statecraft* 9, no. 1 (March 1998): 112–134.
11. The United States National Archive, College Park, MD (hereafter USNA), RG59, Lot 53D84, Box 197, USIS Baghdad Report, 1 January–1 July 1946.
12. Frances Donaldson, *The British Council: The First Fifty Years* (London: J. Cape, 1984), 22–23.
13. USNA, RG84, 2410, Cairo Embassy 1936–55, Box 196, Folder 820.02 U.S.I.S. Reports No. 2 1948, USIS-Cairo October, 1948 Report and Special Report, 24 November 1948.
14. See Peter Partner, *Arab Voices: The BBC Arabic Service 1938–1988* (London: British Broadcasting Corporation, 1988); Frances Donaldson, *The British Council;* Philip M. Taylor, *The Projection of Britain: British Overseas Publicity and Propaganda, 1919–1939* (Cambridge and New York: Cambridge University Press, 1981).
15. Youssef Choueiri, *Arab Nationalism, a History: Nation and State in the Arab World* (Oxford: Blackwell, 2000); Adeed Dawisha, *Arab Nationalism in the Twentieth Century: From Triumph to Despair* (Princeton: Princeton University Press, 2003).
16. USNA, RG84, 2410 Cairo Embassy 1936–55, Box 169, Folder 820.02 I 1947, Tuck to Secretary of State, No. 2533, 19 May 1947, Enclosure: Report on a trip through Palestine, Lebanon and Syria by Mr. Noel Macy, Public Affairs Attaché.
17. USNA, RG59, Lot 53D47, Box 3, OII, Cody to Stone, 13 September 1949.
18. USNA, RG84, 2410 Cairo Embassy 1936–55, Box 171, Folder 820.02 I 1947, Tuck to Benton, 17 April 1947.
19. USNA, RG 84, 2410 Cairo Embassy 1936–55, Box 196, Folder 820.02 USIS Reports (American Propaganda) No. 1, USIS-OIE Report Cairo Egypt, Report of Activities, January 1948.

20. USNA, RG84, 2410 Cairo Embassy 1936–55, Box 169, Folder 820.02 I 1947, Tuck to Secretary of State, No. 2533, 19 May 1947, Enclosure: Report on a trip through Palestine, Lebanon and Syria by Mr. Noel Macy, Public Affairs Attaché.
21. USNA, RG59, Lot 53D266, Box 188, Working Group on Special Materials for Arab and Other Moslem Countries, State Department Transcript of Proceedings, Working Group on Special Materials for Arab and Other Moslem Countries, 1 April 1952.
22. See Frederick Barghoorn, *The Soviet Cultural Offensive* (Princeton: Princeton University Press, 1960); Walter Laqueur, *The Soviet Union and the Middle East* (London: Routledge & Kegan Paul, 1959).
23. USNA, RG84, 2410 Cairo Embassy 1936–55, Box 153, Folder 820.02 General 1946, Tuck to Secstate, No. 2017, 31 December 1946.
24. USNA, RG84, 2410 Cairo Embassy 1936–55, Box 150, Folder 800 (Political Affairs) 1946, Cecil B. Lyon to Secretary of State, 20 July 1946, enclosing memorandum by Philip Ireland, "Soviet Penetration in the Middle East," 16 July 1946.
25. USNA, RG84, 2410 Egypt 1936–55, Box 187, Folder 800 Communism, Department of State to Cairo, 27 July 1948, Committee on Foreign Affairs Report, "National and International Movements: The Strategy and Tactics of World Communism."
26. USNA, RG59, Lot 53D47, Box 12, Address by George Allen to the first meeting of the US Advisory Commission on Information, 7 October 1948.
27. Ibid.
28. For an interesting study of the relationship between the cultural diplomacy program of the US government and private-sector agencies, see Nicholas J. Cull, "Public Diplomacy and the Private Sector," in *The US Government, Citizen Groups and the Cold War: The State-Private Network,* ed. Helen Laville and Hugh Wilford (London and New York: Routledge, 2006), 210–226.
29. USNA, RG306, US Advisory Commission on Information, Reports, 7th Semi-Annual Report of the US Advisory Commission on Information, January 1953.
30. USNA, RG84, 2410 Cairo Embassy 1936–55, Box 195, Carter memorandum, 10 March 1948.
31. USNA, RG59, Lot 62D333, Box 2, PSB D-22, PSB Program for the Middle East, 6 February 1953.
32. USNA, RG306, USIA Publications, Box 170, *News Review,* no. 51, 28 June 1951.
33. Wilbur Eveland, *Ropes of Sand: America's Failure in the Middle East* (London and New York: W.W. Norton, 1980), 125; Mark J. Gasiorowski, *U.S. Foreign Policy and the Shah: Building a Client State in Iran* (Ithaca, NY: Cornell University Press), 128; Helen Laville and Wm. Scott Lucas, "The American Way: Edith Sampson, the NAACP, and African American Identity in the Cold War," *Diplomatic History* 20, no. 4 (Fall 1996): 565–590, here 577.
34. USNA, RG59, 511.74/3-2853, USIS Country Plan - Egypt, 20 May 1953.
35. Dwight D. Eisenhower Presidential Library, Abilene, Ks. (DDE), Whitman File: Name Series, Box 19, Howard to Eisenhower, 2 June 1956.
36. DDE, Whitman File: Name Series, Box 19, Jackson to Whitman, 27 June 1956.
37. USNA, RG306, USIA Inspection Reports, Box 6, Jordan, 10 February 1956.
38. DDE, Sprague Committee Records, 1959–61, Box 19, USIA (2), "The U.S. Information Program Since July 1953," undated.
39. USNA, RG59, Lot 53D84, Box 197, USIS Baghdad Report, 1 January–1 July 1946.
40. USNA, RG59, Lot 53D84, Box 197, Report by J. A. Wilson, "American Colleges in the Near East," March 1946.
41. British National Archive, Kew, London (TNA), FO371/98276/E11345/7, FO minute, 25 January 1952, enclosing memorandum, "United States Economic and Social Interests in the Middle East."

42. Ibid.
43. USNA, RG59, Lot 53D47, Box 41, USIE Country Paper for Syria, August 1950.
44. USNA, RG84, 2410 Cairo Embassy 1936–55, Box 153, USIS-OIC Cairo Report for September 1946.
45. DDE, Whitman File: NSC series, Box 5, 193rd meeting, 12 April 1955.
46. USNA, RG306, USIA Intelligence Bulletins of the Office of Research 1954–56, IB-53-55, "Near East Students at U.S. Colleges and Universities 1950–55," 27 September 1955.
47. USNA, RG306, USIA Publications, Box 170, *News Review,* no. 37, 10 September 1953.
48. The National Security Archive, George Washington University (NSAGWU), "U.S. Propaganda in the Middle East," Doc. 93, Damon to Hadsel, 30 April 1953.
49. NSAGWU, Doc. 90, Dodge to Sanger, 2 February 1953.
50. USNA, RG306, Subject Files of the Office of Administration, Box 1, Folder: Information Centers 1952–1953, Harris to ICD, 17 January 1952.
51. DDE, Jackson Committee Records, Box 6, Correspondence -J(2), Interview with Malcolm Johnson, 9 March 1953, attaching Franklin Publications Inc. pamphlet, undated.
52. USNA, RG306, US Advisory Commission on Information, Books Abroad Advisory Committee, 18th meeting, 10 February 1956.
53. USNA, RG84, 3253 Syria Damascus Embassy General USIS 1955–57, Box 4, USIA Circular CA-481, 16 September 1955.
54. USNA, RG84, 3253 Syria Damascus Embassy General USIS 1955–57, Box 4, Folder H-8 Book Publication Program, Mann to USIA, No. 16, 9 November 1955.
55. The Jackson Committee was an inter-Departmental committee of enquiry commissioned by President Eisenhower in 1952 to investigate the effectiveness and organisation of the US overseas information programme. The Committee was chaired by William Jackson, formerly a deputy director of the CIA and its report, presented in the summer of 1953, led among other reforms to the creation of the United States Information Agency (USIA).
56. DDE, Jackson Committee Records, Box 11, Correspondence XYZ(2), Zanuck to William Jackson, 2 March 1953.
57. USNA, RG59, 611.80/6-1755, "Memorandum for the Chairman, OCB Working Group on NSC 5428, Near East," 17 June 1955.
58. DDE, Jackson Committee Records, Box 14, Report to the President, 30 June 1953.
59. DDE, C. D. Jackson Records 1953–54, Box 1, Jackson to Adams, 19 January 1954.
60. Ibid.
61. See, for example, USNA, RG84, Cairo Embassy 1936–55, Box 153, Allen report, 21 August 1946 and Box 153, American Legation, Cairo to State Department, No. 1742, 23 July 1946, Enclosure No. 1.
62. USNA, RG84, Cairo Embassy 1936–55, Box 153, Allen report, 21 August 1946.
63. USNA, RG306, Special 'S' Reports of the Office of Research 1953–63, Box 3, S-33-53, 'Film Distribution Channels in Egypt', 30 September 1953.
64. TNA, FO 953/373/PME592, Information Department, Baghdad, to Middle East Information Department, 23 July 1948.
65. USNA, RG59 Lot 53D266, Box 188, Jones to Barrett, 15 January 1951.
66. DDE, C.D. Jackson Papers, 1931–67, Box 62, Washburn memorandum, 28 October 1954.
67. USNA, RG306, USIA Publications, Box 170, *News Review,* no. 31, 15 May 1952.
68. USNA, RG59, Lot 52D238 & 53D254, Box 86, Begg to Barry, 4 February 1952. See also Rachel J. Owen, "The Olympic Games and the Issue of Recognition: British

and American Perspectives 1944–1972," unpublished PhD thesis, Aberystwyth University, 2006.

69. USNA, RG59, Lot 60D262, Box 93, USIA Fortnightly Guidance for the NEA Area, No. 17, 23 December 1954 and No. 32, 21 July 1955.
70. USNA, RG84, 2756A Baghdad USIS General Records 1956–58, Box 4, State Department Instruction, CA-7722, 7 May 1955.
71. USNA, RG84, 2410 Cairo Embassy 1936–55, Box 171, Folder 820.02 I 1947, Benton to Tuck, 3 April 1947.
72. USNA, RG84, 3253 Syria Damascus Embassy General USIS 1955–57, Box 5, Folder A1-1 Country Plan, Global and Area Objectives, USIS Damascus to USIA Washington, No. 3, 20 July 1954.
73. Ibid.
74. USNA, RG84, 3253 Syria Damascus Embassy General USIS 1955–57, Box 5, Folder A Administration and General Program, Robert A. Lincoln (Acting Public Affairs Officer, USIS Damascus) to USIA, No. 1396, 2 January 1957.
75. USNA, RG59, Lot 60D262, Box 97, USIA Infoguides 3 July–28 December 1956, USIA Circular No. 552, 30 August 1956.
76. USNA, RG59, Lot 54D202, Box 6, Near East and Africa Information Programs 1947–1951, Department of State Transcript of Proceedings, Meeting: Information Policy Committee, 15 May 1950.
77. USNA, RG59, Lot 53D266, Box 188, Working Group on Special Materials for Arab and Other Moslem Countries, State Department Transcript of Proceedings, Working Group on Special Materials for Arab and Other Moslem Countries, 1 April 1952.
78. USNA, RG59, Lot 53D84, Box 197, Wilson report, "Information and Cultural Services in the Arab Near East," March 1946.
79. USNA, RG59, Lot 53D47, Box 12, George V. Allen address to first meeting of the US Advisory Commission on Information, 7 October 1948.
80. USNA, RG59, Lot 53D47, Box 3, Mohler to Streibert, 24 August 1951.
81. USNA, RG59, Lot 53D84, Box 197, Wilson report, "Information and Cultural Services in the Arab Near East," March 1946.
82. USNA, RG59, Lot 53D47, Box 27, Damon to Block, 17 October 1952.
83. USNA, RG59, Lot 53D84, Box 197, USIS Baghdad Report, 1 January–1 July 1946.
84. USNA, RG59, Lot 188, Box 120, Tyler to Stone, 4 October 1947.
85. USNA, RG59, Lot 53D47, Box 12, Hunt to Barrett, 21 August 1950.
86. USNA, RG59, Lot 53D84, Box 197, Wilson report, "Information and Cultural Services in the Arab Near East," March 1946.
87. USNA, RG84, 2410 Cairo Embassy 1936–55, Box 151, Folder: Lebanon 1946, Wadsworth to Secretary of State, No. 1241, 6 June 1946.
88. USNA, RG84, 2410 Cairo Embassy 1936–55, Box 168, Dorsz to Secretary of State, A-413, 18 December 1947.
89. USNA, RG84, 2410 Egypt Cairo Embassy 1936–55, Box 187, Folder 800 Secret 1948, Memorandum by A.H. Meyer, "U.S. Information Policy as Viewed from Iraq," 8 April 1948.
90. USNA, RG59, Lot 52D365, Box 48, Fisk to Phillips, 19 February 1951.
91. USNA, RG59, Lot 54D202, Box 6, Near East and Africa Information Programs 1947–1951, Transcript of Proceedings, Meeting: Information Policy Committee, Subject: Near East and Africa, 15 May 1950.
92. USNA, RG59, Lot 53D266, Box 188, State Department Transcript of Proceedings, Working Group on Special Materials for Arab and Other Moslem Countries, 1 April 1952.

Bibliography

Barghoorn, Frederick. *The Soviet Cultural Offensive.* Princeton: University of Princeton Press, 1960.

Carruthers, Susan L. "Propaganda, Communications and Public Opinion." In *Palgrave Advances in International History,* ed. Patrick Finney. Houndmills, Basingstoke and New York: Palgrave Macmillan, 2005.

Caute, David. *The Dancer Defects: The Struggle for Cultural Supremacy during the Cold War.* Oxford and New York: Oxford University Press, 2003.

Choueiri, Youssef. *Arab Nationalism, a History: Nation and State in the Arab World.* Oxford: Blackwell, 2000.

Connelly, Matthew. *A Diplomatic Revolution: Algeria's Fight for Independence and the Origins of the Post–Cold War Era.* Oxford and New York: Oxford University Press, 2002.

Dawisha, Adeed. *Arab Nationalism in the Twentieth Century: From Triumph to Despair.* Princeton: Princeton University Press, 2003.

Donaldson, Frances. *The British Council: The First Fifty Years.* London: J. Cape, 1984.

Eveland, Wilbur. *Ropes of Sand: America's Failure in the Middle East.* London and New York: W. W. Norton, 1980.

Gasiorowski, Mark J. *U.S. Foreign Policy and the Shah: Building a Client State in Iran.* Ithaca, NY: Cornell University Press, 1991.

Gienow-Hecht, Jessica C. E. "Shame on U.S.? Academics, Cultural Transfer and the Cold War: a Critical Review." *Diplomatic History* 24, no. 3 (summer 2000): 465–494.

———. *Transmission Impossible: American Journalism as Cultural Diplomacy in Postwar Germany, 1945–1955.* Baton Rouge: Louisiana State University Press, 1999.

Gienow-Hecht, Jessica C. E., and Frank Schumacher, eds. *Culture and International History.* New York: Berghahn Books, 2003.

Haddow, Robert. *Pavilions of Plenty: Exhibiting American Culture Abroad in the 1950s.* Washington, D.C.: Smithsonian Institution Press, 1997.

Hewison, Robert. *In Anger: British Culture in the Cold War, 1945–60.* New York: Oxford University Press, 1981.

Hixson, Walter. *Parting the Curtain: Propaganda, Culture and the Cold War, 1945–1961.* Houndmills: Macmillan, 1997.

Kuisel, Richard. *Seducing the French: The Dilemma of Americanization.* Berkeley: University of California Press, 1993.

Laqueur, Walter. *The Soviet Union and the Middle East.* London: Routledge and Kegan Paul, 1959.

Laville, Helen, and Wm. Scott Lucas. "The American Way: Edith Sampson, the NAACP, and African American Identity in the Cold War." *Diplomatic History* 20 (Fall 1996): 565–590.

Laville, Helen, and Hugh Wilford, eds. *The US Government, Citizen Groups, and the Cold War: The State-Private Network.* London and New York: Routledge, 2005.

Lee, J. M. "British Cultural Diplomacy and the Cold War: 1946–61." *Diplomacy and Statecraft* 9, no. 1 (March 1998): 112–134.

Owen, Rachel J. *The Olympic Games and the Issue of Recognition: British and American Perspectives 1944–1972,* unpublished PhD thesis, Aberystwyth University, 2006.

Partner, Peter. *Arab Voices: The BBC Arabic Service, 1938–1988.* London: British Broadcasting Corporation, 1988.

Poiger, Uta. *Jazz, Rock and Rebels: Cold War Politics and American Culture in a Divided Germany.* Berkeley: University of California Press, 2000.

Rawnsley, Gary D., ed. *Cold War Propaganda in the 1950s.* New York: St. Martin's Press, 1999.

Richmond, Yale. *Cultural Exchange and the Cold War: Raising the Iron Curtain.* University Park: Pennsylvania State University Press, 2003.

Scott-Smith, Giles, and Hans Krabbendam, eds. *The Cultural Cold War in Western Europe, 1945–1960.* London: Frank Cass, 2003.

Shaw, Tony. *British Cinema and the Cold War: The State, Propaganda and Consensus.* London and New York: I. B. Tauris, 2001.

Taylor, Philip M. *The Projection of Britain: British Overseas Publicity and Propaganda, 1919–1939.* Cambridge and New York: Cambridge University Press, 1981.

Vaughan, James R. *Unconquerable Minds: The Failure of American and British Propaganda in the Arab Middle East, 1945–1957.* Basingstoke and New York: Palgrave Macmillan, 2005.

Wagnleiter, Roland. *Coca-Colonization and the Cold War: The Cultural Mission of the United States in Austria after the Second World War.* Chapel Hill: University of North Carolina Press, 1994.

Westad, Odd Arne. *The Global Cold War: Third World Interventions and the Making of Our Times.* Cambridge and New York: Cambridge University Press, 2005.

Part IV

CIVIL SOCIETY AND CULTURAL DIPLOMACY IN JAPAN

Chapter 7

DIFFICULTIES FACED BY NATIVE JAPAN INTERPRETERS

Nitobe Inazô (1862–1933) and His Generation

Yuzo Ota

Cultural diplomacy may be described as any official and unofficial undertaking to promote a national culture among foreigners, when performed by those who identify themselves as part of the national culture at hand. Even in this very broad sense, cultural diplomacy remains a relatively new concept in Japan, having been first employed only in the second half of the nineteenth century, after the period of seclusion that lasted from 1640 to the 1850s.

In Japan before this period, it seems that there was a lack of interest in promoting Japanese culture abroad or to foreigners in Japan. Those who are genuinely convinced of their cultural superiority might believe that their country would naturally attract culturally "inferior" people without any effort on their part to promote it, an attitude that prevailed in premodern China. Japanese indifference to cultural diplomacy in the premodern period was different. This may have been a result of Japan's remoteness from the center of the civilized world, which for Japan at the time was China. Only when an oppressive sense of Chinese cultural superiority became too strong did Japan begin to assert its own. Certainly during the Tokugawa period (1600–1867), some Japanese people—often those who had once admired Chinese culture—started to assert the cultural superiority of Japan over China.

Yamaga Sokô (1622–85), a major thinker of Tokugawa Japan, was a typical example of this movement. He wrote a book in 1669 that

Notes for this section begin on page 206.

argues for Japan's superiority over China, maintaining that Japan, rather than China, was truly "the middle country," the center of the civilized world. He confessed in his autobiography (1675) that he had assiduously read Chinese books and had once thought that "[s]ince our country is a small country, it is inferior to China in every respect."[1] He claimed that adoration of China was the rule rather than an exception among Japanese scholars.[2] We cannot regard Yamago Sokô as a participant in cultural diplomacy, however; he addressed his message only to his own countrymen, whom he wanted to disabuse of the erroneous adoration of China that he had once shared. The same applies to the participants of the National Learning Movement from the eighteenth century, who also asserted the cultural superiority of Japan.

As long as Japan maintained its seclusion policy, there were no practical opportunities to engage in cultural diplomacy. Cultural diplomacy entered the realm of possibility for Japan only when, in accepting the Western rules of international relations, it opened itself to the outside world during the 1850s.

"Cultural Revolution" and a Sense of Identity

My main aim in this essay is to present the difficulties inherent in the work of Japanese cultural diplomats who tried to interpret Japanese culture for a foreign audience. Their work required a very good knowledge of a European language (usually English) that served as a common language with their audience. In this article, I will focus on Nitobe Inazô (1862–1933) and his generation, the first of native Japan interpreters,[3] to illustrate these difficulties.

Nitobe was born a samurai's son in the northern part of Japan a few years before the fall of the feudal Tokugawa regime. He was one of the samurai youths whose family fortunes were affected adversely by the birth of the new government and subsequent abolition of the traditional privileges afforded to the samurai class. Like many samurai young people under similar circumstances, he tried to gain an honorable position in the new society by receiving the best education available at that time. Nitobe left his mark in several different fields—as an agricultural specialist who made a great contribution to the increase of sugar production in Taiwan under Japan's colonial rule; as a university professor who lectured, among other subjects, on colonial policy; as the principal (from 1906 to 1913) of the most prestigious preparatory secondary school in Japan, Dai-Ichi-

Kôtô-Gakkô, which educated many of Japan's elite; and as an under-secretary general of the League of Nations from 1920 to 1926, to name just a few.

Nitobe's generation of native Japan interpreters are of particular interest to us because they most clearly embody some of the inner contradictions that other native interpreters of Japanese life and culture for a foreign audience have also shared to an extent. Under the pre–World War II modern Japanese education system, it was often the case that the better educated a person was, the more alienated he or she would become from Japanese cultural tradition. Lafcadio Hearn (1850–1904), who established himself as the most popular writer on Japan soon after his arrival in Japan in 1890, did not believe that the upper-class Japanese could be of much help in helping others to understand Japan: "From the modernized upper classes nothing is to be learned,"[4] he declared. Basil Hall Chamberlain (1850–1935) was similarly distrustful of the cultural expertise of the Japanese upper classes. "You want flowers arranged? Ask your house-coolie. There is something wrong in the way the garden is laid out? ... Call in the cook or washerman as a counsellor,"[5] he said. It was among the well-educated members of Nitobe's generation, the first generation who could complete their modern-style higher education within Japan, that this alienation from Japanese cultural tradition was manifest, indeed more than with any other generation of educated Japanese who followed them. It is hardly surprising, then, that their work as Japan interpreters was fraught with difficulties.

The problems these men faced could also be regarded as the result of "an immense cultural revolution," to borrow the expression used by Erwin Baelz to describe what he witnessed upon arriving in Japan in 1876.[6] Japan was heavily influenced by the West starting at the beginning of the Meiji period (1868–1912) and subsequently underwent a rapid transformation. This resulted in a perceived devaluation of the Japanese cultural tradition for many people. The break with Japan's past that the elite (i.e., the best educated) members of Nitobe's generation experienced was especially extreme. Having barely completed their primary education, they were exposed to intense Western influences through their "abnormal"[7] education, which forcefully neglected Japanese culture. English was used almost exclusively as the medium of instruction, as opposed to the Japanese and classical Chinese languages through which the Japanese cultural tradition had previously been transmitted. These circumstances made it very difficult for Nitobe's generation to have a clear sense of their cultural identity. It is perhaps, then, inevitable that some would question their legitimacy as interpreters of Japanese culture, as we will see later.

For some Japanese people, Western cultural influence was not just a means to make Japan strong and prosperous: they also heartily admired Western culture. Their admiration, however, often had a "denationalizing" effect. Miyake Kokki (1874–1954), a Japanese painter specializing in Western styles, noted the following in his autobiography in reference to his second visit to Paris: "I was more and more charmed by Paris. I thought that a painter who can live in Paris is the happiest human being. Other Japanese painters in Paris, beginning with Mr. Asai, were also all living as if they were Frenchmen. They also adored everything in Paris, and, although it sounds scandalous, they behaved as if they had completely forgotten their Japanese nationality."[8]

Uchimura, a Japan interpreter of Nitobe's generation, was aware that he had been denationalized to the extent that he once regarded Japan as a "good-for-nothing" among the nations.[9] Nitobe and some of his contemporaries became interpreters of Japanese life and culture when their sense of national and cultural identity began to reawaken despite their intense exposure to Western culture and denationalizing influences. Visiting abroad and experiencing the Eurocentrism of the Westerners was often a catalyst for this reawakening, a concept that is further explored later.

Nationalism and Westernization

Basil Hall Chamberlain said, in the fifth edition of *Things Japanese* (1905): "The Japanese, though they have twice, at intervals of a millennium, thrown everything national overboard, are intense nationalists in the abstract."[10] Indeed, Japanese nationalists were not rare in Meiji Japan. However, they were not primarily cultural nationalists—people whose nationalism was rooted in pride in their culture. They derived their nationalistic pride from other things, such as the astonishing speed with which Japanese people were able to adopt the Western science of navigation, for example, as Fukuzawa Yukichi (1834–1901) did.[11] Pioneers of Western studies in Japan, like Fukuzawa, were already young adults before the end of the Tokugawa period, and their attitudes differed from those of Nitobe's generation. They seemed to have little desire to defend Japanese culture. They were perhaps psychologically less vulnerable than Nitobe's generation, as their exposure to Western culture was neither as intense nor as concentrated in their formative years as it was for Nitobe's generation. They could advocate Westernization without an inferiority complex.

Mori Arinori (1847–89) was the first diplomat to represent Japan in Washington, D.C. (from 1871 to 1873), and was in this respect closer to Fukuzawa than to Nitobe and his generation. Mori was a radical "Westernizer." For example, he advocated the adoption of English as the national language of Japan: "Our meager language, which can never be of any use outside of our islands, is doomed to yield to the domination of the English tongue ... All reasons suggest its disuse,"[12] said Mori in his *Introduction to Education in Japan: A Series of Letters Addressed by Prominent Americans to Arinori Mori* (1873). As the Japanese minister in Washington he naturally had the occasion to speak about Japan to Americans, but he did not seem to take interest in promoting Japanese culture. Kido Takayoshi (1833–77), one of the leading officials of the Meiji government, visited Washington as vice-ambassador extraordinary of the Iwakura mission while Mori was minister. Not only was Kido disgusted with the "frivolous and superficial talk" of Japanese students in the United States and their uncritical stance toward the West, but he also criticized Mori: "I have heard a rumor that Mori himself, though a minister of our country, denigrates the customs of our country publicly in his talks with foreigners. He is not alone. Among Japanese officials in this country not a few have come to think lightly of Japan, as soon as they toured around this country and observed it superficially."[13]

Mori had left Japan as a teenager and lived in Europe and the United States from 1865 to 1868. He became one of the most westernized Japanese people of early Meiji Japan. His deviation from common Japanese views manifested itself, for example, in his advocating the abolition of the samurai custom of carrying two swords in 1869,[14] a time when the majority of the samurai were still fiercely attached to this badge of their status. In contrast, Kido, an older man, had stronger ties to the traditional culture of the samurai class than Mori or the Japanese students in the United States. It is perhaps ironic that those who had a good understanding and genuine appreciation for their national culture usually lacked the language skills necessary to engage in cultural diplomacy as interpreters of Japan. Accordingly, this task was often entrusted to people whose attitude toward Japanese culture was highly ambivalent, if not entirely negative.

Foreign Writers as First Japan Interpreters

Some members of Nitobe Inazô's generation, born around 1860, started publishing books on Japan during the last decade of the nineteenth century. Before this point, those interpreting Japan for a foreign audience were virtually all foreigners themselves rather than Japanese.[15] Previously there was simply not any Japanese scholar who could write a book in English that would have impressed a Western audience. Nitobe's was the first generation that could take full benefit of government-supported schools modeled on Western ones and attend the few institutions of higher education that had come into existence just in time for them to enroll. These changes correlated to a widespread indifference to Japanese cultural tradition at the beginning of the Meiji period. Baeltz, writing in 1876, captured this indifference neatly: "[T]he Japanese have their eyes fixed exclusively on the future, and are indifferent when a word is said of their past. The cultured among them are actually ashamed of it. 'That was in the days of barbarism,' said one of them in my hearing. Another, when I asked him about Japanese history, bluntly rejoined: 'We have no history. Our history begins today.'"[16] Chamberlain also made a similar observation in *Things Japanese* (1st ed., 1890): "The Japanese have done with their past. They want to be somebody else and something else than what they have been and still partly are."[17] It is not surprising that during the first half of the Meiji period, when the indifference of the Japanese to their own culture was particularly noticeable, virtually no major books on Japan intended for a foreign audience were written by Japanese authors. It was a period in which a number of educated Japanese people advised inquisitive foreigners to address their questions to Ernest Satow of the British legation, who in their view was the highest authority on Japanese "history, religions or ancient customs."[18]

The Japanese government appreciated foreign authors who spoke highly of Japan in their books. In 1922 Edward S. Morse was awarded the rarely conferred second class of the Order of the Sacred Treasure.[19] This was most likely due not only to his brief but distinguished service as the first professor of zoology at the University of Tokyo between 1877 to 1879, but also to the consistently rosy picture he painted of Japan in his books and lectures. Morse's abiding enthusiasm for Japan is reflected in an American newspaper article about him, published in 1904: "There is no doubt that [Morse] is and has been enthusiastic over Japan and the Japanese ever since he came in contact with them, about a quarter of a century ago. He has been ready to talk Japan at any hour of the day or night ever since he returned to America."[20]

It is conceivable that the Japanese government supported the work of some foreign authors because of their value to Japan's cultural diplomacy. Lafcadio Hearn, for example, could be regarded as a man who was tacitly recruited as an agent for Japan's cultural diplomacy. Commenting on Hearn's engagement by the University of Tokyo, then called the Imperial University of Tokyo, a Japanese contributor to the *Kobe Chronicle* wrote in 1926: "In June, 1896, Hearn receives the offer of a position as lecturer in the Tokyo Imperial University from Dr Toyama, who was statesman enough to realize the propaganda value of Hearn in days when the word 'propaganda' was not in so much vogue as now."[21] Hearn himself felt that the chief reason that the Japanese government gave him the position was to enable him to "write at ease many books on Japan."[22]

Makeup of Japan Interpreters of Nitobe's Generation

Members of Nitobe's generation emerged as the most conspicuous native interpreters of Japan largely because their education made them more proficient in English than any generation of elite Japanese students before or after them.[23] Saitô Hidesaburô, a member of Nitobe's generation who became a specialist in English linguistics, was clearly aware of the risk to Japanese language and culture, noting: "I learned my English at the expense of my Japanese."[24] This illustrative sentence, which he inserted into his dictionary, was nothing short of a surreptitious confession.

It is therefore unsurprising that some regard members of Nitobe's generation as unreliable interpreters of Japan. I will illustrate why by highlighting a few facts concerning Uchimura, Nitobe's classmate at the Sapporo Agricultural College (the forerunner of Hokkaido University), between 1877 and 1881. As a result of the peculiar education that the elite students of his generation received, he read mainly in English. Uchimura confessed in 1899:

> As for my reading of this year, the majority of books which I have read were books in English. I am not completely incapable of understanding what is written in Japanese or classical Chinese. However, once I acquired the ability to understand English, books in Japanese or classical Chinese somehow ceased to interest me ... I confess that I am a person whose reading is done at the ratio of fifty pages in English to one page in Japanese or classical Chinese.[25]

After the publication of *How I Became a Christian* (1895), his first work written in English, and *Japan and the Japanese* (1894), both of which were eventually translated into several European languages and were read fairly widely, Uchimura continued to publish English-language articles addressed to a foreign audience in newspapers and periodicals such as *Yorozu Chôhô* [Sundry Morning News], *Tokyo Dokuritsu Zasshi* [The Tokyo Independent], *Seisho no kenkyû* [Study of the Bible], and the *Japan Christian Intelligencer.* He thus remained an interpreter of Japanese life and culture almost to the end of his life.

Uchimura's unreliability as an interpreter of Japanese culture, however, can be seen from his comments about *Genji monogatari* [The Tale of Genji], widely acknowledged as the greatest masterpiece of classical Japanese literature.[26] This novel depicted the aristocratic society in Japan around the middle of the Heian period (794–1185) with realism and psychological depth in fifty-four chapters centering around Prince Genij and, in later chapters after Prince Genji's death, a grandson of his and his rival in love, an illegitimate son of Prince Genji's young wife. Its author, Murasaki Shikibu [Lady Murasaki], whose real name we do not know, was the talented daughter of a middle-ranking aristocrat born in the late tenth century. She wrote *The Tale of Genji* as a young widow while serving as a lady-in-waiting in the court of Queen Shôshi. That she was truly a remarkable woman is evident from her penetrating self-reflections and fascinating self-portrait contained in *Murasaki Shikibu Nikki* [Diary of Murasaki Shikibu], a much shorter work.[27] In a book published in 1897, Uchimura wrote the following about Murasaki Shikibu:

> If a work produced by a person, such as she, is a work of literature, it is not a legacy which benefits posterity. Rather it is harmful to posterity. I concede that *The Tale of Genji* may have preserved a beautiful language. However, has it done anything to raise Japanese morale? Not only it has not done anything to raise it, it has made us effeminate and spineless. I would like to eradicate totally such a work from among us.[28]

It is highly probable that Uchimura condemned Lady Murasaki's masterpiece without reading a single page. It is not the kind of work that a person "whose reading is done at the ratio of fifty pages in English to one page in Japanese or classical Chinese" could easily handle. It is perhaps characteristic of Uchimura's generation, which lacked real respect and appreciation for Japan's cultural tradition, that he did not hesitate to summarily condemn *The Tale of Genji* on hearsay, despite the important place it occupies in classical Japanese literature.

Motivations behind Interpreting Japan

Chamberlain, who did not mention any Japanese authors in his article "Books on Japan" (which discusses books on Japan in major European languages) in the first edition of *Things Japanese,* refers to six Japanese authors in the fifth edition.[29] They include Nitobe, Uchimura, and Okakura Tenshin (1862–1913), another contemporary of Nitobe. As for the Japan interpreters of Nitobe's generation, their desire to write about Japan was usually born of their reaction to the conscious/unconscious Eurocentrism or ethnocentrism of Westerners, to which they were exposed in the West. Although they had themselves internalized Eurocentrism to a considerable extent through their education, which neglected the Japanese language and Japanese culture almost completely, they could not remain indifferent to the Westerners' ignorance about Japan and prejudices against Japan when they witnessed them firsthand in the West. Their desire to be treated with respect by Westerners forced them to assert the value of their country and its culture, as they were often treated not as individuals but only as members of the Japanese nation. In the case of Uchimura, we can see in *How I Became a Christian* how his reaction to the "real" West (in his case, the United States) led to his rediscovery of Japan. Uchimura came to have a very rosy image of the United States after his conversion to Christianity, having formed his ideas on the basis of Christian books and what he heard from American missionaries. Accordingly, he was shocked to find racism, greed, and all sorts of other unsavory practices in the United States when he visited in 1884. As his estimation of United States sank, that of his native country rose, as he wrote in *How I Became a Christian:* "But looking at a distance from the land of my exile, my country ceased to be a 'good-for nothing.'"[30]

Uchimura's *Japan and the Japanese* was an attempt to present Japan and the Japanese as favorably as possible. During his stay in the United States, he had been stung by the racism and ethnocentrism of Americans. He found it especially painful to be mistaken for Chinese, who often engaged in menial work in the US around that time, and to be jeered at, as we can see from his American letters.[31] Resentment toward foreigners (in Uchimura's case, primarily

Americans and other Westerners of "Christendom"), rather than the author's real appreciation of Japan and Japanese culture, seems to have motivated him to write the book. One of its reviewers pointed out: "Starting with the first sentence 'Is greatness impossible with Japan?,' the author maintains from the beginning to the end that foreigners treat our countrymen with contempt."[32]

The main part of the book, which was retained in the second edition, consists of biographies of five great men from Japan's past: "Saigô Takamori—A Founder of New Japan," "Uesugi Yôzan—A Feudal Lord," "Ninomiya Sontok—A Peasant Saint," "Nakae Tôju—A Village Teacher," and "Saint Nichiren—A Buddhist Priest." Through these characters, Uchimura attempted to demonstrate the greatness of Japan. He even gave a new title to the second edition, *Representative Men of Japan.* However, the five men he chose were exceptional people, by no means typical of Japan. For example, the following assertion in a letter to his publisher, printed in translation in the German version (published in 1908 and based on the text of the second edition), takes advantage of readers' general lack of knowledge about Japan and assumes that the language barrier will prevent reliability checks against other sources: "The Tojus were our teachers, the Yozans were our feudal lords, the Sontoks were our agricultural leaders, the Saigos were our statesmen who had made me what I was before I was called to worship at the footstool of the divine man of Nazareth."[33] To make an implicit generalization about Japan's past on the basis of a handful of exceptional Japanese figures would not be justifiable if the aim was to represent Japan and the Japanese in a way compatible with historical accuracy and intellectual honesty. That was the method of a propagandist.

Inner Contradictions of Uchimura

Uchimura's *Japan and the Japanese* is the work of a man who was fraught with inner conflicts. His conversion to Christianity, his formative years in Japan in an atmosphere filled with enthusiasm for the West, and the education he received all made his break with Japan's past even more radical than was the case with the majority of his countrymen of Meiji Japan, those to whom Chamberlain was referring when he noted that "the Japanese have done with their past."

Thus Uchimura's disillusionment with the United States and his spiritual return to his own fatherland were by no means the whole story. The United States, which he criticized harshly in *How I Be-*

came a Christian, was still, as he confided to an American friend a few years later, "the very best country in the world" in his eyes.[34] Uchimura glorified Japan's past in *Japan and the Japanese,* implicitly pleading for the preservation of its essence. But at the same time he advocated thoroughgoing Westernization in an English-language article published in 1898: "As we said once and again, Japan stands alone and single-handed as long as she refuses to be Europeanized from the very bottom of her social constitution. Oriental and Asiatic in her view of things, she is not yet of the civilized world ... We believe it lies in the ways of true patriotism that this Europeanization of our land be accomplished as speedily as possible."[35]

Contradictory elements remained with Uchimura until the end of his life.[36] On the whole, the Uchimura who admired Japan's past was more superficial than Uchimura the Westernizer. This is perhaps to be expected, considering that Uchimura, who "learnt all that was noble, useful, and uplifting through the vehicle of the English language," as he confessed in chapter 6 of *How I Became a Christian,* continued to read mainly in English. He could not truly help foreign audiences understand Japanese culture as a whole because he never studied Japanese culture in great depth himself.[37] He remained at the level of a propagandist and a polemical defender of Japan against contemptuous foreigners.

Nitobe, an Apologist for Japan

In the preface to the first edition of his book, *Bushido,* Nitobe writes: "Between Lafcadio Hearn and Mrs. Hugh Fraser on one side and Sir Ernest Satow and Professor Chamberlain on the other, it is indeed discouraging to write anything Japanese in English. The only advantage I have over them is that I can assume the attitude of a personal defendant, while these distinguished writers are at best solicitors and attorneys."[38] Nitobe revealed himself and the nature of this book here, perhaps more than he was aware. It was not an impartial exposition of Japanese thought as suggested by the full title of this book, *Bushido The Soul of Japan: An Exposition of Japanese Thought,* but the work of an apologist who wished to defend the honor of Japan. The method Nitobe used was, as in the case of Uchimura, largely that of a propagandist. The anonymous reviewer of the tenth edition of Nitobe's *Bushido* in the 19 August 1905 issue of the English journal *The Athenaeum* saw this clearly: "He makes out his case by partial statement and wholesale suppression."[39]

The Japanese interpreters of Japan for the foreign audience were not necessarily people who were close to the Japanese establishment. Uchimura, for example, was critical of Meiji government leaders and distanced himself from them. Nitobe, however, had a closer relationship with those in power. Thanks to his appointment to a position with the Government-General of Formosa in 1901, he became acquainted with Gotô Shinpei (1857–1929), then the civil governor under Kodama Gentarô, the governor-general. His connection with Gotô, one of the most important statesmen of modern Japan, was particularly important for Nitobe. In his later years he seems to have utilized cultural diplomacy in promoting Japan's national interests in a more direct way, in tacit cooperation with the Japanese government's political diplomacy. His appointment by the Japanese government as the first Japanese exchange professor in 1911, in accordance with an agreement with six US universities, enabled Nitobe to combine the role of a learned Japan interpreter with a role comparable to that of a Japanese government envoy.

During his year in the United States (1911–12), he often commented on current issues between Japan and the United States in the course of his scholarly lectures, material from which was later collected in *The Japanese Nation: Its Land, Its People, and Its Life* (1912).[40] Titles that he gained over the years include A.M., Ph.D., LL.D., President of the First National College, Japan, Professor in the Imperial University of Tokyo, Exchange Professor from Japan to American Universities, and Author of "Bushido, the Soul of Japan." They must have helped to lend credence to his words. When the *New York Times* reported on Nitobe's first lecture at Columbia University, given on 20 November 1911, the paper featured headlines such as "Dr. Nitobe Answers Hobson and Others," "President of Imperial College of Japan Says His Country Thinks Little of These War Criers," "Japan Always for Peace," and "All Wars In Which She Has Been Engaged, He Says, Were Forced by the Enemy."[41] Nitobe also commented on current affairs outside the host universities, as we can see from the headlines "Japanese Educator Calls Hobson Jingo," "Dr. Nitobe Tells the Japanese Society That the Congressman's War Talk Is Groundless," "His Country For Peace," and "Quotes the Prime Minster as Saying He Is Unalterably Opposed to Any Such Conflict."[42]

Nitobe's Last Visit to the United States (1932–1933)

Almost until the very end of his life Nitobe continued his work as an interpreter of Japan for audiences abroad. The "abnormal" education that had enabled him to become one of the most prominent native Japan interpreters was limited to a brief period of transition, and there were few native Japan interpreters of his generation. By the time Nitobe visited the United States for the last time in April 1932 the situation between Japan and the United States had deteriorated, and up to his departure in March 1933 Nitobe played a role that was, in part, not very different from that of an actual diplomat or spokesperson for the Japanese government. Nitobe's aim was to defend Japan. His lecture entitled "The Manchurian Question and Sino-Japanese Relations" (dated 21 November 1932) and his two radio talks, "Japan and the League of Nations" (8 May 1932) and "Japan and the Peace Pact: With Special Reference to Japan's Reaction to Mr. Stimson's Note Regarding the Pact," (20 August 1932) are examples of his defense of Japan.[43] This discredited him by casting him as an apologist of Japan's militaristic policies in the eyes of many Americans. "An Open Letter to Dr. Inazo Nitobé," published in *The New Republic,* criticized Nitobe: "it is heartbreaking for those who have followed your past career to believe that these statements accurately portray your views ... In view of the present regime in Japan, we could understand a policy of silence on your part, but we cannot understand a policy which uncritically defends Japanese militarism."[44]

Nevertheless, he continued to combine the role of a scholarly Japan interpreter and that of an unofficial envoy in this period.[45] Among the lectures given during this final sojourn in the United States were "Moral Ideas of Old Japan," "Japanese Poetry," "Family Life in Japan," and talks on a number of other subjects that did not concern current affairs, as we can see from *Lectures on Japan: An Outline of the Development of the Japanese People and their Culture,*[46] published posthumously in 1936.

The following quotation, taken from Nitobe's article "On American Attitudes toward Japan" (1933), written in Japanese, reveals implicitly his understanding of the place of cultural diplomacy.

> What is of crucial importance in my view is how the Americans view the Japanese and how they understand our national character. Their view of a concrete event, such as the Shanghai Incident, very much depends on this ... Accordingly, when we explain Japan for the American audience, it is not necessary to confine our attention to current issues between Japan and the United States. An explanation covering Japanese history or a wide range of aspects of Japanese life would likely be of greater lasting value.[47]

Cultural diplomacy supports political diplomacy by providing a favorable image of the country—we may paraphrase Nitobe's words quoted above in this way. This acknowledgment of the relationship between cultural diplomacy and political diplomacy was very likely why he gave lectures on topics unrelated to current issues during his stay in the United States from 1932 to 1933. Cultural diplomacy was, for Nitobe, a mere tool to enhance the prestige of Japan and promote Japan's national interests.

Nitobe's defense of Japan's policies toward China could not convince his American audience. Those who knew Nitobe's past were saddened by what they thought was Nitobe's fall. The author of "An Open Letter to Dr. Inazo Nitobé" was not alone in recalling Nitobe's Geneva days as under-secretary general at the League of Nations by way of contrast. An editor of *The Christian Century,* for example, after mentioning Nitobe's "most sweeping and unqualified approval of everything that Japan has done in Manchuria and Shanghai," said, "it is incredible that the Dr. Nitobe of the Geneva days could have taken such a position."[48]

Nitobe's fall from his "Geneva days" was perhaps more apparent than real. He was a veritable nationalist even during his time in Geneva. Kamiya Mieko (1914–79) witnessed how the Japanese community in Geneva, headed by Nitobe, conducted cultural diplomacy. Shortly after her arrival in Geneva in 1923, Nitobe told Mieko's mother—whose marriage to the Japanese representative of the International Labour Organization (ILO) he had arranged—"Whatever you say and whatever you do, it will be taken as a reflection of the level of Japanese civilization. I would like you to be extra careful and live here in such a way as to never bring shame to Japan."[49] Though still a child, Mieko could not help being struck by what she felt was a superficial effort on the part of the Japanese community in Geneva never to bring shame on Japan and to convey the superiority of Japanese civilization to foreigners.

Nitobe's Weaknesses as a Japan Interpreter

Nitobe also failed to impress the American audience with his endeavors in cultural diplomacy. Following the publication of his *Lectures on Japan* in 1936, which collected his aforementioned lectures and talks from 1932 to 1933, one reviewer commented, "the reader looks in vain for new facts or new interpretations not already known to students of Far Eastern affairs."[50] His understanding of Japanese culture, like that of the majority of the educated elite of his generation, was shallow. This was in fact something of which he was keenly aware, although he did not avow this to his foreign audience. In addition, his attitude toward Japanese culture was often contradictory and ambivalent. His writings on bushido clearly illustrate these two points. Having written *Bushido: The Soul of Japan,* he managed to pass for a great authority on bushido in the eyes of his Western readers. However, Nitobe himself confided to Japanese readers: "As I published a little book on bushido in the past, people tend to regard me as a student or advocate of bushido. However, it would be a great exaggeration to say that I have studied bushido. Accordingly, I do not understand the secret of bushido."[51] Moreover, his feeling toward bushido was ambivalent, as is shown by the following comment on bushido, written in Japanese for a Japanese audience:

> I believe that our ancestors lived with great freedom before the rise of bushido. After the rise of bushido in the Kamakura period, they began to pretend that they were not hungry when they were, that they did not feel pain when they did, and that they were not sad when they were. This did them immeasurable harm by thwarting their natural development as human beings. It was from that period that our countrymen have been developing unnaturally.[52]

Nitobe's *Bushido: The Soul of Japan* received much praise from Western reviewers: "Mr. Nitobé writes with full knowledge of his subject,"[53] and "[o]nly a native writer, like Dr. Nitobe, thoroughly versed in the history and literature, and what is more necessary, imbued with the spirit of the people, can present the case of his country to the European public."[54] These were virtually all comments from reviewers who lacked knowledge of the Japanese language, history, and literature. Accordingly, they were people who could not claim to possess the ability to produce such evaluations, and as such did not suspect that Nitobe's erudition about Japan lacked authority. Chamberlain, who had an excellent knowledge of the Japanese language, was aware that Japanese writers would often take advantage of the foreigner's credulity by hiding behind the language barrier. In "Bushido or The Invention of a New Religion," he asked: "How should he [the foreigner] imagine that people who make such positive statements about their own country are merely exploiting his credulity?"[55]

Concluding Remarks

The difficulties encountered by the Japan interpreters of Nitobe's generation were not unique. True, later generations of elite students did not receive instruction in various subjects from foreign professors in English as they had done. On the other hand, even decades after the schooling of Nitobe and his contemporaries, subjects related to Japanese culture still carried little weight in the education of the Japanese elite. One Dai-Ichi-Kôtô-Gakkô student (and future president of the University of Tokyo) at the prestigious preparatory secondary school where Nitobe served as principal listed the following weekly hours for each subject in the fall term of 1911: English, 9 hours; German, 9 hours; Japanese, 2 hours; Classical Chinese, 3 hours; History, 3 hours; Psychology, 2 hours; Physical Education, 3 hours; Morals, 1 hour.[56] Eighteen weekly hours devoted to two European languages clearly shows the Eurocentric orientation of the education of the future elite, intended to allow Japan to compete with the most advanced academic and cultural achievements in the West. A future professor of the Faculty of Law at the University of Tokyo who took an entrance examination to the Faculty of Law in 1934 recalled that success or failure was still more or less determined by the candidates' performance in the European languages examination, although in that year composition in Japanese was added to European languages as an examination subject for the first time.[57]

In much of the modern Japanese literature that flourished, there is evidence of an internalized Eurocentrism and widespread ambivalence toward their culture on the part of Japanese. A novel entitled *Shin kichôsha nikki* [Diary of a Person Who Has Just Returned from Abroad], by Nagai Kafû (1879–1959), a major twentieth-century writer, illustrates this clearly. It was published in 1909, the year after Nagai himself had returned from a four-year stay in the United States and Europe. In it the hero ruminates on the neglect of his native culture by fellow countrymen:

> The success or failure in the entrance examination to a higher school was determined by marks in English rather than marks in Japanese or classical Chinese. This was an undeniable fact. The Japanese need not know Japan. If you want to get high status and fame in this age of Meiji, you must acquire western knowledge, even forsaking everything Japanese. You must study the western alphabet first, rather than the Japanese letters. During my travel to the West, how many eminent Japanese diplomats did I see whose talent allowed them to write in a European language but who were incapable of writing even letters properly in Japanese![58]

The protagonist finds the Japanese neglect of their culture strange, but this does not prevent him from internalizing Eurocentrism himself.

As we have seen in the case of Uchimura, Eurocentric Japanese would often make a spiritual "return" to Japan once they themselves had encountered the Eurocentrism of the West. Such a return was not limited to the Meiji period. The hero of chapter 3 of *Ryûgaku* [Studying Abroad] (1965), a novel by Endô Shûsaku (1923–96), is a young lecturer in French literature at a Japanese university. While in Japan, he wonders why many of his senior colleagues and friends, upon return to Japan after their studies in Europe, have abruptly transformed into "Japanocentrists." Even before his first day in France is over, he feels that he has gained insight into their psychology because of various humiliating experiences, some due to his poor comprehension of French.[59]

Such a return, however, did not necessarily mean true liberation from internalized Eurocentrism. For example, in 1916 Uchimura condemned English and American missionaries for the continued use of English in their interaction with Japanese people even after having spent years in Japan, taking this as "sure evidence that they have no true love for our souls."[60] Yet his own Eurocentrism is evident on a postcard dated 12 July 1921, sent to his future daughter-in-law, in which only the last sentence, "[y]ou will probably understand English of this level quite well,"[61] was written in Japanese.

The language barrier between Japan and the rest of the world meant that those who participated in cultural diplomacy as native Japan interpreters continued to be a small minority who had somehow managed to acquire a good knowledge of English or whichever language was needed for partaking in cultural diplomacy. For the elite of Nitobe's generation, educated at a time when a Tokyo University official voiced his concern that their graduates "may be proficient only in English and incompetent in Japanese,"[62] the language barrier did not really exist. For the elite students who were educated a few decades later at one of the prewar higher schools before proceeding to a university, English was no longer the medium of instruction, yet they received an enormous amount of instruction in English and another European language to enable them to keep abreast of the latest developments in the West. In terms of both their good command of English and the extent to which Japanese culture was neglected, these students were not as extreme as Nitobe's generation, but they were still much closer to them than the postwar generations educated immediately after the abolition of the elitist higher schools of the prewar days.

The ideal native Japan interpreter is someone who combines an excellent knowledge of English (or another international language) with a deep knowledge and appreciation of Japanese culture. However, these two factors do not often go hand in hand. I suspect that even long after Nitobe's generation, many of the native Japan interpreters shared some of the shortcomings of Nitobe and his contemporaries. This is a primary motivation for revisiting this prototypical generation of native Japan interpreters: their example shows that native interpreters of Japan still needed to establish a more natural and genuine relationship with Japanese culture, a task that remained problematic as long as these individuals continued to feel a tacit sense of cultural inferiority toward the West. Japan's emergence as one of the most affluent countries in the world has, one hopes, liberated Japanese thought and culture from Eurocentrism at last. This should allow the Japanese population to gain a genuine appreciation for their culture, in place of the somewhat superficial appreciation that arose from resentment of Westerners' Eurocentrism and a desire for nationalistic aggrandizement. In the future, Japan may no longer lack people capable of becoming successful participants in cultural diplomacy and astute native Japan interpreters.

Endnotes

1. Japanese names in this article follow the Japanese order with the family name preceding the personal name, except names of authors of publications in a European language. Yamaga Sokô, "Haisho zanpitsu" [Autobiography in Exile], in *Nihonjin no jiden* [Japanese Autobiographies], ed. Saeki Shôichi and Kano Masanao (Tokyo: Heibonsha, 1980–82), supplementary vol.1 (1982), 17.
2. Ibid.
3. The expression "Japan interpreters" in this essay refers to people who explain or discuss various matters related to Japan to audiences outside of Japan.
4. Lafcadio Hearn, *Glimpses of Unfamiliar Japan* (Rutland, VT: C. E. Tuttle, 1976), 663.
5. Basil Hall Chamberlain, "Taste," in *Things Japanese,* 5th ed. (London: J. Murray, 1905), 450.
6. Erwin Baelz, *Awakening Japan: The Diary of a German Doctor, Erwin Baelz,* ed. Toku Baelz (Bloomington: Indiana University Press, 1974), 16. (Reprint of *Erwin Baelz, Das Leben eines deutschen Arztes im erwachenden Japan,* translated by Eden and Cedar Paul (New York: Viking Press, 1932.)
7. "Abnormal" was the adjective that a classmate of Nitobe's (Miyabe Kingo) used to characterize the education his generation of elite students received. See my book *Eigo to Nihonjin* [Use of English Language in Modern Japan], 2nd ed. (Tokyo: Kôdansha, 1995), 164.
8. Miyake Kokki, "Omoi izuru mama" [Just as I Remember], in Saeki Shôichi and Kano Masanao *Nihonjin no jiden* [Japanese Autobiographies], vol. 19 (1982), 196. The English translation is borrowed from my article "Images of Westerners in Japanese Autobiographies," *Asian Cultural Studies,* no. 18 (Tokyo: International Christian University, 1992), 3–20, here 10.
9. Kanzô Uchimura, "How I Became a Christian," in Uchimura Kanzô, *Uchimura Kanzô zenshû* [The Complete Works of Uchimura Kanzô] (Tokyo: Iwanami Shoten, 1980–84), vol. 3 (1981), 92. Hereafter this complete works will be cited as

Works of Uchimura and the publication year of an individual volume will be indicated within parentheses at the first reference.

10. "Japanese People (The Characteristics of)," in Chamberlain, *Things Japanese,* 5th ed., 261.
11. Yukichi Fukuzawa, *The Autobiography of Yukichi Fukuzawa,* trans. Eiichi Kiyooka (New York: Columbia University Press, 1966), 110–111.
12. Mori Arinori, *Mori Arinori zenshû* [The Complete Works of Mori Arinori], ed. Ôkubo Toshiaki (Tokyo: Senbundô Shoten, 1972), vol. 3, 266.
13. Kido's diary entry of the eighth day of the third month, the fifth year of Meiji [15 April 1872]. *Mori Arinori zenshû,* vol. 2, 848.
14. "Heishi kanri no hoka taitô o haisuru wa zuii tarubeki gian" [The proposal that people, with the exception of soldiers and officials, should be free to discontinue carrying their swords], in *Mori Arinori zenshû,* vol. 1, 12–14.
15. We can see this from the fact that Chamberlain mentions no Japanese author in "Books on Japan" in the first edition of Basil Hall Chamberlain, *Things Japanese* (London: Kegan Paul, Trench, Trübner & Co., 1890), unlike in the fifth edition published in 1905, in which he mentions six Japanese authors, including Nitobe, Uchimura, and Okakura (see pp. 72–73 of the fifth edition).
16. Baelz, *Awakening Japan,* 17.
17. Chamberlain, *Things Japanese,* 1st ed., 3.
18. Isabella L. Bird, *Unbeaten Tracks in Japan* (New York: G. P. Putnam's Sons, 1881), vol. 1, 31.
19. As for the statement that the second class of this order was rarely awarded, see Chamberlain, *Things Japanese,* 5th ed., 114.
20. *Sunday Globe,* 14 February 1904, quoted from a clipping found among the Morse Papers in the possession of Peabody Museum, Salem.
21. As quoted in Yuzo Ota, *Basil Hall Chamberlain: Portrait of a Japanologist* (Richmond, Surrey, UK: Curzon Press, 1998), 163. Toyama was the president of Tokyo University in 1897.
22. Letter of November 1896 to Ellwood Hendrick, in Elizabeth Bisland, ed., *The Life and Letters of Lafcadio Hearn* (Boston: Houghton, Mifflin and Company, 1906), vol. 2, 313–314.
23. See Yuzo Ota, "The 'Decline' of English Language Competence in Modern Japan," *Journal of Asian Pacific Communication* 5, no. 4 (1994), 201–207.
24. As quoted in my book, *Eigo to Nihonjin,* 131.
25. "Yo no kotoshi no dokusho" ["My Reading of this Year"], in *Works of Uchimura,* vol. 7 (1981), 483.
26. My criticism of Uchimura's comment that follows is based on my own reading of *Genji monogatari* [The Tale of Genji] in Japanese and the conviction I hold that it is indeed a real masterpiece. See Murasaki Shikibu [Lady Murasaki], *Genji monogatari* [The Tale of Genji], vols. 1–5, ed. Yamagishi Tokuhei (Tokyo: Iwanami Shoten, 1958–1963).
27. See Murasaki Shikibu, "Murasaki Shikibu nikki," ed. Ikeda Kikan and Akiyama Ken in *Makura no sôshi Murasaki Shikibu nikki,* ed. Ikeda Kikan, Akiyama Ken and Kishigami Shinji (Tokyo: Iwanami Shoten, 1958), 403–518.
28. "Kôsei e no saidai ibutsu" [The Greatest Legacy to Posterity], in *Works of Uchimura,* vol. 4 (1981), 271.
29. See endnote 15.
30. *Works of Uchimura,* vol. 3, 92.
31. Printed in *Works of Uchimura,* vol. 36 (1983).
32. Anonymous review, in *Keirin,* no.14 (Sapporo, Feb. 1895), as quoted in my article "Daihyoteki Nihonjin" [On Representative Men of Japan] in *Uchimura Kanzô*

zenshû geppô [Newsletters for the Complete Works of Uchimura Kanzô], no. 11 (Tokyo: Iwanami Shoten, 1981), 2.

33. *Works of Uchimura,* vol. 3, 294.
34. Letter of 13 May 1893 to D. C. Bell, in *Works of Uchimura,* vol. 36 (1983), 378.
35. *Works of Uchimura,* vol. 5 (1981), 395.
36. My book *Uchimura Kanzô: Sono Nihonshugi to sekaishugi o megutte* [World and Nation in Modern Japanese Christianity: The Case of Uchimura Kanzô] (Tokyo: Kenkyûsha Shuppan, 1977) gives numerous examples of his contradictory remarks and tries to interpret them. See, for example, chaps. 2 and 5.
37. In this respect he was not like some Christian authors of more recent times, such as Father Inoue Yôji, whose writings show much more serious preoccupation with Japanese culture and its relationship with Christian faith. See, for example, Inoue Yôji, *Yohaku no tabi: Shisaku no ato* [A Journey of a Margin: Tracks of my Thought] (Tokyo: Nihon Kirisuto Kyôdan Shuppankyoku, 1980).
38. Nitobe Inazô, *Nitobe Inazô zenshû* [The Complete Works of Nitobe Inazô] (Tokyo: Kyobunkwan, 1969–1970), vol. 12 (1969), 8. Hereafter cited as *Works of Nitobe.* The publication year of an individual volume will be indicated within parentheses at the first reference.
39. Review in *The Athenaeum,* no. 4060, 19 August 1905, p. 229. I have already discussed this review in Yuzo Ota, "Mediation between Cultures," in *Nitobe Inazô: Japan's Bridge Across the Pacific,* ed. John F. Howes (Boulder, CO: Westview, 1995), 237–252. See 247–249 for its discussion.
40. Reprinted in *Works of Nitobe,* vol. 13 (1970). Nitobe's titles, quoted a few lines later in the text, are those that are printed in the title page of this book below his name.
41. *New York Times,* 21 November 1911.
42. *New York Times,* 10 December 1911.
43. The lecture and the two radio addresses are printed in *Works of Nitobe,* vol. 15 (1970), 221–233, 234–239, and 240–252.
44. Raymond Leslie Buell. "An Open Letter to Dr. Inazo Nitobé," in *The New Republic,* 25 May 1932, 42–43.
45. Nitobe's letters written in March 1932 suggest that he made his last trip to the US at the request of some Japanese government leader or leaders, although he was not formally sent by the Japanese government. The use of the words "an unofficial envoy" seems to be justifiable. See my book, *"Taiheiyô no hashi" to shite no Nitobe Inazô* [Nitobe Inazô as a "Bridge across the Pacific"] (Tokyo: Misuzu Shobô, 1986), 136–137.
46. Reprinted in *Works of Nitobe,* vol. 15.
47. "Beikoku no tai-Nichi taido ni tsuite" [On American Attitude toward Japan], *Works of Nitobe,* vol. 4 (1969), 467–468.
48. "The Menace of Militarism: Editorial," *The Christian Century* (1 June 1932): 692.
49. Yuzo Ota, *A Woman with Demons: A Life of Kamiya Mieko (1914–1979)* (Montreal and Kingston: McGill-Queen's University Press, 2006), 30.
50. Albert P. Ludwig, "Review of *Lectures on Japan,*" *Pacific Affairs* 10 (June 1937): 220, as quoted in Yuzo Ota, "Mediation between Cultures," 240.
51. "Nogi Shôgun no junshi o hyôsu" [On the Suicide of General Nogi], in *Works of Nitobe,* vol. 4, 452. See Yuzo Ota, "Mediation between Cultures," 242–245 for facts illustrating Nitobe's surprising ignorance about bushido and Japanese history.
52. "Fujin ni susumete," in *Works of Nitobe,* vol. 11 (1969), 176
53. Review in the *Christian Register* (Boston), 19 July 1900, as printed on p. 6 of the Appendix of Inazô Nitobe, *Bushido: The Soul of Japan,* 5th ed. (Tokyo: Shôkwabô, 1904).

54. Review in the *American* (Baltimore), 29 January 1900, on pp. 15–16 of the same Appendix.
55. Quoted from reprint of Chamberlain, *Things Japanese,* 6th ed. (posthumously published in 1939) in *Complete Edition Things Japanese* (Tokyo: Meicho Fukyu Kai, 1985), 90.
56. Based on the diary entry of 1 September 1911, *Yanahara Tadao zenshû* [The Complete Works of Yanaihara Tadao], as quoted in my book *Eigo to Nihonjin,* 213.
57. Maruyama Masao, *Maruyama Masao kaikodan* [Reminiscences of Maruyama Masao], ed. Matsuzawa Hiroaki and Uete Michiari (Tokyo: Iwanami Shoten, 2006), vol. 1, 164.
58. Nagai Kafû, *Shin kichôsha nikki* [Diary of a Person Who Has Just Returned from Abroad], in Nagai Kafû, *Nagai Kafû shû* [Selected Works of Nagai Kafû], vol. 1 (Tokyo Chikuma Shobô, 1969), 205.
59. See Endô Shûsaku, *Ryûgaku* [Studying Abroad], in *Endô Shûsaku shû* [Selected Works of Endô Shûsaku] (Tokyo: Shinchôsha, 1969), 120–128.
60. "Missionaries and Language," in *Works of Uchimura,* vol. 22 (1982), 381.
61. *Works of Uchimura,* vol. 38 (1983), 502.
62. Yuzo Ota, "The 'Decline' of English Language Competence in Modern Japan," 202.

Bibliography

Baelz, Erwin. *Awakening Japan: The Diary of a German Doctor, Erwin Baelz,* ed. Toku Baelz. Trans. from the German edition, Erwin Baelz, Das Leben eines deutschen Arztes im erwachenden Japan, by Eden and Cedar Paul. New York: Viking Press 1932. Reprint Bloomington: Indiana University Press, 1974.

Bird, Isabella L. *Unbeaten Tracks in Japan.* New York: G. P. Putnam's Sons, 1881.

Bisland, Elizabeth, ed. *The Life and Letters of Lafcadio Hearn,* vol. 2. Boston: Houghton, Mifflin and Company, 1906.

Buell, Raymond Leslie. "An Open Letter to Dr. Inazo Nitobé." *The New Republic,* 25 May 1932, pp. 42–43.

Chamberlain, Basil Hall. *Complete Edition Things Japanese.* Tokyo: Meicho Fukyu Kai, 1985.

———. *Things Japanese.* 5th ed. London: John Murray, 1905.

———. *Things Japanese.* 1st ed. London: Kegan Paul, Trench, Trübner & Co., 1890.

Endô, Shûsaku. *Endô Shûsaku shû* [Selected Works of Endô Shûsaku]. Tokyo: Shinchôsha, 1969.

Fukuzawa, Yukichi. *The Autobiography of Yukichi Fukuzawa.* Trans. Eiichi Kiyooka. New York: Columbia University Press, 1966.

Hearn, Lafcadio. *Glimpses of Unfamiliar Japan.* Rutland, VT: C. E. Tuttle, 1976.

Ioue, Yôji. *Yohaku no tabi: Shisaku no ato* [A Journey of a Margin: Tracks of My Thought]. Tokyo: Nihon Kirisuto Kyôdan Shuppankyoku, 1980.

Maruyama, Masao. *Maruyama Masao kaikodan* [Reminiscences of Maruyama Masao], vol. 1, ed. Matsuzawa Hiroaki and Uete Michiari. Tokyo: Iwanami Shoten, 2006.
"The Menace of Militarism: Editorial." *The Christian Century* (1 June 1932): 691–692.
Miyake, Kokki. "Omoi izuru mama" [Just as I Remember], in *Nihonjin no jiden* [Japanese Autobiographies], vol. 19, ed. Saeki Shôichi and Kano Masanao. Tokyo: Heibonsha, 1982.
Mori, Arinori. *Mori Arinori zenshû* [The Complete Works of Mori Arinori], vols. 2 and 3, ed. Ôkubo Toshiaki. Tokyo: Senbundô Shoten, 1972.
Murasaki Shikibu [Lady Murasaki]. *Genji monogatari* [The Tale of Genji], vols. 1–5, ed. Yamagishi Tokuhei. Tokyo: Iwanami Shoten, 1958–63.
———. "Murasaki Shikibu nikki" [Diary of Lady Murasaki], ed. Ikeda Kikan and Akiyama Ken. In *Makura no sôshi Murasaki Shikibu nikki,* ed. Ikeda Kikan, Akiyama Ken, and Kishigami Shinji. Tokyo: Iwanami Shoten, 1958.
Nagai, Kafû. *Nagai Kafû shû* [Selected Works of Nagai Kafû], vol. 1. Tokyo: Chikuma Shobô, 1969.
Nitobe, Inazô. *Nitobe Inazô zenshû* [The Complete Works of Nitobe Inazô], vols. 4 (1969), 11 (1969), 12 (1969), 13 (1970), and 15 (1970). Tokyo: Kyobunkwan, 1969–70.
———. *Bushido: The Soul of Japan,* 5th ed. Tokyo: Shôkwabô, 1904.
Ota, Yuzo. *A Woman with Demons: A Life of Kamiya Mieko (1914–1979).* Montreal and Kingston: McGill-Queen's University Press, 2006.
———. *Basil Hall Chamberlain: Portrait of a Japanologist.* Richmond, Surrey: Japan Press, 1998.
———. *Eigo to Nihonjin* [Use of the English Language in Modern Japan]. 2nd ed. Tokyo: Kôdansha, 1995.
———. "Mediation between Cultures." In *Nitobe Inazô: Japan's Bridge Across the Pacific,* ed. John F. Howes. Boulder, CO: Westview, 1995.
———. "The 'Decline' of English Language Competence in Modern Japan." *Journal of Asian Pacific Communication* 5, no. 4 (1994): 201–207.
———. "Images of Westerners in Japanese Autobiographies." *Asian Cultural Studies* (Tokyo, International Christian University), no. 18 (1992): 3–20.
———. "Daihyôteki Nihonjin" [On Representative Men of Japan]. *Uchimura Kanzô zenshû geppô* [Newsletters for the Complete Works of Uchimura Kanzô], no. 11 (1981). Tokyo: Iwanami Shoten, 1–3.
———. *"Taiheiyô no hashi" to shite no Nitobe Inazô* [Nitobe Inazô as a "Bridge across the Pacific"]. Tokyo: Misuzu Shobô, 1986.
———. *Uchimura Kanzo: Sono Nihonshugi to sekaishugi o megutte* [World and Nation in Modern Japanese Christianity: The Case of Uchimura Kanzô]. Tokyo: Kenkyûsha Shuppan, 1977.
Reports on Nitobe in the US (1911–1912), *New York Times,* 20 November and 10 December 1911.

Reviews of Nitobe, *Bushido: The Soul of Japan* in *The Athenaeum,* 19 August 1905.

Uchimura, Kanzô. *Uchimura Kanzô zenshû* [The Complete Works of Uchimura Kanzô], vols. 3 (1981), 5 (1981), 7 (1981), 22 (1982), 36 (1983), and 38 (1983). Tokyo: Iwanami Shoten, 1980–84.

Yamaga, Sokô. "Haisho zanpitsu" [Autobiography in Exile] in *Nihonjin no jiden* [Japanese autobiographies], ed. Saeki Shôichi and Kano Masanao. Supplementary vol. 1 (1982). Tokyo: Heibonsha, 1980–82.

Chapter 8

"GERMANY IN EUROPE", "JAPAN AND ASIA"

National Commitments to Cultural Relations within Regional Frameworks

Maki Aoki-Okabe, Yoko Kawamura, and Toichi Makita

Introduction

This essay examines the historical commitment of nations to the promotion of international cultural relations within regional frameworks. Historically, state rulers and nations have made efforts to foster international cultural relations; here, these efforts are termed "ICR policy." In the modern era of nation-states, one major pattern of ICR policy has been cultural diplomacy (sometimes also called public diplomacy): the construction of a "national culture" by projecting such culture outward. During the latter half of the twentieth century, a newer trend of interactive ICR policy within different regional frameworks began to emerge.

Region denotes here a group that consists of more than a single nation-state. The members of a region and the nature of the relationship between those members are determined by the perception of the peoples who live within the region. National policymakers and their geopolitical and economic interests play an especially important role in these perceptions. In other words, interaction among people, and the "we-feeling" or collective identity formed as a result of such interaction, are potential factors for region building.[1] ICR policy is closely related with the formation of this "we-feeling,"

Notes for this section begin on page 232.

since cultural programs bring people into contact with the "other" and re/construct the sense of collective self through such contact. Today, regional ICR policy covers various issues ranging from mutual understanding, science, and technology to political issues such as human rights. In this essay, we attempt to correlate such regional cultural policymaking with construction of regional identity. Why do national policymakers foster cultural relations within a regional framework? Is there any common pattern in the development of regional cultural relations? We try to answer these questions by comparing the postwar Japanese commitment in Asia[2] with the case of the Federal Republic of Germany (FRG) in Europe.

There are many different ways of developing cultural relations among peoples, and cultural diplomacy is one specific type of state policy promoting such relations. According to J. M. Mitchell, cultural diplomacy "seeks to impress, to present a favorable image, so that diplomatic operations as a whole are facilitated."[3] In other words, cultural diplomacy is strategic action by a government to spread national culture—it is often less concerned with mutual benefits and promoting understanding and cooperation between nations.

In order to fully understand the nature and implications of Japanese and German commitment to cultural relations within the respective regions, it is not only necessary to examine cultural diplomacy as one-way government action. One should also take account of broader intercultural activities involving societal actors such as grassroots groups, NGOs, municipalities, etc., and governmental efforts to relate, or sometimes even incorporate, such broad societal activities into its own diplomacy. In addition, it is crucial to examine the content of cultural policies. In the postwar years, both the FRG and Japan found it difficult to conduct cultural diplomacy as a simple projection of a positive national image to the rest of the world. Both governments, though in different manners and degrees, also tried to promote interactive cultural programs and cooperative cultural policymaking to promote mutuality among regional members.

Accordingly, in analyzing the cases of the FRG and Japan, we adopt a somewhat differentiated terminology. We use the overarching term "international cultural relations (ICR)" to describe various attempts to bring different cultures into contact across national borders.[4] There are two dimensions of ICR: policy/activity and phenomenal. The former refers to policies and activities that intentionally promote intercultural relations, while the latter refers to the transnational flow of people, goods, money, information, etc. in general, and to changes in societies that occur as a result of such transnational surges. Cultural diplomacy belongs to the policy/activity subcategory of ICR.

Both state and nonstate (societal) actors can carry out ICR policies and activities. Cultural diplomacy is a government foreign policy that is planned and executed to promote national culture abroad, but it need not be the only element of state-level ICR policy. State-level ICR policy may also include interactive cultural programs promoting mutual interest and carried out in a cooperative way. Some governments, especially in non-Western countries, conduct state-level ICR policy not only outward (as part of foreign policy) but also domestically, through inland policies such as educational reform and the adoption of laws and norms that fit "global standards." Societal-level ICR policies and activities comprise various intercultural exchange programs carried out by municipalities, NGOs, grassroots groups, and so on. The interactions facilitated by societal agents, often involving two or more groups, aspire to ideals such as world peace, equality, and understanding. An overview of different levels and dimensions of ICR is illustrated in Figure 1.

After the end of World War II, burdened by defeat and national division, the FRG began to implement ICR policy that was focused on the rehabilitation of national prestige and reconciliation with neighboring nations. In Western Europe, the FRG committed itself to multilateral cultural programs in the Council of Europe, for example, as well as to bilateral exchange programs to improve mutual understanding with neighboring countries like France. Reentering international society constituted a big challenge for postwar Japan as well. The Japanese government, under occupation by the Allies, launched ICR polices with similar motivations. Throughout the cold war period, however, the main target countries of Japanese ICR programs were the United States and the nations of Southeast Asia. Although South Korea and China were, as Japan's immediate neighbors, potentially its best partners for regional cooperation, they were also countries with which Japan had had the most serious problems in the traumatic past and thus were not regarded as counterparts for cultural relations.[5] This slightly unnatural selection of policy targets or partners was supported by the US cold war strategy of keeping Japan in the Western camp. Lacking a regional framework for multilateral cooperation, Japan's cultural relations with other nations were mostly one-sided: Japan was either a provider of money and technology for Southeast Asian populations, or a recipient of grants and programs from the US government and American foundations. Conse-

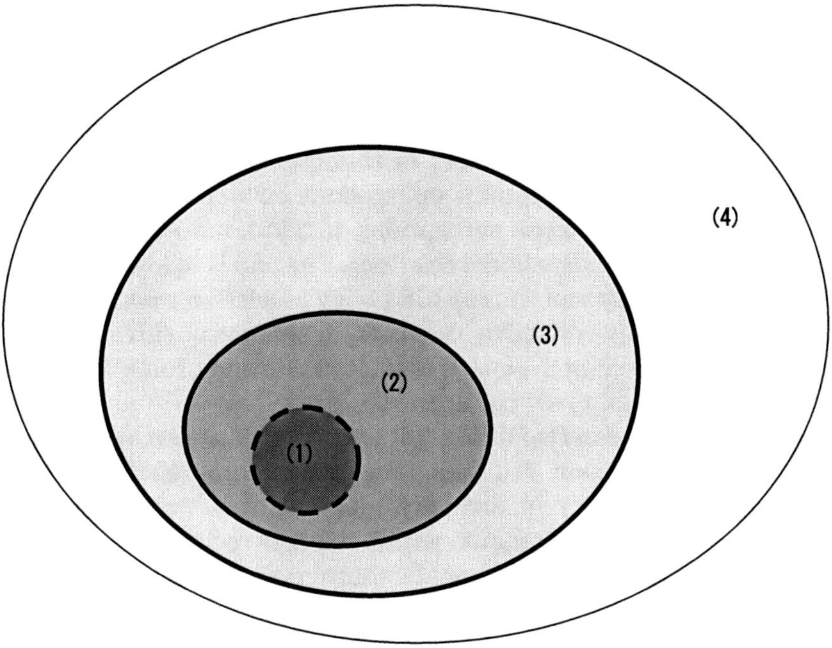

Figure 1 Levels and Dimensions of International Cultural Relations (ICR)

(1) Cultural diplomacy (one-way cultural diplomacy, public diplomacy)

(2) Foreign cultural policy by national governments, including two-way intercultural exchange and internationalization of inland culture-related policies

(3) Intercultural exchange programs by societal actors (municipalities, NGOs, grass-roots groups, etc.)

(4) Transnational flow of people, goods, money, information; internationalization of national societies

(1)+(2)+(3) = ICR as policy and activity (policy/activity dimension

(1)+(2) = state-level ICR policies and activities

(3) = societal-level ICR policies and activities

(4) = ICR as phenomenon (phenomenal dimension)

quently, Japan's policy to promote regional cultural relations shows quite a disproportionate pattern, compared with that of the FRG.

What has kept Japanese policymakers from forging a regional partnership with their immediate neighbors? This anomaly reflects Japanese policymakers' struggle to define how Japan identifies itself in an international context.

Regional Cultural Relations and National Identity

Since the late 1990s, the idea that the perception of agents determines the dynamics of international relations has drawn much academic interest.[6] Some scholars in this constructivist trend have focused on agents' perceptions on relations between self and other. This essay considers such perceptions, in addition to the construction of identity in international relations. The aim is to show that national policymakers can employ ICR policy as a tool for constructing and reconstructing collective identities, to shape a positive national identity by controlling the image of their nation and promoting interactions between different cultures.

Policymakers can also utilize ICR to construct a positive national identity within a region. Promoting regional cultural relations under the concept of "unity in diversity," for example, guarantees the uniqueness of their own nation within a larger regional framework. By taking the initiative in regional cultural policymaking, a country can also promote its positive image. Of course, the direct projection of national cultures by means of cultural diplomacy strengthens national identities, but the promotion of mutually beneficial cultural relations can also be an effective tool.

After the end of World War II, policymakers in the FRG and Japan had to find a way of negotiating their identities as "defeated countries" or "ex-invaders." Under such circumstances it was difficult for either of the two countries to pursue cultural diplomacy as an independent national project, as in the case of France or the United States. Consequently, both the FRG and Japan attempted to transform their negative identities into positive ones through active commitment to ICR policy in collaboration with their regional partners. Nevertheless, as shown later, the two countries' commitments to their respective regional cultural relations varied considerably.

When a country promotes regional cultural relations, the policymakers' blueprint determines the ICR policy concept—the content of cultural programs, the style of policymaking, and so on. In our analysis of regional cultural relations, two aspects of program/policy concepts are of particular interest. The first is the prospective structure of relations among members in the region: whether national policymakers pursue a hierarchical order led by a stronger power, or equal partnership among all the regional members. Cultural diplomacy aimed at impressing other nations with one's national culture is more likely to promote the hierarchical relationship, whereas interactive programs to promote mutual understanding and cooperation are suited to building equal partnership. The second aspect to be noted is the emphasis of regional cultural programs: whether the focus is on the uniqueness and autonomy of the respective units (nations) of a region or on their commonality. The former type of program envisages a region as the type of pluralistic security community described by Karl Deutsch,[7] while the latter type aims to transform a region into a well-integrated community more like a nation-state.

The following sections examine the German commitment to European cultural relations and the Japanese commitment to Asian cultural relations in light of these conceptual aspects, especially the first. The structure of the relationship with other countries of the region proves to be quite different in both cases. This difference in assumed regional structure effectively reflects the contrast of identity formation in Germany and Japan in the postwar period.

German Commitment to European Cultural Relations

Policymakers in the FRG looked to Europe to form the basis of a West German identity. The importance of "Europe as a niche" continued to grow throughout the postwar period, though the perceived role of the FRG within Europe differed according to the time and standpoint of the respective policymakers.[8] Before Germany was divided, major figures of German cultural agencies, some of them had been active in prewar days and had more or less distanced themselves from the Nazi cultural policy, gathered in Wiesbaden to discuss the plan for postwar reconstruction. They regarded cultural relations as a tool for the revitalization of the German nation in Europe. Experts planned to promote research projects on occidental culture (*abendländische Kultur*) and on the history of the European integration movement. They even tried to construct a cultural organization within a European supranational framework to realize such ideas as "German renovation" and the "internal renaissance of the German nation."[9] Once the Federal Republic was founded, these ambitious plans were not carried out, but the FRG soon began to commit itself to multilateral cultural cooperation within a broader regional framework, namely the Council of Europe. Noteworthy is the launch of six European Symposia of History Education (1953–58), which was initiated by Georg Eckert and two other West German historians with the support of the Federal Government.[10]

In the 1960s West Germany formed a partnership with France, and together they began to lead European cultural cooperation. The then Chancellor Konrad Adenauer signed a friendship treaty with France in 1963 and launched bilateral ICR programs between the two nations. Youth exchanges and language learning, as well as other cultural and educational programs, were promoted on a large scale. Aiming for mutual understanding between citizens, these programs involved a wide range of people from both countries. It is worth noting that ordinary French and German citizens had begun various grassroots exchange programs as early as the occupation period; these private exchanges, interactive in their nature, were the predecessors of state-level binational cultural programs.[11]

Thus, West Germany's major ICR policy in postwar Europe began in the form of bilateral exchange programs with neighboring countries, aiming at rapprochement. Public opinion research reported that such programs promoted participants' awareness of being European, especially among young people.[12] In the 1980s, West Germany further enhanced its commitment to European cultural relations under Hans-Dietrich Genscher. Genscher became minister of foreign affairs in the mid 1970s, when the European Commission published a communication to the Council, titled *Education in the European Community*,[13] under the German commissioner Ralf Dahrendorf. The communication advocated the introduction of a "European dimension" to education programs in EC member countries, and the promotion of transnational movement for teachers and students within Europe. It thus aimed to foster a European feeling among individuals in the EC by granting the equal right to education regardless of nationality; according to Dahrendorf, such a right was essential for European citizenship.

In the wake of such initiatives in the 1970s, the FRG continued to actively promote European cultural relations in the 1980s, from the introduction of a statement on cultural cooperation in the Solemn Declaration on European Union in 1983 and the launch of a European media policy together with France, to the adoption of the European Cultural Declaration at the 1984 conference of European cultural ministers in West Berlin. The initiatives were undertaken within various frameworks—the EC, Council of Europe, etc.—and were always cooperative. The inspiration for a comprehensive European identity was rooted in a clear idea: the concept of Europe, which surrounds and sustains Germany, is an essential element of German identity, whether "Germany" here meant West Germany or a hypothetical united Germany. Although the fall of the Berlin Wall and the end of the cold war expanded the realms of Europe both geographically and conceptually, the positioning of self within Europe has remained integral to Germany's pursuit of a national identity. It should be noted, however, that the focal point of German-European cultural relations now seems to fluctuate between the Franco-German axis and the re-emerging *Mitteleuropa* (Central Europe).

The FRG committed itself to the promotion of European cultural relations as a continuous enterprise to develop a German identity in a European context. After the war, Germany struggled to define a sense of self following the defeat and division of the nation; in such a situation, an emphasis on Europe as the base of Germans' collective identity served to strengthen a positive national feeling. Active involvement in the promotion of intercultural relations within a European framework helped Germany to dispel neighbors' fears that it remained the "successor of the Nazis." It eased tensions among regional members, and even contributed to the establishment of regional relations centered on Germany itself.[14] Behind this mutual enforcement of German and European identities was an acknowledgment that determinant problems for postwar Germany have been inextricably linked with geopolitical factors in Europe.

Above all, Germany's grand strategy to commit itself to European cultural relations was manifest in cooperative bilateral cultural relations with those European countries that had experienced tensions with Germany at different moments in history. Overcoming longstanding antagonisms, Germany built a partnership with France whereupon the Franco-German axis gained central importance for the development of European cultural relations and for the construction of a European identity. To the east, Germany had also conducted dialogue since the 1970s with neighboring countries such as Poland, which has since become an important regional cultural partner for Germany.[15] It is important to recognize that the young people who participated in these European dialogue and exchange programs became the leaders of the next generations and themselves promoted regional cultural programs further as key persons in cultural policymaking.[16] Principles of equal partnerships between the parties underlie all these bilateral programs, aiming at co-prosperity by respecting cultural idiosyncrasies.

Japanese Commitment to Cultural Relations in Asia

ICR Policy as a Tool for "Contributing to International Society"

Compared with the West German diplomatic mission, cultural relations between Japan and other Asian nations show distinct features.

The first is an overemphasis on Southeast Asian nations, or more precisely, on members of the Association of Southeast Asian Nations (hereafter referred as ASEAN), as partners (or targets) for cultural relations. While Europe includes Germany geographically, Japan clearly stands apart from Southeast Asia; it is not even a member of ASEAN. Where Germany had Europe, it was conceivable that Japan would look first to Northeast Asia, China, and Korea, and then to Southeast Asian countries, perhaps prioritizing the former group. Japan's commitment to regional cultural relations, however, started and developed in the form of cultural programs targeting Southeast Asian countries.

The second feature is the profound influence of the United States on the region, particularly Japan's compliance with American cold war policies. ICR activities of postwar Japan, at both state and societal levels, began during the US occupation and developed in response to the United States' cultural initiatives. Undergirding the Japanese commitment to regional cultural relations was Japan's peculiar position as junior partner of the United States: the Japanese government had to contribute to security initiatives in Southeast Asia, which was considered an area of Japanese responsibility under the auspices of the United States. In other words, Southeast Asia was a target of Japanese security and economic policy within the framework of the United States' cold war strategy, rather than an equal partner for cooperative contributions to international society or a group of neighboring nations within a regional community.

Early Post-Independence Period: 1950s–1960s

Immediately following the war, Japanese policymakers regarded ICR policy as a means to reenter international society. For example, Naruhiko Higasikuni, who assumed the office of prime minister in August 1945, envisaged establishing the "new Japan as a democratic, peaceful, morally and culturally enlightened nation," and "reconstructing Japan into the supreme contributor to the worldwide disarmament, peace and welfare of mankind."[17] Such aspirations were nationally espoused at that time.[18] Japanese policymakers conceived of ICR policy, at that time also called *bunka gaiko* or cultural diplomacy, as a way of transforming their negative national identity as a defeated country into a positive one as a contributor to the world.[19]

Such a quest to become a contributor to international society, however, could not be brought into action during the occupation. The concept of international contribution took shape only after Japanese national sovereignty was fully restored; this self-identification as "a nation that contributes to the world's well-being" formed the foundation of Japan's ICR policy thereafter. Upon the signing of the San Francisco Peace Treaty in 1951, Japan embarked upon economic interaction with Southeast Asian countries via trade relations, which developed alongside the United States' strategy to build an anti-communist bloc in Asia.[20] In light of a surge in exchanges of goods, money, and people between Japan and Southeast Asia, the Japanese government began to launch ICR projects for these countries. For example, the admission of Southeast Asian students to Japanese universities and the youth exchange program (begun in 1959 by the Management and Coordination Agency of Japan) started as part of Japan's postwar reparations to invaded nations from 1954 onward. As the speeches by prime ministers of this period show, those programs focusing on Southeast Asia were intended as a stimulus to bilateral economic relations, rather than a tool to constitute a regional collective identity.[21]

It is noteworthy that in the early post-independence period, private organizations initiated ICR activities. The International House of Japan (IHJ), the main ICR actor until the government established the Japan Foundation in 1972, illustrates this clearly. The then US Secretary of State John Foster Dulles asked John D. Rockefeller III to accompany him on a visit to Japan and to help frame the new US-Japan cultural relations of the postwar period. Dulles was anxious as to whether Japan would, as in the prewar years, be attracted to China because of its huge market for Japanese products. He wanted to maintain pro-American sentiment in Japan by means of cultural exchange with the United States and its allies. For such a purpose, Dulles thought, activities by a private foundation would be more effective than governmental cultural programs. On Dulles's suggestion, Rockefeller collaborated with Japanese liberals such as Shigeharu Matsumoto in order to establish the IHJ in Tokyo in 1955. Rockefeller's foundation paid half of the construction costs, and the rest was covered by donations on the Japanese side. The Rockefeller Foundation further provided the IHJ with business contacts as well as grants to cover program costs.[22]

The IHJ's ICR activities were more or less similar in style to those of prewar ICR organizations (such as the League of Nation's Intellectual Cooperation Committee) and American private foundations. Major participants of ICR programs were limited to "a handful" who were considered able to exercise influence upon government policies and thus ultimately contribute to international peace. "Asian" counterparts to Western and Japanese intellectuals were recruited from Southeast Asia and South Asia mainly through networks of foundations in the United States.

Shigeharu Matsumoto, a well known journalist, actively committed himself to securing peace between Japan and China during the war, albeit unsuccessfully. After the war he intended to promote two-way dialogue not only with Western countries but also with other Asian countries through IHJ programs, but he could only begin to reestablish cultural relations with China much later, after another visit in 1979. ICR activities in Japan's private sector thus also developed in accordance with the United States' cold war strategy, despite the stated aim of creating horizontal cultural relations with the rest of the world. As a result, Japanese cultural relations toward Asia in early postwar years remained largely disproportionate, both at state and nonstate levels.[23]

Government Initiatives toward Asia: The 1970s

Epochal events in the early 1970s redirected Japanese policymakers to ICR policies. The restoration of proper relations between the United States and China was a prime example. When the United States announced its readiness for President Nixon's visit to China in 1971, Japanese policymakers were shocked, for they had not anticipated this historic event. Together with the emerging economic conflict over textile trading with the United States, it disrupted Japanese policymakers' identity as a primary partner of the United States and prompted them to improve US-Japan relations.

Another shock came from Southeast Asia. Rapid deployment of Japanese corporations, in parallel with a flood of "made in Japan" products in Southeast Asian markets, increased a sense of threat and mistrust of Japan among local peoples. Boycotts of Japanese products in Thailand in 1972, compounded by anti-Japanese riots in Indonesia and Thailand during Premier Kakuei Tanaka's tour of ASEAN member countries in 1974, symbolized the limits of their economy-biased foreign policy. These changes were an incentive for policymakers to develop new ICR policies. Takeo Fukuda, who served as minister of foreign affairs in the early 1970s and became prime minister later in the decade, inaugurated an ICR policy focused on "mutual understanding" between Japan and its counterparts.

The establishment of the Japan Foundation (JF) in October 1972 as a national ICR agency was a major example of Fukuda's initiative for mutually beneficial cultural relations. The Cultural Project Division of the Ministry of Foreign Affairs summarized the purpose of the JF as:

(a) to promote Japan as a peaceful nation in international society,
(b) to promote domestic understanding of other countries and cultures, and
(c) to contribute to the advancement of technology and well-being in developing countries.[24]

At the eighth US-Japan Joint Economic Conference, held in September 1971, Fukuda introduced his idea to establish a cultural agency to enhance mutual understanding between Japan and the United States. Both countries agreed then to promote academic exchange, and the agreement was implemented as one of the first projects of the JF.[25] These events imply that the redefinition of Japanese ICR policies in the 1970s started primarily with the aim of improving Japan-US relations.

The JF targeted Southeast Asian countries as well as the United States.[26] The foundation's inaugural activities included not only arts and humanities projects, but also technological assistance, all of which were explicitly intended as tools to contribute to the world's welfare. Two years after the JF was established, the Ship for Southeast Asian Youth Program, an exchange program for young people in Southeast Asia and Japan, was launched. After his accession to the premiership, Fukuda offered financial support for regional cultural cooperation with ASEAN as a part of his initiative for "heart to heart communication" between ASEAN nations and Japan.[27]

In sum, Fukuda and his advisors in the Ministry of Foreign Affairs rediscovered ICR policy as a tool for moving beyond economy-oriented foreign policy. Together with financial aid, ICR policy was one of the few available diplomatic means that did not provoke antagonism among Asian nations. By promoting initiatives in cultural relations, Fukuda and his government tried to demonstrate that Japan played a "political role" commensurate with its economic power. At the same time, they believed that Japan could contribute to peace and prosperity in Asia as a partner of the United States by assisting cultural and technological development in Southeast Asia. It is noteworthy that Fukuda saw the improvement of US-China relations as an opportunity for Japan to play such a role. In this context, Southeast Asia was regarded as little more than an "area" in which to fulfill a responsibility as junior partner of the United States. Though Fukuda promoted exchange programs aimed at "mutual understanding," the relationship between Japan and Southeast Asian nations remained hierarchical, with Japan as a regional leader that provided assistance to other members.

Japan's determination to play a political role, however, was interrupted in 1979 by the unexpected invasion of Cambodia by Vietnam. As the Soviet Union's invasion of Afghanistan gave rise to international tensions in the so-called second cold war, Japan refrained from playing a significant role in Asia and emphasized its position as a member of the Western camp.

Development of "People to People Diplomacy" at the Local Level: The 1970s

While the Japanese government redefined ICR policy, municipal-level (political) movements created alternative policies, not only in the domestic policy sphere but also in Japan's foreign relations. The first "civil society" discourse to influence Japanese international relations was "people to people diplomacy" or *minsai* discourse, advocated by Kazuji Nagasu. Nagasu, the governor of Kanagawa prefecture from 1975 to 1995, was one of the symbolic figures of so-called progressive municipalities (*kakushin jichitai*) in the 1970s and early 1980s.

Yoshikazu Sakamoto, a leading progressive political scientist, described the period's trend using the term "people to people relations (*minsai kankei*)," which he perceived as a replacement for "international relations (*kokusai kankei*)." He pointed out that in relations among developed countries, the trading of goods and information, as well as human exchange (in our terms, ICR as phenomenon), occurred on a tremendous scale at the private level. Sakamoto held that these "people to people" relations, which were rapidly increasing their predominance over "government to government" relations, could be a post–nation-state phenomenon and the key to international peace in the future. He also stressed that Japan's "people to people" relations with Asia were not sufficient, and thus should be actively promoted by suitable policies.[28]

Influenced by Sakamoto, Nagasu advocated "people to people diplomacy" by regarding citizens as agents of international relations. He also tried to make municipalities as independent as possible from the central government by promoting citizens' participation in local governance and policymaking. Since Kanagawa prefecture was second only to Okinawa in its number of US military bases, conflict with the central government was inevitable; local authorities thus had some legitimacy, Nagasu thought, in pursuing an independent "diplomacy" on behalf of their local residents. Nagasu resisted not only the government's support of US military bases in Kanagawa but also authoritative policies in other areas—for example, the enforcement of requirements that residential foreigners register themselves and be fingerprinted. Further, he enthusiastically gave support—financial and otherwise—to emerging Japanese NGOs, which remained largely ignored by the national government.

Nagasu's "people to people diplomacy" had a great impact on policies of other local authorities. Many of them followed the example of the "advanced prefecture" and began similar initiatives, though they were not as antagonistic toward the central government as Kanagawa had been in the early days of Nagasu's governorship. Later, in the 1980s, the Ministry of Home Affairs actually promoted this movement at the local level and issued guidelines encouraging all local authorities to establish "international exchange associations" (*kokusai koryu kyokai*) and have their own international policy. This boom of constructing local-level international relations resulted in the active engagement of municipalities and grassroots groups in developing ICR programs.

It is particularly significant that it was a politician who initiated Japanese "people to people" (or civil society–oriented) ICR discourse. The notion that NGOs and civil society are important was advocated from above, not from below. True, ordinary citizens created NGOs in Japan in the early 1980s, but the number and size of these NGOs were (and still are) very small, compared with those in other developed nations. Japan was regarded as "underdeveloped" in this way, not just by progressive politicians like Nagasu but also by the bureaucrats themselves. The construction of civil society thus became a nationwide objective to be attained in order to "catch up with the West." In the late 1990s the Japanese government actually started to nurture NGOs by providing them with financial and technical assistance.

According to the philosophy of "people to people diplomacy," local authorities supported civil engagement in ICR activities in the 1970s. These local initiatives to promote ICR were a precursor to the explosive expansion of ICR activities at the societal level in the 1980s, which had a great impact on national-level ICR policies. In this sense, *minsai* discourse, or the Japanese local version of civil society discourse, was indeed a milestone in the history of Japanese ICR. The boom of grassroots ICR, however, was not only a product of *minsai* discourse. Japanese economic achievement, or the birth of an increasingly affluent society by the mid 1980s, was also an important factor that enabled ordinary people to participate in ICR activities.

Silent Change in the 1980s

As the chance for Japan to pursue its political motives in Asia diminished, the weight of regional cultural relations in Japanese foreign policy decreased. Indeed the government's involvement with the JF remained at the same level until 1987.[29] Despite this quantitative stagnation of government financial support, Japanese ICR as a whole experienced a qualitative improvement during the 1980s. This improvement—or transformation—of ICR activities had some distinct characteristics: rapid rise of societal agents, focus on two-way rather than one-way interaction, emergence of issue-oriented projects, and collaboration among agents at different levels.[30]

In the 1980s, various international grassroots organizations, development NGOs, and local governments readily put into practice the ideas and methods for ICR programs that they had acquired through interaction with European and US agencies. The numbers and budgets of such societal actors tripled or quadrupled during the 1980s and early 1990s. Two factors account for this sudden increase in societal agents in ICR. Firstly, the Japanese yen rose steeply after the 1985 Plaza Accord, which depreciated the US dollar in relation to the Japanese yen and German mark by intervening in currency markets in developed countries. Secondly, Japanese overseas travel increased rapidly, and large numbers of Japanese people began to visit and experience foreign countries and cultures. Under these circumstances, it became easier for Japanese societal agencies to realize mutually beneficial ICR through interactive cultural exchange with, or development assistance to, their Asian counterparts, especially those in Southeast Asia. ICR programs also began to show a greater variety of content, from the promotion of goodwill and mutual understanding to issue-oriented cooperation on environment, gender, education, and so on. These collaborative and practical ICR programs marked a departure from conventional national ICR policy, in which Southeast Asian nations had been regarded only as targets of Japan's foreign policy.

New movements at the societal level were soon incorporated into national policies via collaboration between state and societal ICR agencies. The case of the Japan Foundation is a clear example of government-societal ICR collaboration. As is mentioned above, the budget of the JF remained on a plateau at that time. In order to overcome its fiscal limitations, the foundation started working together with societal agencies and outsourcing some of its projects.[31] It established the JF Prizes for Community-Based Cultural Exchange (started in 1985, now renamed JF Prizes for Global Citizenship) and various other new programs in order to promote collaboration with, or support activities of, local and grassroots actors. In turn, these programs worked as channels by which the JF could absorb the methods and ideas of mutually beneficial ICR that had been developed at societal levels. As a result, cross-sector networks comprising state and societal ICR agents grew throughout the 1980s and beyond. The idea of collaboration and interactive programs became a nationwide trend in Japanese ICR activities, and agencies at all levels put such ideas into practice in exchange programs with Asian nations.

Revival and Renewal: Cultural Relations in Asia at the End of 1980s

In the late 1980s, ICR policy toward Asia came back into the national-level spotlight in Japan. On becoming prime minister in November 1987, Noboru Takeshita sent a cultural mission (*bunka* mission) to Southeast Asia.[32] The mission aimed to examine the potential for developing ICR projects with Southeast Asian nations, and its report pointed to the need to promote such projects.[33] Accordingly, Takeshita initiated active cultural policy toward Southeast Asian policy, set up the Japan-ASEAN Comprehensive Cultural Exchange Program, and established the ASEAN Cultural Center with the JF.[34] The mission's report also encouraged Japanese ICR polices in general, as well as Japan's further commitment toward Southeast Asian nations. In January 1988, a year after Takeshita's mission to ASEAN, the premier announced his "Concept for International Cooperation" in a speech during his visit to London. He stated that Japan was willing "to contribute to world peace and prosperity" using three measures: financial and civil support for peacekeeping operations, expanded Official Development Assistance (ODA), and further commitment to ICR policies.

Takeshita's initiative was prompted by a change in international relations in Asia, brought about by the settlement of the Cambodian conflict. In view of the détente among conflicting parties in late 1987, Japanese policymakers envisaged resuming their once abandoned "political role" to broker peace in the region.[35] Policymakers understood that they could no longer remain in the shadows of "the Western camp" watching the other parties construct international order.[36] Thus they once again began to appreciate cultural relations as a tool for international proactivity targeting Southeast Asia.

Immediately following his speech in London, Prime Minister Takeshita organized the Advisory Group on International Cultural Exchange (Kokusai Bunka Koryu ni Kansuru Kondankai).[37] The report issued by the advisory group regarded ICR policy as a tool to contribute to world harmony. On the one hand, it agreed with the basic assumption of Fukuda's initiative in the 1970s: that international cultural exchange and cooperation foster mutual understanding among peoples and enhance the diversity of the world's cultures.[38] On the other hand, the initiative of the late 1980s differed from that of the 1970s in some important aspects. The 1989 report recognized the need to involve various societal agents such as NGOs, local authorities, and individuals active in ICR, and advocated cooperation between public and private sectors. Furthermore, it propounded "academic cooperation in the fields that require global efforts such as environmental conservation" and recommended "enhancing the activities of the ASEAN Cultural Center in order to promote interactive ICR policies among the parties."[39] These elements of the advisory group's report—broadening the areas of cooperation and stressing mutuality—mirrored the concepts and methods that had developed at the grassroots level in the 1980s.

Expanding Asia: Cultural Programs for a "Symbiotic Relationship"

The influence of societal agents was evident in the development of the JF ASEAN Cultural Center. When the center was established in 1990 for the promotion of ASEAN cultures, it merely provided general data and information on Japan and ASEAN with the aim of "maintaining the mutuality of ICR with ASEAN nations."[40] The center's scope of activities broadened further under the Peace, Friendship and Exchange Initiative (Heiwa Yuko Koryu Keikaku) announced by the Socialist Prime Minister Tomiichi Murayama in 1994, as did the range of target countries in its programs. This initiative was the first attempt to address historical issues between Japan and other Asian countries at the national level.[41] As a result, the ASEAN Culture Center was expanded and reorganized into the Asia Center, now to include China and South Korea. While conventional ICR programs launched by the national government, such as the Japan-ASEAN Dialogue (as of 1977), primarily involved consultations with major cultural figures,[42] the Asia Center's intellectual exchange programs took the form of policy-oriented collaboration on specific issues with experts from Japan and other Asian nations. The center aimed to construct and share a "new history" among people in Asia by means of such collaboration between artists and academics.[43] Its ultimate goal was to build a "symbiotic relationship" between nations in Asia.[44] The center's programs, which supported academic research projects and conferences on global issues such as the environment and security, the conservation of Asian cultural heritage, multinational art collaboration (the dramatic performance of *King Lear* in 1997 is a prime example), and so on, aimed to create networking opportunities for Asian intellectuals and artists with the ultimate goal of "symbiosis" in Asia.[45]

Japanese ICR programs within Asia after the late 1980s contrast with earlier ones in three particular aspects. Firstly, later programs stressed commonality, rather than difference, among the participants. Secondly, the regional framework of ICR programs became a broader, more inclusive "Asia" consisting of Japan and Southeast Asia but also Northeast Asian nations. Thirdly, the new programs included various issue-oriented and collaborative projects, which had been less frequent in the former period.

Successive administrations inherited this specialized and cooperative style of cultural relations. For example, the Multilateral Cultural Mission, organized in 1997, consisted of artists and academics from Japan as well as ASEAN countries. These mission members came together to address the conservation of cultural heritage sites in Asian countries, "which are in danger of rapid globalization."[46] With regard to cultural relations with Northeast Asian nations, the Japanese government has become proactive in bilateral programs such as those in the Japan–Republic of Korea National Exchange Year, or the FIFA World Cup co-hosted by South Korea and Japan in 2002. These national ICR programs with Northeast Asian nations furthered the development of broader cultural relations at the grassroots level.[47]

In the meantime, mutual understanding with regard to Japanese, Chinese, and South Korean history has stagnated since the aforementioned Peace, Friendship and Exchange Initiative. Fueled by conflict surrounding the junior high school "history textbook problem,"[48] tensions are mounting between Japan and other Northeast Asian nations.[49]

Unlike the German commitment to European cultural relations, the Japanese commitment to cultural relations within Asia has been neither well organized nor rigidly institutionalized (the JF Asia Center was abolished in 2004 because of the restructuring of the Foundation). It was Japanese local authorities and grassroots actors who developed complex bilateral or multilateral networks across state and societal levels. Some of them brought new ideas and methods into national ICR, complementing the Japanese government's commitment to Asian cultural relations. These ideas and methods have paved the way to more horizontal and equal relationships between Japan and other Asian nations.

Conclusion: "Germany in Europe," "Japan and Asia"

After close examination, it seems that West German and Japanese commitment to regional cultural relations have three features in common. The first is that both countries used regional ICR as a means of rebuilding a national identity in contemporary international society. The function of ICR policy in constructing national identity is evident in the FRG's "grand strategy." Japan's attempt to build an inclusive Asia was quite inconsistent throughout the postwar period, but the government gradually strengthened its commitment to regional cultural relations from the 1990s onward. In both cases, interactive and cooperative cultural programs served to build a horizontal relationship with neighboring countries. The FRG has utilized joint initiatives and multilateral frameworks, promoting dialogues and personal exchanges since the early postwar years. In Japan, interactive ICR activities were developed by societal actors at first, to be joined later by national agencies. The "classic" cultural diplomacy that projects national cultures did not—or could not—play a significant role in building regional partnerships for either country.

Secondly, both cases show that membership in a region is variable, depending on the time period and the nature of the identity pursued. The fluctuation of regional borders appears more prominently in the Japanese case but could be seen in West Germany as well, as the definition of Europe has always been controversial among policymakers. Since the end of the cold war, the Federal government has directed large amounts of money and energy toward cultural exchange programs with Central and Eastern European countries. Today, economic disparity among new and old EU members has cast a pall over the ideal of a "Europe of equal partnership."

The third point is that ICR activities had a multiplying effect in both cases. In the case of the FRG, participants of Franco-German exchange programs became policymakers of the next generations and leading ICR proponents, expanding early initiatives into European-wide cultural exchange programs. The Japanese commitment to regional cultural relations, in contrast, emerged as a reaction to broader ICR developments at a phenomenal level. It was the interaction of people, goods, and information that incited the redefinition of Asia and shaped the cooperative style of Japanese ICR programs. National ICR policy and the government's commitment to Asian cultural relations incorporated these ideas and program styles through interaction with nongovernmental agents.

Meanwhile, it is important to consider the difference between the German and Japanese commitments to cultural relations in respective regions: that is, the perceived structure of relationships between regional members. While the FRG seems to have been successful in embedding itself in Europe based on numerous bilateral and multilateral partnerships with neighboring nations, Japan has looked to build an inclusive Asia founded upon equal partnerships. Throughout the postwar period, Japan maintained its identity as a contributor to peace and prosperity in Southeast Asia, its area of responsibility under the auspices of the United States. It was these unique circumstances that kept Japan from considering Asia to be as essential as Europe is to Germany. In other words, Japan's primary partner in the second half of the twentieth century was the United States rather than China or South Korea, or even the nations of Southeast Asia. Japan's commitment to regional cultural relations with Northeast Asian nations, especially regarding historic issues, was downplayed until the 1990s, and there remain significant gaps in understanding between these neighbors.[50]

Since the late 1980s, Japan has consequently begun to express itself as a member of Asia and tried to construct a self-inclusive region based on collaborative relationships. As Japanese societal agents have done in the past, its national agencies are now developing collaborative projects at different levels with various Asian counterparts. With regard to the economy, for example, the Japanese government pursues free trade area agreements (FTAs) with East Asian countries with the intention of building a regional economic partnership. East Asian nations including ASEAN, China, the Republic of Korea, and Japan have agreed to develop an East Asian FTA in 2005. More recently, the "Asia Gateway Vision," proposed in May 2007 by then Prime Minister Shinzo Abe, clearly emphasizes the importance of situating Japan among horizontal partnerships with Asian nations. The introduction to the report compiled by Abe's strategic committee states that the Asia Gateway must be based on the notion of "Japan in Asia," not "Japan and Asia."[51]

Could Japan belong in Asia at last? It is difficult to be optimistic when faced with this question.[52] Considering the domestic societies in the region, East Asian nations seem far from building a unified regional community. During the administration of Jun'ichiro Koizumi (2001–06), anti-Japanese sentiment rose in China and Korea after the prime minister's visit to the Yasukuni Shrine. Yasukuni is a controversial site because it memorializes all the soldiers who have fought and died for Japan since the beginning of the modern period, including war criminals who were executed after World War II. This episode illustrates that Japanese regional commitment promotes mainly pragmatic cooperation, leaving mutual understanding through dialogue on historical issues far behind.[53] In addition, during the Koizumi administration the Japanese government strengthened Japan-US security relations, furthering the attempt to promote a joint operation of military forces. Koizumi also sent a Japanese Self Defense Force to Iraq in response to the US call for voluntary participation. This operation was the first since World War II to send Japanese troops abroad, and it provoked serious concerns from neighboring Asian countries. It is therefore likely that Japan will remain undecided as to whether to embed itself firmly within the Asian region or to opt for a "special partnership" with the United States.

If Japan is to become a member of the Asian regional community, it must commit itself to regional cultural relations. Above all, Japan should pursue stronger ties with its neighboring nations through joint cultural programs that seek to promote mutual understanding. As the example of West Germany suggests, continuous dialogue, discussion, and exchange between citizens form the basis for building a region of equal partnerships, as best denoted by the phrase "Japan in Asia."

Endnotes

1. Mie Oba, *Asia Taiheiyo Chiiki Keisei e no Katei: Kyokai Kokka Nichi-Go no Identity Mosaku to Chiiki Shugi* [Road to Asia-Pacific: Search of Identities by Japan and Australia as Liminal Nations and Regionalism] (Kyoto-shi: Mineruva Shobo, 2004), chap. 1.
2. In this chapter, "Asia" includes both Northeast Asia (Japan, China, and the Korean peninsula) and Southeast Asia (the contemporary Association of Southeast Asian Nations members).
3. J. M. Mitchell, *International Cultural Relations* (London and Boston: Allen & Unwin, 1986), 5. In the first part of this book, Mitchell distinguishes a "first-order meaning (inter-governmental negotiation of treaties, conventions, agreements and exchange programs)" and "second-order meaning (national diplomacy)" of cultural diplomacy (pp. 3–5). Mitchell himself is actually concerned with the latter meaning and examines national cultural diplomacy throughout his study. This essay is primarily concerned with national cultural diplomacy (Mitchell's second definition), but it also takes into account initiatives by governments to promote cultural relations at multilateral level, especially in regional organizations.
4. For a detailed examination of the term ICR, and the history of academic investigation of ICR, see Yoko Kawamura, "The Study and Practice of International Cultural Relations: A Japanese Approach to International Relations." Paper pre-

sented at the JAIR (Japan Association for International Relations) 50th Anniversary International Conference, Kisarazu, Japan, 2006.

5. In 1910, Japan annexed the Korean peninsula to its national territory. It expanded its influence over mainland China by establishing Manchukuo, its puppet state in Northeastern China. Those experiences of invasion before and during World War II are perceived as national trauma by both North and South Korea and the People's Republic of China, even after its independence in the postwar era. Japan found it quite difficult to initiate cultural cooperation with these neighbors because attempts to do so evoked the image of the cultural assimilation policy of the Great Japanese Empire.
6. Peter Katzenstein, *The Culture of National Security: Norms and Identity in World Politics* (New York: Columbia University Press, 1996); Josef Lapid and Freidrich Kratochwil, *The Return of Culture and Identity in IR Theory* (Boulder, CO: Lynne Rienner, 1996); Alexander Wendt, *Social Theory of International Relations* (Cambridge: Cambridge University Press, 1999).
7. Karl Deutsch et al., *Political Community and the North Atlantic Area: International Organization in the Light of Historical Experience* (Princeton: Princeton University Press, 1957).
8. Peter J. Katzenstein, *Tamed Power: Germany in Europe* (Ithaca, NY: Cornell University Press, 1997), 33.
9. Yoko Kawamura, "Wiesbaden Sagyo Circle: Sengo Doitsu Bunka Koryu Koso ni okeru 'Weimar no Saisei'" [Wiesbadener Arbeitskreis: 'Weimar Renaissance' in Postwar German Conception for Cultural Exchange], Odysseus 3 (1999): 38–51. Documents on the Wiesbaden circle can be found in the files of the Goethe-Institute archive held at the German Federal Archive in Koblenz.
10. With the establishment of the Federal Republic, the West German government also cautiously started its own ICR policy, apart from multi- and bilateral cultural programs. Programs of early postwar German ICR policy put emphasis on the promotion of German language and classical "high culture" in foreign countries, though in later years more cooperative programs were introduced and a broader definition of culture was adopted.
11. John Farquharson and Stephen C. Holt, *Europe from Below: An Assessment of Franco-German Popular Contacts* (London: Allen & Unwin, 1975).
12. Farquharson and Holt, *Europe from Below,* 189–191.
13. The Commission of the European Communities, *Education in the European Community* (Communication from the Commission to the Council presented on 11 March 1974), *Bulletin of the European Communities,* Supplement 1974/03.
14. Markovits and Reich likened united Germany in Europe to hegemony in a Gramscian sense. Andrei S. Markovits and Simon Reich, "Should Europe Fear the Germans?" in *From Bundesrepublik to Deutschland: German Politics after Unification,* ed. Michael Huelshoff, Andrei S. Markovits, and Simon Reich (Ann Arbor: University of Michigan Press, 1993).
15. Masao Nishikawa, *Jikoku Shi wo Koeta Rekishikyoiku* [History Education beyond National History] (Tokyo: Sanseido, 1992), Part II.
16. Barthold C. Witte, who served in the German Foreign Office as culture-specialist and became the head of its Cultural Department under Minister Genscher, was a member of the Student Movement for Transnational Federation (Studentenbewegung für übernationale Föderation e.V., ISSF) in the French zone during the occupation period and participated in a Franco-German university summer course. He recollects such early experiences as a starting point of his career. Personal comment of Witte in an interview in Bonn, 27 April 1996. Ralf Dahrendorf, the aforementioned EC commissioner in the 1970s, also participated in

European cultural dialogues (e.g.. a Wilton Park seminar held by the British Occupation Force) in the early years of his life.

17. Naruhiko Higashikuni, *Ichi Kozoku no Senso Nikki* [War Diary of a Royal Family Member] (Tokyo: Nihon Shuhosha, 1957), 200–201.
18. The Ministry of Foreign Affairs, for example, upheld the renewal of cultural policy together with political and economic reconstruction in the Plan for Voluntary and Immediate Policy Enforcement, which the ministry drew up in 1945 as a counter plan for occupation by the Allies. In their joint work *Theory of Cultural Nation: Power to Make Law,* law scholars Eiichi Makino and Asao Odaka insist on developing the independence and uniqueness of their nation in order to "promote diversity and fairness in the international community."
19. Mamoru Shigemitsu, foreign minister of the Higashikuni administration, regarded the newly independent Southeast Asian nations as partners for establishing a politically and culturally independent and prosperous Asia through nonmilitary measures such as cultural cooperation. See Susumu Sato, "Sengo Nihon Gaiko no Sentaku to Ajia Chitsujo Koso [The Choice of Postwar Japanese Diplomacy and Initiative for Order of Asia]," *Hogaku Seijigaku Ronkyu,* no. 41 (1999): 171.
20. Kenichiro Hirano, "Sengo Nihon ni Okeru 'Bunka'" ["Culture" in the Context of Postwar Japanese Diplomacy], in *Sengo Nihon no Gaiko Seisaku* [Diplomacy of Postwar Japan], ed. Akio Watanabe (Tokyo: Yuhikaku, 1985), 339–374.
21. In the speeches by premiers of this period, the term "culture" always appears in combination with "economy": for example, "cooperation in the economic-cultural field" (Tanzan Ishibashi at the 26th Diet, February 1957), "economic cooperation and cultural partnership" (Shinsuke Kishi at the 27th Diet, November 1957), "active exchange both in the economic and cultural field with friends" (Hayato Ikeda at 39th Diet, September 1961). See Hirano, "Sengo Nihon," 351.
22. Takeshi Igarashi, "Sengo Nichi-Bei Bunkakoryu Keikaku no Taido" [Stirring of the Post War US-Japan Cultural Exchange Program], in *Senryo to Nihon Shukyo* [Occupation and Religion in Japan], ed. Fujio Imon (Tokyo: Miraisha, 1993).
23. For the American influence on the construction of postwar ICR institutions in the Japanese private sector, see also Toichi Makita, "Liberal na Kokusai Bunka Koryu" [Liberal International Cultural Relations], in Sengo Nihon Kokusai Bunka Koryu Kenkyukai (Study Group on International Cultural Relations of Postwar Japan), *Sengo Nihon no Kokusai Bunka Koryu* [International Cultural Relations of Postwar Japan] (Tokyo: Keiso Shobo, 2005). Toshihiro Menju, a Japanese specialist of grassroots exchange, describes the impact of American philanthropy on the development of postwar Japanese ICR at the grassroots level up to the mid 1970s: Toshihiro Menju, "The Development of Grassroots International Exchange in Japan and the Impact of American Philanthropy," in *Philanthropy and Reconciliation: Rebuilding Postwar U.S.–Japan Relations,* ed. Tadashi Yamamoto, Akira Iriye, and Makoto Iokibe (Tokyo: Japan Center for International Exchange, 2006).
24. MOFA (Ministry of Foreign Affairs) Cultural Project Division, (*Gaimusho Bunka Jigyobu*), *Kokusai Koryu no Genjo to Tenbo (1972)* [Current Situation and Prospect of International Exchange (1972)] (Tokyo, 1973), 13–14. This is a preparatory report for the establishment of the JF. The report introduces financial assistance to the Japan Study Center project from eleven universities in the US and Canada.
25. MOFA Cultural Project Division, *Kokusai Koryu,* 18.
26. MOFA Cultural Project Division, *Kokusai Koryu,* 12, stressed the importance of Southeast Asia as a target for Japanese ICR policy and pointed out the urgent

need to correct a "wrong image of Japan" as "economic animals." Fukuda and the diplomats who assisted him had similar opinions. See for example Takehiko Nishiyama, "ASEAN no Genjo to Wagakuni tono Kankei" [Present Situation of ASEAN and Its Relationship with Our Country], *Keizai Kyoryoku,* no. 130 (1978): 12–19. Foreign Minister Fukuda expressed his opinion on this point in a speech at the Lower House Foreign Affairs Committee on 15 March 1972. See Kokusai Koryu Kikin Jugonenshi Hensan Iinkai (Compilation Committee for Fifteen Years' History of Japan Foundation), *Kokusai Koryu Kikin Jugo Nen no Ayumi* [Fifteen Years of Japan Foundation] (Tokyo, 1990), 235.

27. On his visit to Southeast Asian nations in 1977, Fukuda offered to fund ASEAN's regional cultural cooperation as a part of his heralded initiative to support ASEAN. For information about its impact on development of ASEAN regional cultural cooperation, see Maki Aoki-Okabe, "Chiiki Bunka Kyoryoku wo Meguru Bunka Shokuhen: ASEAN Bunka Kyoryoku ni Taisuru Ikigai Shutai no Eikyo" [Acculturation of Regional Cultural Cooperation: The External Influence upon Regional Cultural Cooperation by ASEAN], in Sengo Nihon Kokusai Bunka Koryu Kenkyukai, *Sengo Nihon.*
28. For details see Kazuji Nagasu and Yoshikazu Sakamoto, *Jichitai no Kokusai Kouryu* [International Relations of Local Governments] (Tokyo: Gakuyo Shobo, 1983).
29. See Kokusai Koryu Kikin Jugonenshi Hensan Iinkai, *Kokusai Koryu Kikin Jugo Nen no Ayumi,* 222–223; Bunka Koryu Kenkyukai (University of Tokyo Study Group on International Cultural Relations), *Nihon ASEAN Kokusai Bunka Koryu, Bunka Kyoryoku Jigyo no Rekishiteki Tenklai no Keii, Genjo, Kadai* [Historical Development, Present Situation and Challenge of Japan–ASEAN International Cultural Exchange and Cooperation Projects], report commissioned by the Japan Foundation Asia Center (Tokyo, 1999), 29.
30. Masaru Sakato, "Kokusai Koryu Kikin no 25 Nen: Jigyo Seikaku to no Tenkai" [25 Years of the Japan Foundation: Development of Its Programs, etc.], *Kyorin Daigaku Fuzoku Kokusai Kankei Kenkyujo Kenkyu Nenpo,* no. 2 (1999): 135–158.
31. See Kokusai Koryu Kikin Jugonenshi Hensan Iinkai, *Kokusai Koryu,* 50.
32. The mission consisted of major figures in the business community, renowned academics, major cultural figures, and directors of national/nonstate ICR agencies. For details, see Sengo Nihon Kokusai Bunka Koryu Kenkyukai, *Sengo Nihon,* 64.
33. Japan Foundation, *Kokusai Bunka Koryu Gannen he no Kitai* [Hope for The Epoch of International Cultural Exchange] (Tokyo, 1988), 32–37.
34. Ministry of Foreign Affairs (*Gaimusho*), *Waga Gaiko no Kinkyo 1987* [Diplomatic Blue Book 1987] (Tokyo, 1987).
35. MOFA, *Waga Gaiko no Kinkyo 1989* [Diplomatic Blue Book 1989], (Tokyo, 1989), 144–146 and Sakutaro Tanino, "Saikin no Asia Josei to Nihon no Taio" [Recent Situation in Asia and Japan's Response], *Sekai Kezai Hyoron* 32, no. 5 (1988): 22–39, 35 eloquently express these aspirations to revive a "political role" in Southeast Asia.
36. Takakazu Kuriyama, "Gekido no 90 Nendai to Nihon Gaiko no Shintenkai" [Turmoil in the 1990s and New Development of Japanese Diplomacy], *Gaiko Forum* 3, no. 5 (2005): 12–21.
37. Takeshita's group was the first advisory group on ICR policy in history to be directly organized by a Japanese prime minister.
38. Kokusai Bunka Koryu ni Kansuru Kondankai [Advisory Group on International Cultural Exchange], *Kokusai Bunka Koryu ni Kansuru Kondankai Hokoku* [Report of Advisory Group on International Cultural Exchange] (Tokyo, 1989), 2.

39. Ibid., 8–9.
40. Japan Foundation, *Kokusai Bunka Koryu Gannen he no Kitai,* 35.
41. Bunka Koryu Kenkyukai, *Nihon ASEAN Kokusai Bunka Koryu,* 35.
42. Ibid., 47.
43. Kokusai Bunka Koryu ni Kansuru Kondankai, *Atasashii Jidaino Kokusai Bunka Koryu* [Report on International Cultural Exchange in New Age] (Tokyo, 1994), 8.
44. Maho Sato, "Asia ni Okeru Chiteki Koryu no Kokoromi" [Attempts for Intellectual Exchange in Asia], in *Kokusai Bunka Shinkokai kara Kokusai Koryu Kikin e: Kokusai Koryu Kikin Ron* [From Kokusai Bunka Shinkokai to Japan Foundation: Introduction to Analysis of Japan Foundation], FY 1999 Report of the Research by Grants-in-Aid for Scientific Research (Basic Research B), Project "Empirical and Sociological Research of Globalization, Cultural Exchange and Culture Industry," no. 10410055 (Tokyo, 1999), 118.
45. Maho Sato, "Asia ni Okeru Chiteki Koryu no Kokoromi," 119; 121.
46. Joint Secretariat of ASEAN-Japan Multilateral Cultural Mission, *The Report of the Joint Secretariat of ASEAN-Japan Multilateral Cultural Mission, Japan-Singapore* (Tokyo, 1998).
47. Much of the grassroots ICR in Asia was encouraged by the exchange of popular culture in the region. Japanese *manga,* Korean television dramas, and Chinese cinema are rapidly becoming popular among Asian nations. For example, the Korean drama *Winter Sonata,* broadcast on a national Japanese television channel in 2004, sparked a "Korean boom (*Hanryu*)" and brought about a 15 percent increase in Japanese tourists to South Korea in 2005. Though such transnational movements are more phenomenal than intentional, international cultural relations in a broader sense propel ICR policies. Meanwhile, pop culture does not necessarily fill the perceptional gap on political and historical issues between nations. As in the example of anti-Japanese mobs in Beijing after the final Asia Cup football match between Japan and China in 2004, pop cultural exchange sometimes fuels the antipathy of countries.
48. The history textbook problem (*rekishi kyokasho mondai*) is a conflict between Japan and other Northeast Asian nations over the interpretation of the Japanese invasion of China and Korea, and the application of the interpretation to the Japanese educational curriculum. The conflict intensified in 1982 and was revived in 2001 by the publication of an "ultra-nationalistic" textbook that cleared censorship by the Japanese Education Ministry.
49. For example, 30 percent of respondents in an internet questionnaire by the Chinese online portal *Shanghai Searchina* answered that current China-Japan relations are "less favorable," while only 12 percent felt them to be "favorable." Moreover, about 70 percent of the respondents pointed out that the most important issue in future Sino-Japan relations would be the "history problem." *Searchina Marketing News,* 9 January 2004 (internet news accessed on 1 December 2005). The website of Searchina Marketing News was later integrated into "Searchina" portal, <http://searchina.ne.jp/>.
50. Dialogue with China and Korea over historic issues is promoted by private initiatives of historians, teachers, etc. In recent years, public bilateral projects of joint study on history have been launched with South Korea (2002) and with China (2006).
51. See Strategic Committee for Asia Gateway, *Asia Gateway Kousou* [Asia Gateway Vision], 16 May 2007.
52. Japanese effort to enhance regional economic integration in East Asia is contested by China's counter initiative. In the prior negotiation of the East Asian FTA agreement, there was reportedly a serious difference of opinion between

China and Japan about the membership of the community ("ASEAN + 3" or "ASEAN + 6"). Though the contest was a diplomatic one over a new regional framework, domestic opinion in China expressed resentment against a regional integration initiated by Japan. *Mainichi Shinbun*, 9 December 2005.

53. In 2003, Premier Koizumi organized the Advisory Group on Cultural Diplomacy, which submitted a report the following year. This report, in contrast to the conventional Japanese vocabulary, adopted "cultural diplomacy" (*bunka gaiko*) as the key term instead of "international cultural relations" (*kokusai bunka koryu*), related ICR policy (cultural diplomacy) closely to the strategy of general foreign policy, and regarded East Asia as a main target region together with the "Middle East Islam region." The report proposed the "promotion of dialogue on common issues" with countries in East Asia but skipped the historical problems and mentioned only current issues such as environment and welfare. Overall, the report stresses the necessity of promoting the dispatch (*hasshin*) or export of Japanese "cool" culture abroad. See Advisory Group on Cultural Diplomacy (Bunka Gaiko no Suishin ni Kansuru Kondankai), *"Bunka Koryu no Heiwa Kokka" Nippon no Sozo wo* [To Make Japan a "Peaceful State Promoting International Cultural Exchange"] (Tokyo, 2004), 20–21.

Bibliography

Aoki-Okabe, Maki. "Chiiki Bunka Kyoryoku wo Meguru Bunka Shokuhen: ASEAN Bunka Kyoryoku ni Taisuru Ikigai Shutai no Eikyo [Acculturation of Regional Cultural Cooperation: The External Influence upon Regional Cultural Cooperation by ASEAN]." In Sengo Nihon Kokusai Bunka Koryu Kenkyukai (Study Group on International Cultural Relations of Postwar Japan), *Sengo Nihon no Kokusai Bunka Koryu* [International Cultural Relations of Postwar Japan]. Tokyo: Keiso Shobo, 2005.

Bunka Gaiko no Suishin ni Kansuru Kondankai [Advisory Group on Cultural Diplomacy]. *"Bunka Koryu no Heiwa Kokka" Nippon no Sozo wo* [To Make Japan a "Peaceful State Promoting International Cultural Exchange"]. Tokyo, 2004.

Bunka Koryu Kenkyukai (University of Tokyo Study Group on International Cultural Relations). *Nihon ASEAN Kokusai Bunka Koryu, Bunka Kyoryoku Jigyo no Rekishiteki Tenklai no Keii, Genjo, Kadai* [Historical Development, Present Situation and Challenge of Japan-ASEAN International Cultural Exchange and Cooperation Projects]. Report commissioned by the Japan Foundation Asia Center. Tokyo, 1999.

The Commission of the European Communities, ed*ucation in the European Community* (Communication from the Commission to the Council presented on 11 March 1974). *Bulletin of the European Communities*, Supplement 1974/03.

Deutsch, Karl W. et al. *Political Community and the North Atlantic Area: International Organization in the Light of Historic Experience.* Princeton: Princeton University Press, 1957.

Farquharson, John E., and Stephen C. Holt. *Europe from Below: An Assessment of Franco-German Popular Contacts.* London: Allen & Unwin, 1975.

Higashikuni, Naruhiko. *Ichi Kozoku no Senso Nikki* [War Diary of a Royal Family Member]. Tokyo: Nihon Shuhosha, 1957.

Hirano, Kenichiro. "Sengo Nihon ni Okeru 'Bunka'" ["Culture" in the Context of Postwar Japanese Diplomacy]. In *Sengo Nihon no Gaiko Seisaku* [Diplomacy of Postwar Japan], ed. Akio Watanabe. Tokyo: Yuhikaku, 1985.

Igarashi, Takeshi. "Sengo Nichi-Bei Bunkakoryu Keikaku no Taido" [Stirring of the Post War US-Japan Cultural Exchange Program]. In *Senryo to Nihon Shukyo* [Occupation and Religion in Japan], ed. Fujio Imon. Tokyo: Miraisha, 1993.

Japan Foundation, *Kokusai Bunka Koryu Gannen he no Kitai* [Hope for The Epoch of International Cultural Exchange]. Tokyo, 1988.

Joint Secretariat of ASEAN–Japan Multilateral Cultural Mission. *The Report of the Joint Secretariat of ASEAN-Japan Multilateral Cultural Mission, Japan-Singapore.* Tokyo, 1998.

Katzenstein, Peter J. *Tamed Power: Germany in Europe.* Ithaca, NY: Cornell University Press, 1997.

———. *The Culture of National Security: Norms and Identity in World Politics.* New York: Columbia University Press, 1996.

Kawamura, Yoko. "Wiesbaden Sagyo Circle: Sengo Doitsu Bunka Koryu Koso ni okeru 'Weimar no Saisei'" [*Wiesbadener Arbeitskreis*: "Weimar Renaissance" in Postwar German Conception for Cultural Exchange]. *Odysseus* 3 (1997): 38–51.

———. "The Study and Practice of International Cultural Relations: A Japanese Approach to International Relations." Paper presented at the JAIR (Japan Association for International Relations) 50th Anniversary International Conference, Kisarazu, Japan.

Kokusai Bunka Koryu ni Kansuru Kondankai (Advisory Group on International Cultural Exchange). *Atasashii Jidaino Kokusai Bunka Koryu* [Report on International Cultural Exchange in New Age]. Tokyo, 1994.

———. *Kokusai Bunka Koryu ni Kansuru Kondankai Hokoku* [Report of Advisory Group on International Cultural Exchange]. Tokyo, 1989.

Kokusai Koryu Kikin Jugonenshi Hensan Iinkai (Compilation Committee for Fifteen Years' History of Japan Foundation). *Kokusai Koryu Kikin Jugo Nen no Ayumi* [Fifteen Years of Japan Foundation]. Tokyo, 1990.

Kuriyama, Takakazu. "Gekido no 90 Nendai to Nihon Gaiko no Shintenkai" [Turmoil in the 1990s and New Development of Japanese Diplomacy]. *Gaiko Forum* 3, no. 5 (May 2005): 12–21.

Lapid, Yosef, and Friedrich Kratochwil. *The Return of Culture and Identity in IR Theory.* Boulder, CO: Lynne Riener, 1996.

Makita, Toichi. "Liberal na Kokusai Bunka Koryu" [Liberal International Cultural Relations]. In Sengo Nihon Kokusai Bunka Koryu Kenkyukai, *Sengo Nihon.*

Markovits, Andrei S., and Simon Reich. "Should Europe Fear the Germans?" In *From Bundesrepublik to Deutschland: German Politics after Unification,* ed. Michael Huelshoff, Andrei S. Markovits and Simon Reich. Ann Arbor: University of Michigan Press, 1993.

Menju, Toshihiro. "The Development of Grassroots International Exchange in Japan and the Impact of American Philanthropy." In *Philanthropy and Reconciliation: Rebuilding Postwar U.S.–Japan Relations,* ed. Tadashi Yamamoto, Akira Iriye, and Makoto Iokibe. Tokyo: Japan Center for International Exchange, 2006.

Mitchell, J. M. *International Cultural Relations.* London and Boston: Allen & Unwin, 1986.

MOFA (Gaimusho). *Waga Gaiko no Kinkyo 1987* [Diplomatic Blue Book 1987]. Tokyo, 1987.

———. *Waga Gaiko no Kinkyo 1989* [Diplomatic Blue Book 1989]. Tokyo, 1989.

MOFA Cultural Project Division (Gaimusho Bunka Jigyobu). *Kokusai Koryu no Genjo to Tenbo (1972)* [Current Situation and Prospect of International Exchange (1972)]. Tokyo, 1989.

Nagasu, Kazuji, and Yoshikazu Sakamoto. *Jichitai no Kokusai Kouryu* [International Relations of Local Governments]. Tokyo: Gakuyo Shobo, 1983.

Nishikawa, Masao. *Jikoku Si wo Koeta Rekisikyoiku* [History Education beyond National History]. Tokyo: Sanseido, 1992.

Nishiyama, Takehiko. "ASEAN no Genjo to Wagakuni tono Kankei" [Present Situation of ASEAN and Its Relationship with Our Country]. *Kezai Kyoryoku,* no. 130 (1978): 12–19.

Oba, Mie. *Asia Taiheiyo Chiiki Keisei e no Katei: Kyokai Kokka Nichi-Go no Identity Mosaku to Chiiki Shugi* [Road to Asia-Pacific: Search of Identities by Japan and Australia as Liminal Nations and Regionalism]. Kyôto-shi: Mineruva Shobô, 2004.

Sakato, Masaru. "Kokusai Koryu Kikin no 25 Nen: Jigyo Seikaku to no Tenkai" [25 Years of the Japan Foundation: Development of Its Programs, etc.]. *Kyorin Daigak Fuzoku Kokusai Kankei Kenkyujo Kenkyu Nenpo,* no. 2 (1999): 135–158.

Sato, Maho. "Asia ni Okeru Chiteki Koryu no Kokoromi" [Attempts for Intellectual Exchange in Asia]. In *Kokusai Bunka Shinkokai kara Kokusai Koryu Kikin e: Kokusai Koryu Kikin Ron* [From Kokusai Bunka Shinkokai to Japan Foundation: Introduction to Analysis of Japan Foundation], FY 1999 Report of the Research by Grants-in-Aid for Scientific Research (Basic Research B), Project "Empirical and Sociological Research of Globalization, Cultural Exchange and Culture Industry," no.10410055. Tokyo, 1999.

Sato, Susumu. "Sengo Nihon Gaiko no Sentaku to Ajia Chitsujo Koso" [The Choice of Postwar Japanese Diplomacy and Initiative for Order of Asia]. *Hogaku Seijigaku Ronkyu,* no. 41 (1999): 165–196.

Sengo Nihon Kokusai Bunka Koryu Kenkyukai (Study Group on International Cultural Relations of Postwar Japan), with editorial supervision of Kenichiro Hirano. *Sengo Nihon no Kokusai Bunka Koryu* [International Cultural Relations of Postwar Japan]. Tokyo: Keiso Shobo, 2005.

Strategic Committee for Asia Gateway, *Asia Gateway Kousou* [Asia Gateway Vision], 16 May 2007.

Tanino, Sakutaro. "Saikin no Asia Josei to Nihon no Taio" [Recent Situation in Asia and Japan's Response]. *Sekai Kezai Hyoron* 32, no. 5 (1988): 22–39.

Wendt, Alexander. *Social Theory of International Politics.* Cambridge: Cambridge University Press, 1999.

INDEX

D

R

V

CPSIA information can be obtained at www.ICGtesting.com
Printed in the USA
BVOW02s0023080813

327722BV00004B/12/P

9 781782 380795